ABE Adult Basic Education
ESL, GED, diploma & academic skills

District 196 Community Education
Grace ABE Site
7800 W. County Road 42
Apple Valley, MN 55124

tel. 952-431-8316
www.district196.org/abe

2691705336

A NEXTEXT COURSEBOOK

INTRODUCTION TO

Sociology

Authors

Ethel Wood   Judith Lloyd Yero

nextext

Author Affiliates

Ethel Wood, Princeton High School, Princeton, New Jersey

Judith Lloyd Yero, formerly of Carl Sandburg High School, Orland Park, Illinois, is currently director of Mindsight Educational Services, Hamilton, Montana

Cover and interior illustrations: Eric Larsen

Printed in China

ISBN-10: 0-618-11868-3
ISBN-13: 978-0-618-11868-7

7 — 0940 — 09

Table of Contents

Chapter 3
SOCIAL STRUCTURE AND GROUP BEHAVIOR
43

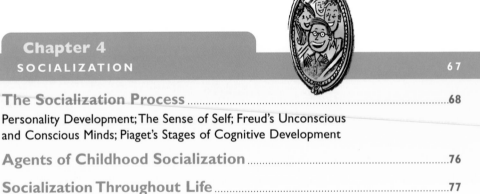

Chapter 4
SOCIALIZATION
67

Chapter 5
DEVIANCE AND CRIME
85

Chapter 6
SOCIAL STRATIFICATION AND CLASS
103

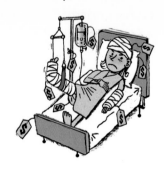

SOCIOLOGY FEATURES

The World of Sociology

In this chapter, you will learn about:

- **the sociological approach**
- **what sociologists do**
- **the development of sociology**
- **sociology today**

On the children's television show "Sesame Street," Ernie considered what would happen if he hit his sister, who had hit him. "She will cry," he thought. "Mother will come running. I will be blamed for hurting her, and I will be punished." In deciding what to do, Ernie used a sociological approach. He saw himself as part of a larger group, the family. And he used his observations of how different members of that group behave to form a conclusion.

Sociologists focus on patterns of human group behavior. People within a family behave in predictable ways based on their roles in the family. Sociologists look at how sports fans behave, how workers and bosses behave, how criminals behave. They look at the many different groups in a society and examine the interactions of people within them.

Sociology is one of the social sciences. Sociologists conduct research and apply their findings to current social problems. They may make policy recommendations to a government or help group members work effectively. Sociology has developed since the mid-1800s. Today, a variety of perspectives influences how sociologists think.

The Sociological Approach

Sociologists study human interactions in many ways. For example, they might examine interactions among family members historically. What patterns do we see in family interactions today compared to those a century ago? Sociologists might take a cross-cultural approach. How do interactions among family members in India differ from those in the United States?

What Sociology Is

Sociology, a word first used in 1824 by the French philosopher Auguste Comte, means "the study of society." Sociologists systematically study social behavior in human groups and look for patterns. They focus on the influence of social relationships on people's behavior and attitudes. They are interested in group behavior; they examine the behavior of individuals in terms of the roles they have in the group.

As a field of study, sociology has a very broad scope. The range of topics it examines is almost endless, since human interactions and behavior take place in a wide variety of groups and circumstances. Sociologists might study:

* Beliefs.
* Values.
* Rules.
* Ways of organizing families.
* Educational systems.
* Religions.
* Political systems.
* Economic systems.
* The roles people play.

Patterns in Human Behavior

Most people tend to see events in their lives as intensely personal. You fail a test. You practice hard on a school athletic team. You have a fight with your girlfriend or boyfriend. Each event is yours alone. Yet many other people have similar experiences. Sociologists study such events and look for the things outside the individuals that influence their behavior.

To a sociologist, the personal event of test failure might be part of a larger pattern. Sociologists ask big questions such as, "Do the values encouraged by U.S. high schools support athletic achievement more strongly than academic achievement?" A fight between boyfriend and girlfriend might trigger, "What societal influences make it difficult for young couples to stay together today?"

Social Facts

Sociologists see patterns in people's behavior that relate to things outside of them, such as where they live, what religious and racial group they belong to, and what their income is. They use **social facts** to explain the patterns. A social fact is any social activity or situation that can be observed and measured. Examples of social facts include:

* Attendance at sporting events.
* Crime patterns.
* Patterns of religious affiliation.
* Marriage rates.
* Unemployment and underemployment rates.
* Patterns of educational level reached.

The Sociological Imagination

Why study sociology? C. Wright Mills, a U.S. sociologist, gave a famous answer in 1959. He said that you can enrich your life when you come to possess **sociological imagination** or vision. Sociological imagination is a way of looking at the world that sees the connections among the seemingly private concerns of individuals and important social issues.

According to Mills, we are bewildered if we don't understand how our personal situations fit in with the "real world." To understand their lives and the human condition, people with sociological imagination ask questions about **three** basic areas:

1. **Society:** What is the particular structure of this society as a whole? What are its

Durkheim's Early Research

The pioneering French sociologist Emile Durkheim introduced the concept of social facts in 1895. In his work *The Rules of Sociological Method*, he argued that observation (not just abstract theory) of social (not psychological) factors was necessary to make the study of sociology a science.

In his famous 1897 work *Suicide*, he demonstrated that one of the most personal of all events was influenced by outside patterns, and thus the suicide rate was a social fact. Durkheim found that there were higher rates of suicide among divorced, rather than married, people and among Protestants rather than Catholics. He also found that people undergoing changes in economic conditions, whether good or bad, were more likely to commit suicide than those living in stable economic situations, even poverty.

essential components, and how are they related to one another?

2. **History:** Where does this society stand in human history? What came before, and how is the society changing? How is it different from societies of the past?

3. **People:** What kinds of men and women exist in this society today, and how are they changing? In what ways does the society influence them? How are they free, and how are they repressed?

The answers to these questions can help people apply societal patterns to understanding individual events. It doesn't matter whether a person is a scholar, a student, or just a curious observer. Sociological imagination lets individuals "step out of themselves" and understand much more about their worlds.

Sociology and the Other Social Sciences

The **social sciences** are a group of related disciplines that study various aspects of society and human relationships. They include **seven** areas:

1. Anthropology.
2. Economics.
3. Geography.
4. History.
5. Political Science.
6. Psychology.
7. Sociology.

The social sciences overlap. Many social scientists today shift back and forth among the disciplines in order to better understand the forces that help shape human lives. However, each field has a distinctive point of view. (See the chart opposite).

What Sociologists Do

The sociological imagination can be developed by anyone who studies sociology. Simply learning how to put one's self in the position of another person is an aspect of developing sociological imagination. But what do professional sociologists do?

* *Teach.* Many sociologists become high school teachers or faculty in colleges and universities. They advise students, conduct research, and publish their work. Over 3,000 colleges offer sociology courses.

* *Advise.* Sociologists work for the business, nonprofit, and government worlds as directors of research, policy analysts (people who develop policy recommendations), consultants, human resource managers, and program managers.

* *Research.* Practicing sociologists with advanced degrees are involved in research analysis, survey research, urban planning, community development, and criminology (the study of crime).

* *Counsel.* Some sociologists have specialized training as counselors, therapists, or program directors in social service agencies.

People who do not become professional sociologists study sociology because it offers valuable preparation for careers in journalism, politics, public relations, business, or public administration—fields

The Social Sciences		
Discipline	**Studies**	**Focuses on**
Anthropology	The origin, behavior, and physical, social, and cultural development of human beings.	Cultures.
Economics	The human production, distribution, and consumption of goods and services.	Theory and management of economies or economic systems.
Geography	Earth and its features and the distribution of life, including human life, on the planet.	Patterns of activity as they are distributed on Earth.
History	The record of past human events—civilizations, social activity and interaction of societies, people, ideas, and forces that changed societies.	Change and the past.
Political Science	Government and its processes, principles, and structures; also political institutions and politics.	How governments work.
Psychology	Mental processes and behavior in humans and animals and how they are affected by the individual's physical states, mental states, and the external environment—including other living things.	Individual behavior.
Sociology	Human social behavior and groups.	Groups in society, how they work, and what it means to be a member of a given group.

that require working with diverse groups and an understanding of society. Many students study sociology because they see it as a base for such professions as law, education, medicine, social work, and counseling.

Conduct Research

No matter what their job titles are, sociologists rely on systematic, thorough research. They use various techniques, such as experiments, observations, and surveys. Reliable sociological research must meet two types of standards: It must reflect the scientific method and it must be ethical.

The Scientific Method

How do sociologists ensure that their research accurately describes an aspect of society? One standard they follow is the **scientific method**, a systematic, organized series of steps that emphasize objectivity and consistency. There are **five** basic steps in the scientific method:

1. **Define the Problem.** The first step is to state as clearly and precisely as possible what you hope to investigate. Do you want to know whether crime rates in the United States are rising? If so, what kinds of crime? Over what time period? A thorough sociologist would not just define the problem as "crime," but would carefully define exactly what information he or she is seeking.

2. **Review the Literature.** The next step is to review research that has already been done in the area. What patterns concerning crime rates have other sociologists found? When were the studies done? Based on what you find, what is a logical "next step" to take in furthering research on crime rates?

3. **Formulate a Hypothesis.** The next step is to formulate a hypothesis. A **hypothesis** is a prediction about the relationship between two or more **variables**. Variables are measurable traits that change under different conditions. Researchers often predict that a change in one variable—an **independent variable**—will cause a change in another—a **dependent variable**. You can test a hypothesis by conducting research.

4. **Design a Research Plan and Collect the Data.** The researcher then designs a plan for collecting data that will either support or disprove the hypothesis. The plan can include such details as what questions to ask, how to gather data, how to measure changes in the variables, and how to organize the data for analysis. Once the plan is set, you follow it to conduct your research and organize the data you acquire.

"Hi. I'm doing a survey. Do you have a few minutes to answer some questions?"

5. **Analyze the Data and Develop a Conclusion.** What do the data reveal? Do the data show a relationship between the variables? If so, your hypothesis may be supported. If your hypothesis is not supported, you need to offer reasons or make recommendations for further research.

EXAMPLE: Suppose you realize you've been hearing a lot about theft from video stores—more than you used to—and it seems worst in the big cities. How would you use the scientific method to investigate? See the chart below.

Using the Scientific Method

Step 1: The Problem

"How has the incidence of video store theft changed in the three largest U.S. cities in the last five years? What affects that change?"

Step 2: The Literature

Last year, several sociologists published articles on theft rates in the three largest U.S. cities. You read the articles and decide how your research can build on what they reported.

Step 3: Hypothesis

Based on reviewing the literature, you wonder whether the population density in a city (the independent variable) affects the rate of video store thefts (the dependent variable). Your hypothesis: "Rates of video store theft increase as population density increases."

Step 4: Research Plan

You list the information you need: crime statistics (arrests? convictions? 911 calls?) and people-per-square-mile data. You devise a procedure for gathering data from city records and decide to organize your data into graphs.

Step 5: Analysis and Conclusion

Do the data show a relationship between increased population density and an increase in the incidence of video store theft? If so, your hypothesis is supported and you say so. If your hypothesis is not supported—for example, if the incidence of video store theft went down as population density increased—you would need to explain why you think the data show this. You might want to suggest the kind of further research that could explain it.

Using the Scientific Method

How many people actually use the scientific method? Even if we never conduct our own research, all of us read or hear about social research. We hear hypotheses about the causes of such social facts as higher crime rates, changing unemployment rates, and political preferences. How can we know if the research is reliable? If you study the research carefully to see how well the researchers used the scientific method, you may form an opinion about the reliability of their conclusions.

Ethical Concerns

Studying human beings is not exactly the same as studying rocks or plants. Whereas rocks can be cut open, scraped, and left on a lab table almost indefinitely, humans can't be treated that way. People have feelings and rights to privacy. Researchers in sociology must consider **ethics**, principles of conduct concerning what is good or moral or right.

EXAMPLE: A 1978 study of fatal car crashes provides an example of ethical concerns in sociological research. Sociologist William Zellner hypothesized that single-occupant fatal car crashes are sometimes suicides disguised as accidents. When Zellner was interviewing family and friends of the victims, he did not reveal his hypothesis because he was afraid that no one would talk to him. Instead, he said that his goal was to reduce the number of future accidents by learning about the emotional characteristics of accident victims.

Zellner concluded that about 12 percent of single-occupant crash victims were actually "autocides." His findings had implications for society. For example, if autocides involve the death of innocent bystanders, it is important to know how they might be prevented. However, you might ask whether Zellner's research method was ethical. Did he deceive his interviewees? What right did he have to invade their privacy?

The ASA Code of Ethics

In order to set uniform ethical standards for social research, the American Sociological Association (ASA) publishes a Code of Ethics. It includes **five** general principles. How do you think Zellner's research measures up against these principles?

1. **Professional Competence.** Sociologists make a commitment to only conduct research for which they are qualified by education, training, or experience. They consult with other professionals when necessary.

2. **Integrity.** Sociologists are honest, fair, and respectful of others and do not knowingly make statements that are false, misleading, or deceptive.

3. **Professional and Scientific Responsibility.** Sociologists follow the highest scientific and professional standards and accept responsibility for their work.

4. **Respect for People's Rights, Dignity, and Diversity.** Sociologists respect the rights, dignity, and worth of all people. In all work-related activities, sociologists acknowledge the rights of others to hold values, attitudes, and opinions that differ from their own.

5. **Social Responsibility.** Sociologists apply and make public their knowledge in order to contribute to the public good. When undertaking research, they strive to advance the science of sociology.

Apply Sociology

Sociologists often apply sociological knowledge to existing social situations. There are **three** main ways in which sociological research and everyday reality intersect.

1. **Understanding Issues.** Sociology can help us better understand today's issues, from capital punishment to health care.

2. **Overcoming Traditional Barriers.** Because sociological research is objective, sociology can speak to all people, not just to the dominant members of a society or group.

3. **Coming Up with Solutions.** If we better understand today's problems, we have the tools to help solve them.

The Development of Sociology

In the Middle Ages, Europe was changing. For many centuries people's lives had been pretty much the same—lords owned the land, knights fought to protect it, and serfs worked to keep the fields productive.

European Roots

Starting around 1500, Europe joined other parts of the world in a vast global trade exchange. Knowledge from Asia and the Islamic countries sparked a scientific revolution that helped create the technology needed for exploration and worldwide contacts. Economic changes led to changes in political and social thinking.

The new way of thinking was boldly dubbed the **Enlightenment,** an era in which scientific knowledge was applied to human society. Enlightenment thinkers believed that they could solve social, political, and economic problems using human reason. During the late 1700s and early 1800s these beliefs inspired political revolutions in many places, including the United States, France, and almost all of Latin America.

Over the same time period, new knowledge prompted an **Industrial Revolution.** Beginning in England, new machines and factory organizations transformed the lives of ordinary people. Amidst all these dramatic changes, the discipline of sociology was born.

Key Figures

Many philosophers became interested in the changes in human lives that they believed resulted from the revolutions. Among the most influential early sociologists were these **five:**

1. **Auguste Comte (1798–1857)**

   Sociology begins with the French philosopher Auguste Comte.

   BACKGROUND: The French Revolution of 1789 had overthrown the government of French kings, who had ruled with absolute power for centuries. It set France into a topsy-turvy spin between old and new styles of government.

   Comte observed the rise and fall of the revolutionary general and emperor, Napoleon. Comte wondered what his science could contribute toward understanding what was going on. He asked himself, "How can France ever regain stability?" and "What patterns exist between order and chaos?" The theory he developed reflects these concerns.

   CONTRIBUTION: Comte believed that sociologists should be concerned with **two** basic problems:

   i. **Order.** What forces (such as kings or economic prosperity) bring order to a society?

   ii. **Change.** What forces (such as new Enlightenment ideas) bring change? Comte theorized that any social change could best be understood by this analysis. The social world, he believed, could be studied with the same scientific accuracy as the natural world.

2. **Herbert Spencer (1820–1903)**

   Whereas Comte was influenced by the events following the French Revolution, English philosopher Herbert Spencer wrote in response to conditions caused by the Industrial Revolution.

   BACKGROUND: As he watched industrialization take hold in England, Germany, and the United States, Spencer pondered the nature of social change. He asked, "How can sociologists explain who will become rich and powerful in this new age and who will be left behind?"

   CONTRIBUTION: Spencer found answers in the work of Charles Darwin, who developed the theory of natural selection. According to Darwin, the evolution of any species is a natural process: The individuals least suited

▲

Auguste Comte was the first to use the word *sociology.*

RESEARCH

Harriet Martineau's Work

Harriet Martineau (1802–1876) was largely responsible for translating Comte's work into English and spreading it to many nations outside France. She also published studies of early 19th-century U.S. society in her book *Society in America*. She differed from many scholars of her day in that she promoted active involvement in solutions to social issues. She believed that intellectuals and scholars should advocate change to solve social problems. She spoke out in favor of women's rights, the emancipation of slaves, and religious tolerance.

▲
Herbert Spencer developed the theory known as Social Darwinism.

to their environments are weak and die out, while the individuals best suited to their environments survive, thrive, and reproduce.

Spencer believed that this concept of "survival of the fittest" could explain social change as well. He believed the Industrial Revolution led to progress, and that through natural competition, the best aspects of society would survive over time. Spencer's theory is known as **Social Darwinism**. His ideas support the view that government should not interfere in the economic and business activities of a society. In the United States, libertarians and laissez-faire economists have been influenced by Spencer.

Did You Know?

An Uncluttered Mind

Both Auguste Comte and Herbert Spencer refused to read any works by other social thinkers, including each other. Comte called this practice "cerebral hygiene," believing that others' work would pollute his own mind. Spencer's refusal to read the work of others came at a high price, since he often declared his own hypotheses as the "truth" without knowing that others had proved him false.

Karl Marx viewed societies in terms of their economies.

▼

3. Karl Marx (1818–1883)

The German Karl Marx also reacted to the social conditions created by the Industrial Revolution. However, he saw exploitation and misery where Spencer saw order and positive change.

BACKGROUND: Marx saw people working for low pay in filthy, unsafe factories, who at night went home to miserable, crowded slums that had been built up around the places where they worked. He attributed these conditions to some historical economic facts.

CONTRIBUTION: Marx believed that the organization of the economy is basic to society, and that political, social, and religious beliefs grow out of the economic structure.

He viewed society as divided into two groups—those who control the economy and those who don't. In capitalism, where free competition is allowed, greed and self-interest drive some individuals to seize control. The worker becomes the victim of the factory owner. It is to the owner's advantage to pay the worker as little as possible.

Marx advocated a "revolution of the proletariat [workers]" to overcome the unfair advantages of the rich. He believed that eventually the whole capitalistic system would disappear and a new "communist" system would take its place—one in which the inequalities among members of society would be removed.

4. Emile Durkheim (1858–1917)

At the turn of the 20th century, most students of society learned sociology from people who called themselves "philosophers." One hugely influential "philosopher" was Emile Durkheim, a professor at the University of Bordeaux in France.

BACKGROUND: Like Comte and Spencer, Durkheim was interested in questions of order, such as "What forces keep a society together?" and "What influences pull society apart?"

CONTRIBUTION: Durkheim thought of answers to these questions in terms of **function**. If an element of society fulfills a true function, or purpose, it must be important in keeping things orderly. Likewise, its removal would cause disorder.

Emile Durkheim studied the functions served by social institutions.

EXAMPLE: The problems that followed the French Revolution came about because kings served a purpose—they organized wars and trade and their armies kept peace within the country. When the king was removed, these functions were interrupted. Over time, French citizens found a way to meet these functions in other ways (today they have a very strong president), but until they did, the society was in disorder.

To Durkheim, the best way to analyze society was by examining the functions different institutions serve. He was particularly interested in the function of religion in society, because he believed that shared beliefs and values hold society together.

5. Max Weber (1864–1920)

German philosophers also made major contributions to the early development of sociology. One of the most famous, Max Weber, was interested in the interactions of society and the individual.

BACKGROUND: Weber examined the role individual beliefs and feelings played in society. He argued that society could not be understood by *objective* measurement. That might work for determining accurate weights and heights, but not for people and societies.

CONTRIBUTION: To fully understand behavior, Weber believed sociologists must learn the *subjective* meanings people attach to actions.

▲

Max Weber focused on individuals and their interactions.

EXAMPLE: You cannot objectively measure a handshake. Instead, you must understand its subjective meaning. Does it signify friendship? Formality? Aggression? Until you can answer these kinds of questions, you cannot understand a society. Weber called this type of understanding *verstehen*, the German word for "understanding."

Weber also developed the concept of the **ideal type**, a model that can be used to measure reality. In using an ideal type, a researcher examines many examples of an aspect of a society and identifies what he or she believes to be its essential features.

EXAMPLE: Suppose that you are studying marriage. You would look at many marriages and come up with a list of typical characteristics. You might start your model of marriage with some-

thing like this: A man and a woman commit to sharing a life together, and many marriages produce children. (The characteristics in the model may vary according to the society.) Your list becomes the ideal type. Using the ideal type, you can examine "real" marriages and better understand their variations.

The Development of Sociology in the United States

American professors who studied Comte, Spencer, Marx, Durkheim, and Weber soon joined the ranks of prominent European sociologists and made their own contributions, many of which we will discuss in this book.

Major U.S. Sociologists

Some of the most famous U.S. sociologists include:

* George Herbert Mead.
* Charles Horton Cooley.
* Talcott Parsons.
* C. Wright Mills.
* Robert Merton.

The Chicago School

One distinctive characteristic of U.S. sociology has been its emphasis on practical solutions to social problems. This attitude reflects an American belief that ideas are important only if they are accompanied by actions. The "Chicago School" of sociology has long been associated with the development of solutions to social problems through social reform.

EXAMPLE: Sociologist Jane Addams established *settlement houses* in poor areas of Chicago in the early 1900s. Their purpose was to assist underprivileged people and, at the same time, develop a society with more equal opportunities for all. Addams, along with black journalist and educator Ida B. Wells, prevented the implementation of a racial segregation policy in the Chicago schools.

In more recent years, the University of Chicago has been a center of urban study that focuses on studying its own city.

Sociology Today

The great theorists who helped develop the field of sociology illustrate the wide variety of possible ways to view society. Comte looked at order and change. Spencer compared change in societies to evolutionary change in living organisms. Marx viewed social change as full of conflict and inequality, but Durkheim saw orderly, functional transitions. Weber concentrated on the relationship between society and the individual. The ideas of these men, as well those of many 20th-century thinkers, have shaped sociological theory today.

Theoretical Perspectives

A perspective is a way of seeing things. In everyday life, some people seem to be eternally optimistic. Others seem to see trouble even when none exists. We all have different points of view, and sociologists are no exception. Today, **three** major

theoretical perspectives illustrate different ways to approach the study of society:

1. **The Functionalist Perspective.**
   People who view society from the **functionalist perspective** like to compare societies to organisms. Every part has a function, and, overall, a society tends to operate smoothly. If something doesn't fit in, the functionalist believes that it will be eliminated naturally, or just won't be passed on to the next generation. Herbert Spencer and Emile Durkheim heavily influenced this perspective.

   How does a functionalist explain why crimes such as murder and robbery exist? Functionalists know that at any given time, some parts of the system don't work well. Crime is a **dysfunction.** Something is a dysfunction if it inhibits or disrupts the working of the system as a whole. It can be a negative result of an activity. A dysfunction threatens the stability of a society. Societies must develop ways to contain dysfunctions so that normal health and stability may be maintained.

   Functionalists also compare **manifest functions,** which are apparent and conscious, to **latent functions,** which are often unconscious, unintended, or hidden.

   EXAMPLE: A school system has the manifest function of teaching the basic knowledge and skills needed to be successful in our society. It has the latent function of passing on mainstream culture and uniting people to core values.

Which are more important—manifest functions or latent functions? A functionalist would explain that institutions exist in harmony with the rest of society when they fulfill many functions, both manifest and latent.

2. The Conflict Perspective. Sociologists using the **conflict perspective** concentrate on aspects of society that encourage competition and change. They don't necessarily emphasize violent conflict. They are also interested in peaceful

U.S. Culture Connection

The McDonaldization of Society

In his book *The McDonaldization of Society,* sociologist George Ritzer claims that "the principles of the fast-food restaurant are coming to dominate more and more sectors of American society as well as of the rest of the world." Ritzer believes that this industry's goals affect far more than hamburgers. They have shaped the human environment, from airports to education.

According to Ritzer, **four** goals of "McDonaldization" are:

1. **Efficiency.** Rational calculation of the most cost-effective method of production (for example, determining the smallest number of kitchen crew members needed to meet the demand for food).

2. **Calculability.** Measurement of outcomes based on quantity rather than quality focusing on how many hamburgers are sold, not on customer satisfaction.

3. **Predictability.** Organization of the production process to guarantee uniformity of product and standardized outcomes (your hamburger tastes the same wherever you buy it).

4. **Control.** Substitution of more predictable nonhuman labor for human labor (cash registers that display what was ordered and calculate change due).

Do you think McDonaldization exists? What could be some examples?

negotiations between groups. Conflict theorists may identify groups that have different interests, such as various political groups or people from different parts of an organization, and study how they work out their differences. They see the potential for conflict in the different points of view of groups that naturally compete with each other.

According to conflict theorists, social conflict arises from competition over limited resources. Once a group gains control of wealth or power, it sets rules that benefit its members and denies benefits to other groups. You may recognize the influence of Karl Marx on this perspective. Most conflict theorists today, however, are not Marxists. They simply see conflict as a part of everyday life in all societies.

3. **The Interactionist Perspective.** Both functionalists and conflict theorists look at the parts of society as they relate to other parts. In contrast, sociologists who adopt the **interactionist perspective** study the ways individuals respond to each other. Interactionists view society as a collection of small interactions; they are much more interested in the small parts than in society overall. They observe and record the intentions and meanings conveyed by individual actions. They

pay attention to what people say, but they focus just as much on nonverbal communication. Their intellectual forebear is Max Weber.

The interactionist perspective emphasizes the role played by **symbols** in daily life. Members of a group or a society understand the social meanings of the symbols they share. For example, a team mascot may be used as a symbol of your school, and all the students know what the mascot means.

Comparing Perspectives

	Functionalist	Conflict	Interactionist
Nature of Society	It is stable, made up of interrelated social structures that work in harmony.	It is made up of competing interests, each seeking to meet its own goals.	It is made up of interacting individuals and groups, all sharing common symbols.
Level of Analysis	Analyzes the entire society.	Analyzes the entire society.	Analyzes interacting individuals and groups.
View of the Individual	Sees individuals socialized to perform functions in society.	Sees individuals as shaped by power, conflict, and authority.	Sees individuals shaping their own social worlds through interaction.
View of Social Change	Predicts that change will be in a direction that reinforces the health of the society.	Sees change as constant, often forced, sometimes with positive consequences.	Sees change reflected in symbols and social interactions.
Possible View of a U.S. School	Observes manifest functions such as teaching, latent functions, such as social and athletic opportunities.	Observes inequalities among schools based on different resources; sees problems within schools based on the interactions of groups.	Observes common symbols and finds verbal and nonverbal communications most interesting.
Forebears	Emile Durkheim Herbert Spencer	Karl Marx	Max Weber

The Power of Sociology

Sociology welcomes the study of many topics, and it encourages its students to examine their social worlds with fresh eyes. Sociologists look at society through different lenses, all of which are useful. The kind of understanding gained from a study of sociology can help people solve problems as personal as a brother's relationship with his sister or as broad and intricate as world hunger.

Chapter I Wrap-up
THE WORLD OF SOCIOLOGY

Sociology is the study of society. Sociologists use social facts and employ the sociological imagination. These tools help them design and conduct research; they also help them apply the results of research in society.

Sociology began as a branch of philosophy. European thinkers such as Auguste Comte, Herbert Spencer, Karl Marx, Emile Durkheim, and Max Weber proposed different theories about how society could be studied and understood. In the United States, early sociologists combined research with a strong interest in working to solve social problems such as poverty.

Today sociologists employ one or more broad approaches to the nature of society. The three main approaches are the functional, conflict, and interactionist perspectives.

Sociology

conflict perspective—point of view in sociology that emphasizes competing interests, power, and inequality. *p. 16*

dependent variable—in research the trait or behavior that changes in response to an independent variable. *p. 6*

dysfunction—activity that threatens the stability of a society. *p. 15*

Enlightenment—18th-century philosophical movement that emphasized the use of reason to examine doctrines and traditions. It led to a scientific approach to social, political, and economic problems and inspired revolutions in the United States, France, and Latin America. *p. 9*

ethics—principles of conduct concerning what is good, moral, or right. *p. 8*

function—work or purpose of an aspect of society that meets a social need. *p. 13*

functionalist perspective—point of view in sociology that emphasizes stable, inter-related social structures, each meeting a social need. *p. 15*

hypothesis—prediction about the relationship between two or more variables. *p. 6*

ideal type—model that can be used to measure reality. *p. 14*

independent variable—in research, the factor on which dependent variables depend. An independent variable is not affected by the activity being investigated. *p. 6*

Industrial Revolution—from about 1750 to 1850, the dramatic change from an agricultural to an industrial society that came about from increased use of machines. *p. 9*

interactionist perspective—point of view in sociology that emphasizes inter-acting individuals and groups. *p. 17*

latent function—unconscious, unin-tended, or hidden work or purpose (of an aspect of society). *p. 15*

manifest function—open, intended, and conscious work or purpose (of an aspect of society). *p. 15*

scientific method—systematic, organized series of research steps that emphasize objectivity and consistency. *p. 6*

Social Darwinism—Herbert Spencer's theory that society will evolve through a process of natural selection, and those aspects that best serve society will survive. *p. 11*

social fact—social activity or situation that can be observed and measured. *p. 3*

social sciences—related disciplines that study human behavior: anthropology, economics, geography, history, political science, psychology, and sociology. *p. 4*

sociological imagination—way of looking at the world that sees connec-tions among the private concerns of individuals and social issues. *p. 3*

sociology—science that studies social behavior in human groups. *p. 2*

symbol—something that stands for or represents something else. *p. 18*

variable—measurable trait that is subject to change under different conditions. *p. 6*

Culture

In this chapter, you will learn about:

- the components of culture
- cultural diversity and change
- American values

You walk into a youth center in a new town. There are people everywhere, hanging around a lobby desk, going through doors, buying things from vending machines. You can hear a basketball game going on and music playing. How do you know what to do first? You might ask yourself, "What are the rules in this place?"

Rules—most people don't like them very much. Still, human beings usually function within a framework of rules that serve as guidelines for living. Because there are an incredibly large number of possible ways for humans to go about their lives, a set of rules helps us organize ourselves in relation to other people.

In this chapter you will learn about the collection of rules called culture. A culture can be described by its values, norms, symbols, and knowledge. While there are some cultural universals, there is also much cultural diversity, and cultures change over time. Americans have held some traditional cultural values since the founding of the country, yet new American values are emerging even today.

What Culture Is

The rules that guide our behavior collectively are known as culture. Humans begin learning the rules of culture almost as soon as they are born, and they continue to be shaped by them all their lives. Culture is both basic and complex.

Every society, from the simplest to the most complex, has culture. **Culture** includes a society's beliefs, history, knowledge, language, customs, moral principles, and skills. It also consists of the objects people make and use that reflect their ways of life.

Culture and Society

Culture and society are not the same, even though it is almost impossible to talk about one without the other. A **society** is a large number of people who:

* Live in the same area.
* See themselves as separate and different from people outside their territory.
* Participate in a common culture.

A society consists of social interactions among people who think of themselves as similar. That doesn't mean that differences don't exist within a society.

Did You Know?

Heredity and Culture

Culture is the set of things that society, not biology, passes on to the individual. However, the division between biology and culture is not clear cut.

Biology determines basic human needs and capacities. The hunger drive, for example, is biological. It makes us all want to eat. But what, how, and where we eat is determined by our culture.

How much of human behavior is inherited, and how much is learned? What is the dividing line between culture and biology?

Is the formation of families biologically or culturally based? What about crime? Is it provoked by biological aggression, or is criminal behavior shaped by the culture? Sociologists do not agree about the answers to these questions.

You might think that the behaviors that don't vary from one culture to another are the inherited ones. However, even this isn't as logical as it seems. For example, virtually all people in all societies use fire, but no one argues that the knowledge of how to use fire is inherited.

EXAMPLE: People who live in San Francisco may see themselves as different from those who live in Chicago, but they see inhabitants of both cities as part of the U.S. society. If they travel to Chicago, they will probably be able to get around all right because the rules—or the culture—would be familiar.

Cultural Traits

The smallest unit of a culture is the cultural trait. A **cultural trait** is a single object, action, or belief.

EXAMPLES: A wedding ring, a handshake, the belief that washing one's hands helps prevent the spread of germs—these are cultural traits.

Cultural traits usually combine to form culture complexes. A **culture complex** is a set of interrelated traits.

EXAMPLE: All people eat, and many cultural traits surround this action. In the United States, the culture complex for eating would include knives, forks, spoons, plates, and all the customs that surround their use.

Cultural traits and complexes vary from one culture to another, but they usually are organized around a limited number of cultural patterns. People in many cultures prefer to eat a large meal at noon, whereas Americans prefer a large evening meal. The French prefer strong coffee, whereas most Americans enjoy a weaker brew. Soup is a staple breakfast food in many cultures. Yet some characteristics of eating are widely shared among cultures. People usually eat alone, with family members, or in small groups of people they know well.

Material and Nonmaterial Culture

Culture consists of concrete objects that can be seen and touched. Culture also consists of beliefs, values, and behaviors that cannot be touched. **Material culture** refers to the set of concrete objects created

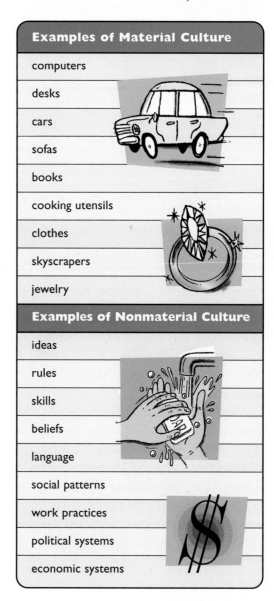

Examples of Material Culture

computers

desks

cars

sofas

books

cooking utensils

clothes

skyscrapers

jewelry

Examples of Nonmaterial Culture

ideas

rules

skills

beliefs

language

social patterns

work practices

political systems

economic systems

or used by the people of a culture. Single objects of the material culture are called *artifacts*. **Nonmaterial culture** is composed of abstract human creations.

The two categories of culture are intertwined. For instance, the material objects created to make our lives easier or better, such as computers and cars, require that we learn particular skills to use them. The chart on page 23 gives examples of material and nonmaterial culture.

Real versus Ideal Culture

Did you ever see someone run a red light or cross the street midway between two intersections? People who break the rules usually know what the rules are. People may agree about what should and shouldn't be done, but they don't always do as their culture directs.

The *ideal culture* is a collection of cultural beliefs that define what people in a culture should do and what they say they do. Most Americans would say you should cross streets at the corners. Even when someone confesses that he or she often jaywalks, that person almost certainly understands the "ideal" behavior.

Sociologists are interested in both the ideal culture and the *real culture* that is reflected by people's actual behavior as it appears to an observer.

Sociologist's Perspective

Ideal versus Real Voting Patterns

Most Americans believe that as citizens of a democracy they have the responsibility to select public officials by voting in elections. How does this ideal behavior compare to the real?

When researchers at the University of Michigan asked Americans if they had voted in the 1996 presidential election, 72 percent said that they had voted. In contrast, according to the U.S. Bureau of the Census, only 48.8 percent of all eligible voters actually voted in the same election. Ideal and real culture are often very different.

Key Elements of Culture

Although cultural traits and complexes vary from society to society, all cultures consist of the same key elements: values, norms, symbols, and knowledge and beliefs.

Values

We each have our own personal values that shape our behavior. One person may value physical fitness and concentrate on running or working out in the gym. Another may value contributing to the community and may spend time helping out in the senior center. Whatever the differences in their personal values, if these two are part of the same culture, they share a general set of objectives as members of their society.

Cultural values are a collection of what is considered good, desirable, and proper in a culture. They reflect what people in a culture prefer as well as what they find important and morally right. Values are broad, abstract concepts that form the foundation for a whole way of life. The types of values held by a society help determine almost everything else about the culture.

Norms

Two people greet each other as they pass on the sidewalk. One says, "Good morning, how are you?"

"Good morning. How do you like this beautiful weather?"

"I love it. We'd better enjoy it while we can!"

What are they doing? What does their exchange mean? They are acknowledging their acquaintance according to the norms of U.S. society.

Norms are the guidelines people follow in their relations with one another. They are shared standards of desirable behavior. Every society has many norms. These range from small things (Don't eat peanut butter from a knife) to major things (Do not kill another human being). Norms are divided into **two** categories according to the strictness by which they are enforced:

1. Folkways refer to everyday habits and conventions that people obey without giving them much thought.

EXAMPLES: replying to invitations and writing thank-you notes for gifts. People who violate folkways may be considered eccentric or rude, but as a rule they are tolerated.

2. **Mores** are norms that have powerful moral significance attached to them. Mores provoke intense reactions if they are broken.

   EXAMPLES: prohibitions against incest, murder, and stealing.

Prohibitions against a society's most important mores are called **taboos**. Violators of taboos usually are considered unfit to socialize with others, and they may be exiled or executed.

A society enforces norms with laws and sanctions.

* **Laws** are written rules of conduct that are enacted and enforced by governments. Laws may formalize folkways (no littering) or may relate to major mores (laws against murder and robbery).

* **Sanctions** are rewards or punishments. Rewards are called *positive sanctions,* and punishments are called *negative sanctions.*

   * *Informal sanctions* are given by individuals or groups.

      EXAMPLE: Employee-of-the-week award (positive), grounding for a child who breaks a family rule (negative).

   * *Formal sanctions* are given by organizations or regulatory bodies, such as governments, police, corporations, and schools.

      EXAMPLES: Fines for traffic violations (negative), suspensions from school (negative), medals for athletic performance (positive).

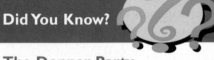

Did You Know?

The Donner Party

Cannibalism violates a major taboo in U.S. society, and those who practice it achieve a certain notoriety. A famous example is the Donner Party, a group of U.S. migrants to California in 1846–1847. They left Illinois under the leadership of George Donner. After considerable difficulty crossing the deserts of Utah, they were trapped by heavy snows in the Sierra Nevada Mountains in November. Forced to camp for the winter at a small lake (now named Donner Lake), they suffered enormous hardships, and members of the group resorted to cannibalism in order to survive. Although the California courts penalized none of the survivors, other settlers shunned them. The Donner name remains forever associated with their grisly deeds.

Symbols

Suppose you want your friends to know about your new dog. How would you go about it? Would you take your dog to school? Probably not. You have the ability to convey the news by using symbols. You may use words, and you may even draw a picture. **Symbols** are commonly understood gestures, words, objects, sounds, colors, or designs that have come to stand for something else.

Different cultures use different symbols to stand for the same object, so there is no obvious, natural, or necessary connection between a symbol and what it stands for. If you speak English, your new pet is a "dog," but if you speak Swahili, it would be a "mbwa." Some symbols, such as many traffic signs, are understood by people who speak many different languages. Symbols can be divided into **two** categories:

1. **Language** is the organization of written or spoken symbols into a standardized system with rules for putting the symbols together. Language not only allows people to communicate about present interests and needs, but also allows them to reflect on the past and imagine the future. The study of language can reveal much about a culture.
   EXAMPLES: The language of the Samoans, who live on an island, includes very precise information about fishing and boating in the Pacific. The language of Eskimos makes many fine distinctions about different kinds of snow. Arabs have hundreds of words to describe

Across Cultures

The Meaning of Circles

The circle is a central symbol for the Oglala Sioux of North America. They believe the circle to be sacred because the Great Spirit caused many things in nature to be round—the sun, the moon, even the stems of plants. The Oglala make their tipis circular, they camp in a circular formation, and they sit in a circle at ceremonies.

camels and horses. Americans distinguish among sedans, convertibles, sports utility vehicles, and vans.

2. **Signs** are nonverbal. In some ways signs are more flexible than language because they can communicate across languages. People in many cultures use their hands to make commonly understood signs.
   EXAMPLES: During World War II, Winston Churchill's famous "V" formed with two fingers symbolized victory for the Allies. The different positions of a Buddha statue's hands and fingers may convey teaching, calm, and caution as well as many other messages.

Knowledge and Beliefs

Knowledge is an element of culture that attempts to define what exists, or the reality of the world. It includes those things people understand as members of the culture as well as the particular kinds of knowledge needed to function in the culture.

EXAMPLE: A culture's history and sciences are part of its knowledge. In a highly technological society such as ours, principles of mathematics, engineering, and physics are very important.

A culture also has **beliefs**. These are its theories and ideas about the nature of the physical and social world. Not all beliefs can be proven. Sociologists are interested in how people decide what to count as knowledge and what to count as beliefs.

Elements of Culture

Values	*Broad, abstract, and basic ideas that reflect what is desirable, proper, good, preferred, important, and right.* Cultures value such ideas as: ✳ Freedom of expression. ✳ Strong families.	✳ Competition. ✳ Loyalty to a leader. ✳ Religious beliefs.
Norms	*Guidelines; shared standards of behavior.* Folkways—group habits and conventions, such as: ✳ Greetings. ✳ Child-raising customs.	Mores—moral standards such as: ✳ Taking care of the homeless. ✳ Honesty. Laws, such as: ✳ Marriage and divorce laws. ✳ Laws against murder. Sanctions, such as: ✳ Raises and promotions. ✳ Fines.
Symbols	*Commonly understood gestures, words, objects, sounds, and designs that stand for something else.* Examples include: ✳ Words. ✳ Maps.	✳ Diagrams. ✳ Traffic signs. ✳ Logos. ✳ National anthems. ✳ Emergency vehicle sirens.
Knowledge and Beliefs	*Culture's definition of reality.* Examples include: ✳ History. ✳ Science. ✳ Medicine.	✳ Skills needed to perform the work of the society. ✳ Ways of doing things. ✳ Ways of making things.

Cultural Variety

Each culture is different from all others, partly because it has adapted to meet the special circumstances of a particular group of people in a particular place.

EXAMPLE: A group of people living on a tropical island will eat the fruit that grows there and learn to catch and eat fish in the surrounding ocean. They obviously will not hunt seals and polar bears.

Cultures may also vary according to the society's social circumstances, such as its technological development, language, beliefs, and history. These factors help determine how a group organizes to meet basic human needs. When we study the variation among cultures, we look at **three** things: cultural universals, cultural diversity, and change inside cultures.

❶ Cultural Universals

Can you imagine a culture that doesn't have families, music, or some type of housing? Almost all cultures have these elements. Features that are common to all cultures are called **cultural universals**.

Some of the similarity among cultures comes from universal human needs. We are all basically alike physically—we must eat, find shelter, take care of children, and deal with aging and ill parents. Every human community begins with these same circumstances.

Another cause of cultural similarities can be found in the dynamics of group life. Groups must organize in order to function, and almost all have some form of leadership.

EXAMPLES: Chiefs, priests, mayors, prime ministers—all are cultural responses to the need for leadership.

Groups must also teach their organization to newcomers and children.

EXAMPLES: Family members, day care centers, schools, community colleges, libraries, and even the Internet meet these needs.

❷ Cultural Diversity

Although cultural universals can be identified, there is still great diversity among the world's many cultures. This diversity is often evident within a single nation, with some groups holding cultural beliefs and customs that differ from those of the majority.

Subcultures and Countercultures

Almost no country has a single set of accepted norms and values. Although people share a cultural tradition, all cultures contain diversity. **Subcultures** form when people share some broad cultural traditions but also follow values and norms that are unique to their group.

EXAMPLES: Subcultures may spring up around some occupations or places of work, such as among hospital workers. Subcultures may be defined by racial or ethnic groups, regions of a country—the South, the Midwest—or age groups—teenagers, senior citizens.

Complex modern societies depend on various subcultures—such as the military, the police, teachers, and religious leaders—for many functions. (We use the term *subculture* for such a group when we are discussing the values and behaviors their

Cultural Universals

In 1945, anthropologist George Murdock published a list of over sixty cultural universals. The manner in which these cultural features are expressed varies from culture to culture.

Examples of Cultural Universals	
Athletic sports.	Language.
Bodily adornment.	Laws.
Cooking.	Marriage.
Dancing.	Medicine.
Decorative art.	Music.
Family.	Myths and legends.
Food habits, taboos.	Personal names.
Funeral ceremonies.	Religious rituals.
Games.	Social status.
Gift giving.	Surgery.
Housing.	Tool making.
Inheritance rules.	Visiting.

members share that are particular to their group.) Subcultures are often seen as strengthening a society and making it more interesting. However, sometimes subcultures intend to challenge the values of the larger society. When a group rejects the values and norms of the larger culture and replaces them with a new set, the subculture formed is called a **counterculture**.
EXAMPLES: Gangs, hippies, skinheads, militia groups.

Ethnocentrism

Ethnocentrism—a term coined in 1906 by sociologist William Graham Sumner—is the tendency to assume that one's own culture and way of life are "normal" and superior to all others. Perhaps because we learn so much of our culture without really thinking about it, most people have some degree of ethnocentrism. We tend to see our own group as the defining point of culture. The consequences of such views are sometimes enormous.

Conflict theorists say that ethnocentrism leads to conflicts between groups in a society. For example, in the United States, ethnocentrism has led to conflict between black and white Americans because it promotes stereotypes based on prejudice. Ethnocentrism can also be seen as a cause of war among nations. On the other hand, functionalists note that ethnocentrism promotes group pride and can help make a country strong.

Ethnocentrism: A Two-Way Street

Sociologists often look for culture-centered behavior and views. One way to spot ethnocentrism is to compare two or more groups' descriptions of each other. Consider the following descriptions by Native Americans and Europeans, written in the early days of European settlement of North America:

> "We know now who they are; these Wapsinis [white people] who then came out of the sea to rob us of our land; starving wretches! With smiles they came, but soon became snakes or foes . . . They were allowed to live with us . . . as our friends and allies . . . But alas they brought also fireguns and fire water, which burned and killed. Also baubles and trinkets of no use; since we had better ones. . . . [They] said more land, more land we must have, and no limits could be put to their steps and increase."

—From the traditional history of the Lenni Lenape, the Delaware Indians

> "In respect to us, they are a people poor, and, for want of skill and judgment in the knowledge and use of our things, do esteem [value] our trifles before things of great value . . . [It] may be hoped, if means of good government be used, that they may in short time be brought to civility and the embracing of true religion."

—From Captain Arthur Barlowe's account of a voyage to Virginia, 1585

Cultural Relativism

The opposite of ethnocentrism is **cultural relativism**, the argument that behavior in one culture should not be judged by the standards of another. Cultural relativism is the view that people's behavior and values should be viewed from the perspective of their own culture. This view emphasizes that different social contexts produce different norms and values. Practices such as polygamy (multiple wives) and bullfighting must be studied within the contexts of the cultures in which they are found.

While cultural relativism does not suggest that we must unquestionably accept every cultural practice, it does require an effort to evaluate norms and values in the light of their source.

❸ Change

What do the U.S. cultures of the 18th and 21st centuries have in common? Although we certainly can identify some common elements—a representative government, the English language, immigrants—many things are different. Our population, means of travel and communication, values, and economy have all changed. Slavery is gone.

Across Cultures

Culturally Correct or Murder?

In 1989, a New York judge acquitted a Chinese immigrant of the most serious charges against him after he beat his wife to death with a hammer. He was sentenced to only five years' probation largely because the judge took cultural relativism into consideration.

The immigrant found out that his wife was having an affair, and, according to an expert on Chinese culture who testified at the trial, husbands in China often severely punish their wives for such behavior. According to the judge, the defendant took his Chinese culture with him when he immigrated to the United States.

The Brooklyn district attorney, Elizabeth Holtzman, disagreed and angrily asserted that "Anyone who comes to this country must be prepared to live by and obey the laws of this country."

What do you think?

All cultures change, continually, sometimes very slowly and at other times with sudden, jolting events.

Stability and Change

Every culture needs stability in order to run smoothly, even to survive. A society's stability rests largely on its ability to convince its members to conform, partly by applying sanctions but also through **internalization of norms**.

People begin to learn the norms of their society so early in their lives that it often doesn't occur to them that they might break them. They also expect the other people around them to follow norms. Internalization is the process by which an individual makes society's norms a part of his or her own set of attitudes and beliefs. We internalize folkways—such as eating with a knife and fork or driving on the right side of the road—as well as mores—such as only marrying one person at a time or refraining from eating human flesh. Most of us do not do these things simply because we fear punishment. When norms are internalized, a person conforms to society's expectations without need of punishment or reward.

Despite the need for stability, a society cannot stay the same forever. Many forces combine to bring about change. Some are as simple as the desire for something different. Some change comes about from a significant invention, such as the electric light or the computer. Other changes may be catastrophic, such as conquest by a people of another culture.

Types of Change

Change can occur in both material and nonmaterial culture, and it can begin in many different ways. A change in one area of life usually means that other areas will be altered as well. Changes can occur in **two** areas.

1. **Changes in Values and Belief.**

   "I found the mind of a female, if such a thing existed, was thought not worth cultivating. I disliked the trouble of thinking for myself and therefore adopted the sentiments of others—fully convinced [that] to adorn my person and acquire a few little accomplishments was sufficient to secure me the admiration of the society I frequented."

   —Eliza Southgate, in a letter to her cousin, May 1801

   Seventeen-year-old Eliza Southgate revealed that she had internalized some values and beliefs that characterized U.S. society 200 years ago. Education for girls who had schooling was usually limited to reading, writing, and simple arithmetic. Well-to-do families would sometimes send their daughters to a "finishing school," where they were taught the social skills of a hostess.

   Over the years since 1801 these U.S. values and beliefs have changed dramatically. Women's rights advocates formed an ongoing social movement. This long-term, conscious effort to promote social change helped bring about new values and ideas.

Today the beliefs that women will not work outside the home and that they need little education have vanished. Many areas of life, from education to business to politics, have changed in response. Thus change in values and beliefs can spread to other areas so that the entire society is transformed.

2. **Changes in Technology.** Many people find great delight in keeping up with new gadgets and integrating them into their lives. Most of us, however, don't stop to think about how the effect of new material objects ripples through society. Gadgets are the result of **technology**—the knowledge and tools people use to shape and mold their environments for practical purposes.

Technological change can occur in **two** ways:

i. **Discovery** involves recognizing new phenomena in the universe and/or developing a new understanding of elements that are already known.

EXAMPLES: As astronomers have developed more powerful telescopes and used satellites and rocket technology, they have contributed to our understanding of Earth and its place in the universe. Likewise, discoveries of new vaccines and treatments for diseases have contributed to better health and longer lives for many people.

ii. **Invention** results when existing cultural items are combined into a form that did not exist before.

Technology and Cultural Lag

Sociologist William F. Ogburn made some observations about cultural change based on the division of material culture from nonmaterial culture. According to Ogburn, material culture changes more readily than nonmaterial culture. So material culture usually changes first, and the nonmaterial culture must adjust to accommodate it.

Cultural lag refers to the time in between the changes, when the nonmaterial culture is still adapting to new material conditions. Ogburn acknowledged that change can occur the other way around—with nonmaterial culture changing first—but he believed that this pattern occurred much less often.

Although inventions take place in areas outside technology, technological inventions often bring about significant change. **EXAMPLE:** The invention of atomic weapons brought about a change in the organization and functions of armies, and, perhaps even more importantly, changed the whole world's attitude toward war. It also resulted in a myriad of other changes, such as nuclear power plants, that can bring inexpensive power to cities across the country.

Ways of Changing

Cultural change often takes place through **diffusion**, the spreading of cultural items from group to group or society to society. Diffusion can occur in many ways—through exploration, military conquest, missionary work, mass media, or tourism.

EXAMPLE: Long ago, the Chinese invented thin noodles. Marco Polo brought them back to his native Italy, where they were called *spaghetti*. Italians brought spaghetti to the United States, where it has become a staple of the American diet.

Diffusion leads to **acculturation**, the modification of the culture of a group as a result of contact with a different culture.

Many other factors may bring about cultural change, including the physical environment, population, and wars. The chart on page 36 gives examples of how cultures change.

Across Cultures

African Cattle Ranches

Modern countries sometimes try to help others around the world by sharing technological knowledge. But this diffusion doesn't work when knowledge of the local customs and beliefs is ignored.

In one African project, planners ignored advice from locals not to create cattle ranches in the project area because they would conflict with customs of the native inhabitants. In protest, thousands of people tore down fences, burned pastures, and rustled cattle because the ranches were built on their ancestral lands. The guerrilla activities continued until foreign managers were replaced with locals, who used traditional agreements between villages to end the rustling.

Examples of Cultural Change				
Diffusion	**Acculturation**	**Environment**	**Population Shift**	**War**
Marco Polo carries noodles from China to Italy.	Italians begin eating noodles. When they migrate to the United States, Americans' diets change.	A volcano's eruption ruins the land for farming. There is widespread poverty.	Declining birth rates lead to school closings. Entire towns disappear in some communities.	Farmers become soldiers.
The explorers of the Americas bring smallpox, which nearly wipes out some native groups.	Potatoes brought to Europe from the Americas become a staple food, and the European population experiences huge growth.	The discovery of gold in Colorado in 1849 produces boom towns and encourages immigration from China.	Population increases lead to overcrowding and shortages of food and supplies. Famines occur.	Refugees take their customs to new countries.

Toward a Global Culture

Technological innovations of the 20th century, such as communications technology, radio, television, motion pictures, and the Internet, have allowed such increased contact among nations that some people think we are headed toward a global culture. If a common global culture emerges in the future, today's nations may someday function more like subcultures than separate cultures.

Many people believe that the Internet will speed creation of a global culture. There are few restrictions on who provides information on the Internet and who gets it, so that people from all cultures and all walks of life (those who have computers and Internet access, that is) can have equal access to information and communication.

Internet Statistics

The Internet is growing much faster than anyone ever imagined. In 1998 the number of people connected to the Internet was about 37 million. The figure had grown by mid-2000 to about 332 million worldwide. The growth, however, is geographically uneven. Only about 1% of those connected in mid-2000 lived in Africa.

American Values

Each country has its own blend of cultural values that makes it different in some ways from all others. Some values have shaped the United States for many generations, whereas others are emerging and changing as our culture changes.

Traditional American Values

Traditional American values have influenced many generations of Americans. These include success, work, moral concern and humanitarianism, efficiency, progress, equality, freedom, and patriotism.

Success

In American culture, whether one succeeds or fails is believed to be due largely to one's own efforts. We are encouraged to believe that anyone who works hard and takes advantage of opportunities can make it to the top. As there is only so much room at the top, this value may leave many people feeling as if they have failed. In midlife, many Americans redefine "success" for themselves.

Work

Most Americans believe they should work hard, and laziness is generally frowned upon. We talk about people having a "work ethic" when they work hard.

Moral Concerns and Humanitarianism

Americans usually have strong opinions and tend to base their judgments on their sense of right and wrong. Americans differ, however, on the degree to which a common morality should be applied to all.

"Religious freedom is my immediate goal, but my long-range plan is to go into real estate."

Basic American Values

In his influential 1970 book *American Society*, sociologist Robin Williams offered a list of basic American values that have remained relatively stable through time: achievement, efficiency, material comfort, nationalism, equality, and the supremacy of science and reason over faith. Of course, not all people in the United States agree on one set of values, so Williams's list is controversial. However, other sociologists and anthropologists, including Talcott Parsons and Margaret Mead, have researched the same topic and have come up with very similar basic American values.

Examples of Values	
achievement	material comfort
efficiency	nationalism
equality	supremacy of science and reason over faith

Despite their belief that individuals are responsible for their own success, Americans have a soft spot for people in need of assistance. They seem to be most generous when people are harmed by situations that they cannot control.

Efficiency

Americans stress the efficient and practical. "Saving time" is a value that drives many lives—do what you have to do in the most efficient way possible so that you will get more done.

Progress

Americans are optimists. We believe our history is one of ongoing progress. We believe that progress will make our lives better, and that we can continue to improve and perfect our way of life. Some critics say that progress in the United States is blind—that we build skyscrapers, factories, and roads without any regard for their effects on the physical environment. On the other hand, the quality of people's lives in many areas has improved as a result of developments in medicine and technology. The belief in progress is closely tied to the idea that science can and eventually will overcome all natural and human-made difficulties.

Equality

"All men are created equal." This phrase from the Declaration of Independence means that the basic American value of equality has been there since the beginning of our country. Without a belief in equality and confidence in the ability of the average person, a democratic form of government would not make sense. On the other hand, by *equality* Americans mean that every individual has (or should have) equal opportunity. This ideal has not yet been realized, but we are working on it.

Across Cultures

Americans in Paris

Americans traveling to Paris often return home with tales of abuse at the hands of the French people. Americans criticize the French for being snobbish and rude. In return, the French often claim that Americans are boorish, loud, and disrespectful of their culture.

Part of the conflict rests in the difference between French and American values regarding efficiency and practicality. Many Parisians value a long, relaxing visit to a sidewalk café; Americans often take their coffee and run. Parisians name their streets after literary figures, artists, and philosophers; Americans frequently number their streets or name them after trees. Differences in values shape people's lives and influence their views of others.

Freedom

Perhaps there is no greater American value than freedom. By freedom, Americans generally mean freedom from governmental controls. We believe we should be free to reach the goals we choose, speak our minds freely, associate with whom we wish, travel where we wish, and be safe from our government spying on us or taking our things unlawfully.

Patriotism

Americans are inclined to believe that the United States is a better, stronger country than all the rest, and that the American way of life is superior to all others. Patriotism implies pride in one's country and its values, but it is also closely connected to ethnocentrism.

Changing American Values

The preceding list of traditional values is not exhaustive. You might think of others you believe most Americans hold. What about consumerism? Are we a nation of consumers? Do we place a high value on having "stuff"? What do you think?

Over time new values emerge as the culture changes. Because they are new, these values are often hard to identify. However, scholars have pointed out that a new cluster of closely related values has appeared in recent years:

* Self-fulfillment.
* Narcissism.
* Hedonism.

Self-fulfillment

Much emphasis has been placed in recent years on **self-fulfillment,** on the commitment to thoroughly developing one's talents and potential. Sociologist Robert Bellah says that values only have meaning if a person's "inner self" is in tune with them.

Evidence of this value of self-fulfillment is apparent in the growth of the "self-help" movement. Health clubs, diet centers, magazines, books, seminars, and web sites all challenge people to improve themselves and to experience life to its fullest. Self-help books have become big business for publishers across the country because of this new emphasis on self-improvement.

Psychologist and survey researcher Daniel Yankelovich views the shift toward self-fulfillment as positive. He believes that an emphasis on self-fulfillment will balance the ill effects that come from the traditional success value—the belief that satisfaction comes only from material gain.

Narcissism and Hedonism

Some sociologists believe that the emphasis on personal fulfillment borders on **narcissism**, or extreme self-centeredness. In "getting in tune with ourselves," we forget about others. A closely related concept is **hedonism**, or the pursuit of pleasure above all other values.

Sociologist's Perspective

Habits of the Heart

"Individuals are each in his or her own way confused about how to define for themselves such things as the nature of success, the meaning of freedom, and the requirements of justice." So writes sociologist Robert Bellah in *Habits of the Heart*. Bellah has identified a restlessness in U.S. society that relates to a struggle to interpret the meaning of traditional values, such as success, freedom, individualism, and equality.

Chapter 2 Wrap-up
CULTURE

A culture is the system of values, norms, symbols, and knowledge a society shares. It is made up of cultural traits that combine into culture complexes. Culture is both material (objects) and nonmaterial (abstract creations), both ideal and real.

Sociologists have identified cultural universals that all cultures share. Yet cultures are diverse as well. Cultures can change through diffusion and acculturation and in response to environmental changes, population shifts, and war.

When a culture changes, its values, beliefs, and technology change. U.S. culture has both traditional and emerging values.

acculturation—process of acquiring the culture of a group or society other than one's own. *p. 35*

beliefs—theories and ideas about the nature of the physical and social world. *p. 28*

counterculture—group that rejects the values and norms of a larger culture and replaces them with a new set. *p. 30*

cultural relativism—principle that behavior in one culture should not be judged by the standards of another. *p. 32*

cultural trait—single object, action, or belief produced by a culture. *p. 23*

cultural universals—features of societies that are common to all cultures. *p. 29*

cultural values—collection of what is considered good, desirable, and proper in a culture. *p. 25*

culture—system of values, norms, symbols, and knowledge that a society shares. *p. 22*

culture complex—set of interrelated cultural traits. *p. 23*

diffusion—process by which cultural items are spread from group to group or society to society. *p. 35*

ethnocentrism—tendency to assume that one's own culture is normal and superior to all others. *p. 30*

folkways—everyday habits and conventions of a people. *p. 25*

hedonism—pursuit of pleasure above all other values. p. 41

internalization of norms—largely subconscious process in which a culture's norms become part of an individual's own set of attitudes and beliefs. *p. 33*

knowledge—element of culture that attempts to define what exists or the reality of the world. *p. 28*

laws—written rules of conduct enacted and enforced by governments. *p. 26*

material culture—set of physical objects (artifacts) constructed by the people of a culture. *p. 23*

mores—traditional rules of a people or a society that have powerful moral significance attached to them. *p. 26*

narcissism—extreme self-centeredness. *p. 41*

nonmaterial culture—abstract creations by the people of a culture, such as ideas, rules, and beliefs. *p. 24*

norms—guidelines, including folkways and mores, that people in a culture follow in their relations with one another. *p. 25*

sanctions—rewards and punishments. *p. 26*

self-fulfillment—thorough development of individual talents and potential. *p. 40*

society—large number of people who live in the same area, see themselves as separate and different from people outside their territory, and participate in a common culture. *p. 22*

symbols—commonly understood gestures, words, objects, sounds, colors, or designs that stand for something else. *p. 27*

subculture—group of people who share some of the broad traditions of a culture but also follow values and norms that are unique to them. *p. 29*

taboo—prohibition against one of society's most important mores. *p. 26*

technology—knowledge and tools people use to shape and mold their environments for practical purposes. *p. 34*

CHAPTER 3

Social Structure and Group Behavior

In this chapter, you will learn about:

- **characteristics of social structure**
- **social structures and society**
- **the nature of groups and organizations**
- **social interaction**

How do you answer the question, "What did you do today?" You probably respond by describing events that made the day different from others, such as making an "A" on an English test or seeing an old friend. You probably would not elaborate on brushing your teeth or eating lunch. Yet it is the routine and usual events of our lives that provide the structure for human society.

From a sociologist's point of view, the daily patterns that include ordinary interactions are more significant than unique events. These patterned behaviors, which often occur in groups and institutions, form the social structure that allows a society to continue, even though its individual citizens die. Analyzing social structure, behavior in groups, and interactions among people and groups helps us understand the way people live in society.

Characteristics of Social Structure

Social structure refers to the way in which a society is organized into predictable relationships. A social structure consists of a network of lasting, orderly relationships among people. One way sociologists look at these relationships is in terms of statuses and roles.

What Is Status?

For sociologists, **status** describes an individual's position within a large group or society and the relation of that person to others in the group. Every member of the group has a status. Also, everyone belongs to many different groups, so we all have many statuses. As we move through life, our statuses change as the groups we belong to and our circumstances change. **EXAMPLE:** A new baby, while very much loved and treasured, is not regarded with respect, and we don't ask that baby for his or her opinion about where the family should go on vacation or anything else. *Baby* is the term that describes that individual's status in the family. His or her status will change with age. When grown, the adult has probably formed a new family and has a very different status from the baby, and such terms as *wife, husband,* and *parent* can describe the new status.

Sociologists often categorize statuses into **two** types, based on whether they are assigned by society or achieved by an individual.

1. **Ascribed statuses** are assigned to a person by society without regard for the individual's talents or abilities. A person's gender, race, and ethnicity can affect his or her status in the groups to which he or she belongs. So, as we've seen, can one's age.
   EXAMPLES: *Senior citizen* is a status that a person cannot change. So, too, are such statuses as *son, daughter, niece,* and the like. Ascribed statuses have significant social meanings in a culture: They often grant privileges to some and restrict privileges for others.

2. **Achieved statuses** come through traits, talents, actions, efforts, activities, and accomplishments.
   EXAMPLE: You have the status of *student.* If you take an after-school job, you will become an *employee,* a status gained through your own efforts. In simple, family-based societies, achieved statuses are limited: *warrior, farmer, magician, trading partner.* However, in a complex society such as ours, the list of achieved statuses is almost endless.

Status is a sign of our social structure. A status shows how people are related to each other, and we know what is expected of us when we recognize each other's status.

Master Status

When one status plays a major role in shaping a person's life, it is called a master status. For children and teenagers, master status is usually defined by age. For example, you are an "11th grader" or a "16-year-old." In addition, a master status could be "football player," "good history student," or "violinist." For adults, marital status, parenthood, economic resources, and employment may provide identity-defining statuses.

What Are Roles?

Do you behave the same way around your parents as when you are with your friends? You probably alter your behavior because you know that your parents expect certain things and your friends expect others. Every status carries with it socially defined **roles,** or expected behavior patterns.

Learning and Playing Roles

We learn how to perform roles by observing and interacting with others who already understand them. **EXAMPLE:** From the age of four or five, American children are taught the role behaviors associated with their status as students. They learn to raise their hands, walk down the hall, ask permission to go to the bathroom, do homework, and pay attention in class.

Every person plays many roles at any particular time in life, and roles change as statuses change.

Expectations and Performance

Think about the mothers you know. Do any two treat their children in exactly the same way? Almost certainly not. No two people who occupy the same status perform their roles identically. Instead, roles provide the script for individuals to express themselves in their own ways.

Role expectations are the behaviors expected of someone in a particular role. These expectations are determined by the society and are similar within a culture. In reality, people's *role performance* may vary widely, and may not match the behavior expected by society. Students do not always do their homework, and children do not always obey their parents. Parents, in turn, may mistreat or neglect their children.

Reciprocal Relationships

All roles have **reciprocal roles**, or roles that are part of the interaction between related statuses.

EXAMPLES: An employee has an employer, a parent has a child, a doctor has a patient, and a coach has athletes. No one can fulfill one role without the existence of the other.

Role Strain and Role Conflict

Even if you wanted to fulfill all the role expectations society places on you, it isn't always possible. **Role strain** may occur when conflicting demands are built into a role.

EXAMPLE: Employees of the National Park Service help visitors enjoy the natural beauty of the parks. They conduct tours, explain the plants and wildlife, and encourage people to explore nature. However, with increasing numbers of tourists visiting the parks, park employees must turn people away, prohibit them from taking their cars on park roads, and supervise their activities so that the ecosystem is not destroyed. Park employees, then, can feel role strain from carrying out these conflicting aspects of their job.

Role conflict occurs when incompatible expectations arise from two or more statuses held by the same person. Fulfillment

Policing the Police

Criminologist Aogan Mulcahy studied the role conflict experienced by internal affairs officers from police departments in four cities in the southwestern United States. These officers were responsible for investigating accusations of misconduct on the part of other officers. As a result, they experienced conflict between their roles as colleagues and as police inspectors. They reported being snubbed by other officers, who would avoid riding elevators or eating with them. Some reacted by going out of their way to compliment other officers on

their work, and others took pride in their belief that they were "real cops." In all cases, the internal affairs officers made special efforts to reduce the discomfort of their role conflict.

of the roles associated with one status may directly violate the roles linked to another. EXAMPLE: Soldiers may experience intense role conflict. Young men who have been brought up to feel that killing is wrong are expected to fire guns and activate missiles. The behaviors expected of them as good members of society are in conflict with those expected of them as military people.

Social Structures and Society

Every society has a structure or organization. In addition to the statuses people hold and the roles they play, the social structures of a society's institutions help define that society. Different types of societies have different statuses, structures, roles, and institutions for performing the functions that help people meet basic needs.

Social Functions

If they are to survive, societies must help their citizens by organizing basic functions, such as:

* *Arranging activities* so that people get the goods and services they need.
* *Protecting people* from external threats, such as attack from other countries, and internal threats, such as crime.
* *Replacing people* who die or migrate.
* *Transmitting knowledge* of statuses, roles, and norms to new members (immigrants and children).
* *Motivating people* to perform their roles by assigning meaning and purpose to social activities.

Social Institutions

All societies have **social institutions**, established patterns of beliefs and behaviors that meet basic social needs. Our social institutions are the ways we perform the social functions listed above. Social institutions vary according to the complexity of the society, but all societies have them.

* *Families* usually take responsibility for raising the young and teaching children about proper roles, statuses, and norms.
* *Education* in a complex society becomes an institution separate from the family, specializing in transmitting more advanced knowledge or helping students relate successfully to people and institutions outside the family.
* *Economic institutions* specialize in helping people obtain goods and services. In simple societies, they may be tied closely to family roles, with work activities different for men than for women.
* *Governments* run the affairs of a society, provide laws and justice, and meet a number of social needs that cannot be handled by families alone.
* *Military institutions* provide protection from groups outside the society and may also be used as a tool of a government's expansion plans.
* *Religious institutions* guide members in understanding the meaning of life.

Types of Societies

One way to identify and compare types of societies is to classify them according to how they use technology. Technology—the machines, equipment, and skills or techniques we work with—helps differentiate societies. We can organize societies from the simplest to the most complex. The simpler a society, the less division of labor or specialization of tasks. The more complex a society, the more specialized the occupations. Also, the more complex society has a greater reliance on a

Types of Societies			
	Hunting/Gathering	**Pastoral**	**Horticultural**
Relative Size	Small	Medium	Medium
Location and permanence	Small, widely dispersed groups continually move to seek and find resources.	Small groups of individuals move regularly to graze herds of animals.	Villages last at least a few years; people move frequently to fertile ground for growing crops.
Distinguishing product or achievement	Simple tools, baskets, pots, clothing, and dwellings made from plants, stones, animal skins, and bones.	Domesticated animals.	Food grown from crops; small permanent and semi-permanent villages.
Other features	Almost all group members are related; gender and kinship define authority and statuses; decisions are based on general agreement.	Kinship defines roles and status. Domesticated animals provide a steady source of food and materials for clothing and shelter. Group size increases. Priests and other leaders emerge.	Emerged 10,000 to 12,000 years ago; people stay in one area and trade with or make war on groups in other areas. Groups begin to include unrelated "strangers."

complicated technology that requires increasingly higher levels of education among its citizens to create and operate it.

Some types of societies are described in the following chart.

Agricultural	Industrial	Postindustrial
Larger	Largest	Largest
Permanent villages and cities are built, the largest in river valleys, whose flood waters provide fertile soil and whose currents provide a means of travel.	Nations are formed and in turn form alliances with other nations.	Postindustrial nations have global influence.
Cities, temples, plumbing, roads, defensive walls, writing, philosophy, history, literature.	Manufactured goods, electric power, cars, airplanes, TVs, telephones.	Production of information; service-oriented economies; nuclear power; space exploration.
Appeared about 5,000 years ago; developed governments, laws, economic systems, trade, religious institutions, armies, and written language. Populations number in the hundreds of thousands or more and include foreigners.	Began in the 1800s; standard of living rises enormously and rapidly; job specialization increases; warfare can be waged on a worldwide scale.	From the mid-1900s; services are emphasized over goods; science and education continue to improve standards of living; social groups cross national borders through increased communication technologies; warfare has the potential to destroy world civilization.

Gemeinschaft and Gesellschaft

In the late 19th century Ferdinand Tönnies, a German sociologist, classified societies into two basic types. *Gemeinschaft* means "community," and the *gemeinschaft* society is typical of rural life. People with similar backgrounds and life experiences live in small communities where almost everyone knows one another. Social interactions are intimate and familiar, and people are committed to and have a sense of belonging to the larger group. *Gesellschaft* means "society" or "association." The *gesellschaft* society is characteristic of modern urban life. Most people are strangers and have little in common with other members of the community. Relationships are based on practical tasks and are impersonal, such as that between a customer and a sales clerk or among business people at a company meeting. In such societies, Tönnies suggested, individual goals are more important than group goals.

The Nature of Groups

Groups and organizations are components of the overall social structure of all societies. In a hunting and gathering society, the most significant groups are bands—combinations of families that gather together seasonally to forage for foods. In contrast, postindustrial societies have a complex web of groups and organizations that support the overall social structure. For both types of society, groups are made up of people interacting with one another and with other groups.

What Are Groups?

For sociologists a **group** is any number of people with similar norms, values, and expectations who regularly interact. People in groups have interrelated statuses and roles.

The simplest of all social groups is a dyad, or a two-member group. A married couple is a dyad. Dyads generally allow the closest relationships. However, the group is destroyed when one member leaves. A triad, or three-member group, stays intact if it loses a member.

Generally, groups must be small enough for members to interact regularly in a direct and familiar way. As the size of a group grows, the nature of the interactions changes significantly. In a larger group, each member has less time to speak and must listen to more points of view.

..AND FURTHERMORE.... MY FELLOW SENATORS, WE MUST CON-TIN-YUH to BLAH... BLAH ... BLAH BLAHHH.. BLAH BLAH BLAH BLAH..

zzZzz... SNORRRK!

Characteristics of Groups

Groups may have different sizes, but they share **three** characteristics:

1. **Structured Interaction.** To be a group, people must form lasting, structured patterns of interactions. Group interactions are different from the interactions of **aggregates**—collections of people who just happen to be in the same place at the same time. People in an aggregate, such as patients in a doctor's waiting room, may make comments to one another, but they don't expect to gather again in the future. A group of people establishes *patterns* of interactions, so that even though they may not see one another for days or weeks, when they reassemble, they interact in familiar ways.

   EXAMPLES: Depending on the size and intimacy of the group, interaction may take many forms. In a close family, members often communicate nonverbally because they know one another so well. In an office with 30 employees, group members might interact through memos, meetings, and e-mail. In both cases, patterns of interaction are established.

2. **Common Goals and Norms.** Group members share common goals.

   EXAMPLES: A family goal may include having children who go to college. The school's French Club members may be working toward a trip to France. Professional organizations seek to establish standards for their members so that the reputation of all is protected.

Common Identities Among the Plains Indians

For hundreds of years, Native American tribes in the Central Plains of North America found various ways to forge common identities among their widely scattered members. Many formed "age sets" that included all the men born during a certain time. Each age set had distinctive dances, songs, possessions, and privileges. Members of each set pooled their wealth to buy admission to a higher level. For most Plains societies, an important step for boys was to gain warrior status as they became young men. Later, they played roles in government and eventually would become "elders" with special ritual responsibilities. Even though they lived in different villages or moved in separate bands, they were bound with a common identity at each stage of their lives.

Along with the common goals of group members are the common norms they share.

EXAMPLE: For a sports team, group norms probably include attending practice, working out, and cooperating with teammates.

No matter what goals and norms a group defines, they are commonly understood and supported by all group members. As groups grow larger, they generally develop **coalitions**, alliances of a few people within the group toward a common goal.

EXAMPLE: A city council is debating whether or not to allow a transmitting tower near a school building. Some council members may form an informal coalition to get the tower approved.

A coalition may become relatively permanent if the members share many similar goals over a period of time.

3. **Common Identity.** Members of a group share a sense of belonging that encourages a common identity.

EXAMPLE: College students who have left their families for the first time may join sororities and fraternities that provide new "sisters" and "brothers." They may announce their new identities by wearing shirts with the Greek symbols of their group.

A shared identity further separates a group from an aggregate. In an aggregate, no sense of belonging or common identity develops.

Relationships Within Groups

Groups help people meet their needs in many ways. Social relationships form within groups when the interaction among people continues long enough for a relatively stable set of social expectations to develop. These social relationships may be put into **two** categories:

1. **Instrumental Relationships** focus on accomplishing goals, and they are generally seen as means to an end.

2. **Expressive Relationships** are valued for their own sakes and have no goal beyond the pleasure each person takes in the relationship.

Most relationships that we have are both instrumental and expressive, and most groups combine elements of each.

How Do Groups Work?

There are many ways to study what groups do. Among them, sociologists have found it useful to look at how decisions are made within the group and at how leaders are chosen and how they behave.

Decision-making Processes

Groups develop decision-making processes that give them a life of their own. Generally, groups make decisions in one of **two** ways:

1. **Decisions Are Made by Nearly all Group Members Participating as Equals.** It is not usual for voting to take place. When a question comes up, the decision will be made after group discussion in which every member has a chance to speak.

Sociologist's Perspective

Sociograms

Sociologists sometimes try to understand how a group works by constructing a sociogram—a diagram that shows relationship patterns among group members. A sociogram is usually constructed by asking each member of a group to identify a "best friend" or the person with whom he or she would most like to do something, such as go to the movies or eat lunch. The results are collected and charted. Sociograms are helpful to sociologists in identifying group leaders, cliques (subgroups), and individuals who are isolated.

Alison, Kelly, and Sandy form a "clique." Michelle is not a member of Sandy's clique. Nicole is isolated. She knows Michelle and Alison but is not part of a group with either girl.

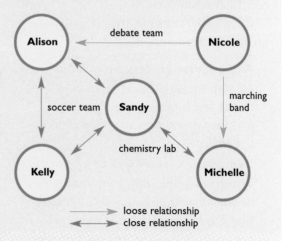

Discussion continues until most members can agree. The final decision is a group consensus.

2. **Decisions Are Made by One or Two Leaders.** Leaders may be elected or formally selected, but they often lead simply because the other members are willing to follow them. This willingness may be based on a judgment of the leader's ability or on an emotional response to some personality characteristic.

Leadership

When a group first forms, one or more central figures—or leaders—emerge fairly quickly. According to a study by R. F. Bales in 1951, a leader of a new group tends to be both the "best liked" and the one with the "best ideas." However, Bales's research showed that as a group develops, two types of leaders emerge: (1) the "best liked," or an emotional leader who helps keep the group solid and harmonious, and (2) an "idea" person who is practical and coordinates activities.

Once leaders emerge, they usually take on one of **three** leadership styles:

1. **Authoritarian Leaders** are suited to accomplishing tasks. They value efficiency and time-saving techniques, and they give orders that they expect to be obeyed.

2. **Democratic Leaders** seek to forge agreement within the group through discussion and give-and-take interaction. Democratic leaders are generally not as efficient as authoritarian leaders.

3. **Laissez-faire Leaders** adopt a "hands-off" approach and make little or no attempt to organize members or to coordinate decision making. This leadership style is usually the least effective because most groups need at least some direction and guidance.

No one leadership style is always best. In some circumstances, saving time and being efficient are very important, and in others, consulting all members of the group may take priority.

EXAMPLES: If a group is under immediate attack by an enemy, people need to act quickly, and they generally respond best to a leader who barks clear, concise orders. On the other hand, a group engaged in a neighborhood clean-up project probably will respond better to democratic leadership and decision making.

Types of Groups

Sociologists distinguish among types of groups: primary and secondary groups, in-groups and out-groups, and reference groups. The picture opposite illustrates the type of groups described below.

Primary and Secondary Groups

Groups may be categorized based on the nature of the relationships that exist within them. **Primary groups** are based on intimate, face-to-face association and cooperation. People usually identify closely with their primary groups, such as family, close friends, or business partners. The relationships last for a long time and usually have emotional depth.

Types of Groups

Secondary Group

Primary Group

In-Group

Out-Group

Reference Group

High School In-Groups and Out-Groups

The tendency to see in-groups in a more positive light than out-groups often leads people to believe that their in-groups are superior. Since one person's in-group is another person's out-group, conflict is bound to occur. The conflict may be mild and relatively harmless, such as when school grade levels compete at a pep rally to see who can show the most support for sports teams.

However, when some students identify the out-groups of others negatively, such as "jocks," "nerds," or "eggheads," the members of those groups understandably develop feelings of resentment. Sometimes such feelings can erupt in violence. It has been suggested that some school shootings—such as the one at Columbine High School in 1999—are the result of conflicts between in-groups and out-groups.

Secondary groups, on the other hand, are formal, impersonal groups in which there is little social intimacy or mutual understanding. They are usually larger than primary groups or of shorter duration. Social relationships are generally superficial.

Group relationships are usually "more or less" primary or secondary, not absolutely so. Secondary groups can change into primary groups, and vice versa. For example, groups in the workplace are often secondary, but primary relations can develop within them. If the work group is stable over time, it may evolve into a primary group.

In-groups and Out-groups

An in-group is any group to which people feel they belong. The in-group may be as narrow as one's family ("We" went on vacation last summer), or as broad as a nation ("We" defeated the Germans in World War II). The existence of an in-group means that an out-group also exists— a group referred to as " they" or "them." People tend to see the world in terms of out-groups and in-groups.

Reference Groups

Sociologists use the term **reference group** to refer to any group that individuals use as a standard for evaluating themselves. Reference groups are not always groups to which we belong. For example, high school students may model their behavior on that of a group they would like to join. The reference group's influence may be so strong that a student will begin behaving like its members.

Reference groups play major roles in shaping our opinions of ourselves. For example, a beautiful girl may consider herself to be ugly because she compares herself to much-admired movie stars. Reference groups change as people get older and life circumstances change. When young people go to college, their reference groups usually shift from people they knew in high school and their neighborhoods to people they encounter in college.

Conforming to Group Judgments

How many of us will follow our convictions in the face of opposing opinions? Solomon Asch (1951) was interested in the effects of group pressure on people's opinions and tested this question in a famous experiment. He brought groups of seven to nine male college students into a classroom and asked them to look at two white cards, one with a single line and one with three lines of different lengths. All students had to identify out loud which line on the second card was the same length as the line on the first card. The trick was that all but one of the students were in league with the researchers and had been coached to select the wrong answers. The uncoached student was always asked for his answer after almost everyone else had answered.

Even though the answers were obviously wrong, more than one third of the time the uncoached students did not trust their own eyesight and went along with the group. A tally of all of the students tested showed 37 percent agreed with the false judgments of the group. When the subjects were asked to judge the length of the lines away from the influence of the group, they made errors only 1 percent of the time.

Formal Organizations

When secondary groups become large and complex, sociologists call them **formal organizations**. These groups are deliberately created to achieve specific goals, and their members work together to support their objectives.

Voluntary Associations and Bureaucracies

Organizations take many shapes and forms. Some are **voluntary associations**, such as sports teams, hobby clubs, and charitable organizations. Some voluntary associations are informal, in that they rely on voluntary participation and contributions and may have few or no written rules.

Nearly all of the formal organizations sociologists study, however, are **bureaucracies**—large, hierarchical organizations. The members of a bureaucracy work for hire. Virtually all large companies are bureaucracies, as are most modern governments.

Weber's Model

Max Weber was one of the first sociologists to think about the concept of bureaucracy. He wrote in Germany during the early 20th century, when capitalism was spawning more and more large businesses. Weber saw bureaucracy as a sensible way for complex businesses and governments to organize. Bureaucracies, Weber said, are set up to achieve specific goals. A bureaucracy's members have assigned tasks (a division of labor) that are narrowly defined. For example, one office worker may handle only letters of complaint, another only letters requesting information.

According to Weber, bureaucracies have the following characteristics:

* *A hierarchical chain of command;* the top bureaucrat has ultimate control, and authority flows from the top down.
* *A clear division of labor* in which every individual has a specialized job.

Did You Know?

Red Tape

The term *bureaucracy* often brings to mind long rows of identical desks staffed by people working with identical equipment, endless forms and procedures, and a special, complex vocabulary. The term *red tape* describes some of the hassles that people experience in dealing with large organizations: standing in long lines to get paperwork done, being transferred from one office to another when trying to get information, having to fill out long forms. This term comes from the ribbon that English civil servants once used to tie up and bind legal documents.

* *Clearly written, well-established, formal rules* that all people in the organization follow.
* *A clearly defined set of goals* that all people in the organization strive toward.
* *Merit-based hiring and promotion;* no granting of jobs to friends or family unless they are the best qualified.
* *Job performance that is judged by productivity,* or how much work the individual gets done.

Weber's characterization was intended to sharply distinguish the bureaucracy from more informal types of social organizations, such as primary groups. Weber's features of bureaucracies make up an ideal type that serves as a model to measure characteristics of actual organizations. The more an organization conforms to the model, the more it can be regarded as a bureaucracy.

The Value of Bureaucracies

Max Weber saw value in the ability of bureaucracies to reach their goals with speed and efficiency. Other sociologists have suggested that bureaucracies are the best way to organize large numbers of people to achieve broad, large-scale goals, such as the mass production of goods at reasonable prices. Bureaucracies provide order by clearly defining job responsibilities and rewards. Bureaucracies also provide social stability, because the organization goes on when individuals leave.

The Problems of Bureaucracies

In spite of their values, bureaucracies are widely criticized. Many critics say that bureaucrats, the people who work in bureaucracies, tend to lose sight of the organization's purpose. They develop rituals that follow written rules and regulations, and thus creativity in the organization is squelched. Critics decry the "red tape" that results because each worker has such a limited knowledge of the overall workings of the bureaucracy, he or she can't really help the customer (or citizen) who is trying to get a response to even the simplest request.

Sociologists have developed several principles or rules to describe the operation of bureaucracies and the interactions

"Just take a seat until one of our agents is available to mire you hopelessly in paperwork."

of people within them. **Three** of these rules or principles are very critical of bureaucracies.

1. **The Peter Principle.** Laurence Peter states that "in a hierarchy, every employee tends to rise to his or her level of incompetence." Peter argues that people who do good work at one bureaucratic level are likely to be promoted to the next level. They continue to be promoted until they do not do good work. This process leaves people working beyond their level of competence.

2. **The Iron Law of Oligarchy.** This rule, developed by sociologist Robert Michels, describes the tendency of bureaucracies to result in oligarchies, or concentration of power in a few people at the top of a hierarchy. Orders flow from the top down, so most people in the hierarchy have no say in how things are run. Those who have power use it to promote their own interests over the interests of the organization. Decisions are made far from the place in the organization where problems occur, and those with hands-on knowledge are often left out of problem-solving activities.

3. **Parkinson's Law.** This law says "work expands to fill the time available for its completion." The criticism is that bureaucracies are inefficient, as bureaucrats waste time doing jobs that do not need to be done.

As a result of these criticisms, large business, government, and not-for-profit organizations have hired sociologists to work with them to overcome some of these problems. Sociologists and other business consultants encourage business leaders to "empower" their employees to solve problems where they occur, to break down hierarchical structures in favor of more democratic ones, and to include employees in writing mission statements for their organizations and in setting their own objectives for their work.

Interaction

We have examined the overall social structures of societies and their component parts—groups and organizations. The smallest and most intimate level of social structures is that of **social interaction**, the way in which people respond to one another. Whenever people take one another into account in what they do, they are engaged in some kind of social interaction.

Symbolic Interactionism

Symbolic interactionism is a kind of interactionist perspective. It stresses the meaning that social interactions have for individuals and groups and how those interactions help them interpret the world. Symbolic interactionists emphasize the influence that particular situations have on social behavior. They argue that when two people meet, they constantly evaluate each other's behavior and react accordingly.

Social interaction is a very delicate and complex process.

George Herbert Mead, an early-20th-century U.S. sociologist, is widely regarded as the founder of the interactionist perspective. Mead was interested in observing the most minute forms of communication—head nodding, smiles, frowns—and in understanding how such individual behavior was influenced by the larger context of a group or society. Although Mead never published a book, his students at the University of Chicago edited volumes of his lectures and published them after his death.

Two Approaches to Social Interaction

Once Mead's teachings became known, other sociologists began to focus carefully on social interaction that occurs in small groups. Sociologists Erving Goffman and Harold Garfinkel provide us with two distinctive methods of studying social interaction.

1. **Goffman's Dramaturgy.** Goffman theorized that many of our daily activities might be explained as self-conscious efforts to control the impression we make on others. His method is known

U.S. Culture Connection

Kissing as Dramaturgy

At the beginning of a romance, impressions are very important. Dramaturgy often governs social interactions at this stage. In the novel *The Bell Jar*, author Sylvia Plath describes a shy, studious girl's nonchalant reaction to her first kiss.

"While he kissed me, I kept my eyes open and tried to memorize the spacing of the house lights so I would never forget them.

"Finally, Buddy stepped back. 'I guess you go out with a lot of boys,' Buddy said.

"Well, I guess I do. . .

"'Well, I have to study a lot.'

"So do I, I put in hastily. I have to keep my scholarship after all. Still, I think I could manage to see you every third weekend.

"I was almost fainting and dying to get back to college and tell everybody."

as dramaturgy, which compares every-day life to the setting of the theater and stage. Just as actors project certain images, all of us seek to present particular features of our personalities while we hide other qualities. So, in class you may project a serious image; at a party, you might try to look relaxed and friendly.

2. **Garfinkel's Ethnomethodology.** Ethnomethodology is a social interaction theory that focuses on the rules underlying ordinary activities. For ethnomethodologists, the central task of sociology is to study the process by which members of a society construct meaning and rules. In the 1960s, Garfinkel devised a technique for uncovering rules. His method is based on the premise that by *breaking* rules and interpreting reactions, we can better understand the rules' importance.

EXAMPLE: In one experiment, Garfinkel asked students to pretend to be guests when they went home to their families—addressing a father as "Mr. Smith"

Forms of Social Interaction

	Exchange	Competition
Description and kinds of rules	Interactions are based on reciprocity, give and take, shared values and trust; rules are informal.	Groups or individuals oppose each other to reach a goal that only one can achieve; rules agreed to in advance govern the interaction.
Examples	Greetings, taking turns in conversation, making and keeping dates.	Sports events, college admissions, winning customers.
Pros	Through repetition of rewarding exchanges, relationships are built and maintained.	Groups are motivated to accomplish their goals, and group unity is achieved.
Cons	Uneven exchange may cause one party to quit.	Can produce stress; lack of cooperation or inequality among group members can keep group from winning.

or not speaking until spoken to.
Of 49 families, 46 were upset with the student and tried to restore family relations. This reaction suggested that the role of "child" in the family was very important. In other experiments students broke other norms, for instance, asking "What do you mean?" to a simple statement like, "I had a flat tire." Each violation of the rules of interaction produced confusion and often anxiety and anger.

Forms of Social Interaction

Like statuses, roles, groups, and institutions, regular patterns of interaction are a part of a social structure. The most common forms of social interaction are:

* Exchange.
* Competition.
* Conflict.
* Cooperation.
* Accommodation.

These are described in the chart below.

Conflict	Cooperation	Accommodation
Groups attempt to control each other by force; rules don't exist, are minimal, or are ignored.	Groups join forces to reach a common goal; rules can be built into a process.	Cooperation and conflict are balanced; rules include negotiation and compromise and may include mediation and arbitration.
Fights between gangs, wars, legal disputes, some arguments.	Workers building a house, city dwellers pulling together after a disaster.	Workers' strikes and labor negotiations, truces between nations, compromises.
Solidarity and cooperation within the group are strengthened; hidden problems may be highlighted, leading to social change.	Jobs get done, rewards are shared.	A difficult goal is achieved and conflict ends, at least temporarily.
Chaos, suffering, destruction of lives and property result.	Lack of individual achievement may bother some.	Difficult to achieve; if resolution is not balanced, conflict may break out again.

Networking and Technology

Advances in technology are creating new types of social networking. We don't need face-to-face contact for knowledge sharing anymore. Whether we are looking for jobs or for companionship, we can network through our computers. Electronic job boards, e-mail, and chat groups are all examples of new ways to network. The Internet and other technological changes have profound implications for social networking. No longer are people bound by geography and social circumstance to find their contacts.

Social Networks

All people in a society are linked to many groups through a variety of social interactions. We all know people in different social circles, and these people broaden our contacts outside our immediate primary and secondary groups. This connection is known as a **social network**, a series of social relationships that link a person directly to others and, as a result, indirectly to still more people. Social networks may limit interactions by including some and excluding others, but they also may broaden an individual's contacts with other people and resources.

You may have heard of "networking" in connection with finding employment. **EXAMPLE:** You might look for a summer job by asking your best friend's father if his firm is hiring summer employees.

Networking is a good thing for the person who gets a job. It is also good for the company looking to attract bright, talented young people to its ranks. But people without good connections may feel the system is unfair.

The structure of a society can be understood as relationships among people and groups. Every person has several statuses, plays multiple roles, and is a member of various groups.

Social institutions organize the functions of a society to meet the needs of its citizens. Different types of societies can be described by how their members carry out basic functions.

Groups afford their members structured interactions, common goals and norms, and shared identity. Different groups have different methods of making decisions and function best with different kinds of leadership. Each person is a member of primary and secondary groups, in-groups and out-groups, and reference groups. Some groups are formal organizations, and some of these are bureaucracies.

Interaction among individuals is generally studied by sociologists using the interactionist perspective. Interaction among groups can take the form of exchange, competition, conflict, cooperation, or accommodation. Social networks encourage interaction among people connected to each other through various groups.

Sociology

achieved status—position that comes through the traits, talents, actions, efforts, activities, and accomplishments of an individual. *p. 44*

aggregate—collection of people who just happen to be in the same place at the same time and do not have a lasting pattern of interaction. *p. 51*

ascribed status—position assigned to a person by society for reasons unrelated to the individual's unique talents or abilities. *p. 44*

bureaucracy—large, hierarchical organization of employees in which each member has an assigned task. *p. 58*

coalition—alliance of a few members within a group to achieve a common goal. *p. 52*

formal organization—impersonal, large group deliberately created to achieve specific goals. *p. 58*

group—two or more people with similar norms, values, and expectations who regularly interact. *p. 50*

more Sociology Words to Know

primary group—group based on intimate, face-to-face association and cooperation. *p. 54*

reciprocal roles—corresponding roles, such as husband/wife or doctor/patient, that define the patterns of interaction between related statuses. *p. 46*

reference group—group that individuals use as a standard for evaluating themselves. *p. 57*

role conflict—friction caused when two or more statuses held by the same person have incompatible expectations. *p. 46*

role strain—friction caused when conflicting demands are built into a role. *p. 46*

roles—expected behavior patterns that people exhibit in relation to a group or to society. *p. 45*

secondary group—formal, impersonal, often temporary group in which there is little social intimacy. *p. 56*

social institution—established pattern of beliefs and behaviors that meets basic social needs. *p. 47*

social interaction—way in which people respond to one another. *p. 60*

social network—series of social relationships that link a person directly to others and, as a result, indirectly to still more people. *p. 64*

social structure—way in which a society is organized into predictable relationships. *p. 44*

status—position or social standing of an individual within a group or society. *p. 44*

voluntary association—relatively informal organization based on voluntary membership. *p. 58*

CHAPTER 4

Socialization

In this chapter, you will learn about:

- the socialization process
- agents of socialization in childhood
- socialization throughout life

Have you ever observed a newborn baby? If so, perhaps it occurred to you that the creature before your eyes was like nothing else you had ever seen. Your reaction would be correct—newborns have little resemblance to the babies they become six months later or the children they develop into by the age of three. Human newborns are wholly dependent on adults for their survival.

Humans gain their independence only after a long childhood and a great deal of learning. We have much to learn—the values, beliefs, and norms of our society, the physical, mental, and social skills we'll need, and how to perform the roles society expects of us. Personality development leads to a sense of self, which changes throughout life—in childhood, in adolescence, in adulthood, and even at the end of our lives.

The Socialization Process

The special kind of learning that sociologists call **socialization** is the process by which we learn to become members of society. We do this as we make the rules and norms of the society our own and learn to perform our social roles, guided by the expectations of others. Socialization is a lifelong process; however, it is most intense during childhood. Our first socialization experiences, usually with immediate family members, shape our personalities and teach us the skills for survival.

Personality Development

Personality includes all the relatively stable patterns of thinking, feeling, and acting that distinguish one individual from another. The socialization process helps shape an individual's personality. During childhood, people experience rapid physical, emotional, and intellectual growth. However, personality development continues throughout life. Many traits remain the same as a person ages.

Heredity and Environment

Is an individual's personality shaped primarily by heredity or by the environment

---

Did You Know?

The Importance of Language

Other species have ways of communicating, but they do not have the intellectual ability to create and use the complicated set of symbols necessary for human language. Dogs may bark to go out or sit in response to a hand signal, but we can't teach them to read and write. Porpoises appear to contact one another with different sounds, but even the most admiring researchers can't compare their communication system to human language. Since language is the chief medium of human learning, the socialization process would be impossible without it.

in which he or she grows up? This question has been the subject of much debate. **EXAMPLE:** During the 19th century, researchers reacted to Charles Darwin's theory of natural selection by emphasizing **instincts**, or inherited behavior patterns. The "herding instinct" was used to explain the fact that people live in communities, and the "maternal instinct" explained mothering.

EXAMPLE: Late in the 19th century, a Russian physiologist named Ivan Pavlov conducted an experiment with dogs that illustrated how learning could affect instincts. Pavlov showed that a dog could learn to associate the ringing of a bell with food and to salivate whenever it heard the bell, whether or not it saw food at the same time.

Over the next few decades, some researchers discounted heredity totally, claiming that environment alone shapes infants.

EXAMPLE: The American psychologist John B. Watson claimed that he could train an infant to become anything he wanted— artist, lawyer, or thief—no matter what the child's ability or ancestry.

Today, most social scientists believe that both heredity and the environment shape human personality. One area of study is particularly interested in this relationship. **Sociobiology** is the study of the biological bases of social behavior. It assumes that particular forms of behavior become genetically linked to a species if they contribute to the species' fitness to survive. Sociobiologists place a strong emphasis on the biological basis of human behavior. For them, even such varied cultural behaviors as ways of practicing religion or choosing mates are determined by biological factors.

Birth Order

How much do brothers and sisters affect your personality? Does it matter if you are an only child or an oldest, middle, or youngest child? Research indicates that **birth order** does shape children's personalities.

* *Only Children* appear to endure much pressure to achieve and excel. As a result, they tend to be overactive, seeking to be involved socially, especially in leadership roles. They also tend to worry more than children with siblings (brothers and sisters) about almost everything.
* *Oldest Children* have many traits of only children, since they had no siblings until the second child was born.

Research indicates that firstborn children are more likely to be cooperative, cautious, and achievement-oriented than their siblings.

* *Later Children* tend to be better in social relationships and to be more affectionate, friendly, and creative than their siblings. They may not be as driven to achieve as the oldest child, but they may gain recognition for their sensitivity and sense of humor.

Sociologist's Perspective

Anna of the Attic

What would children be like if they had no socialization experience? For obvious reasons, researchers don't usually experiment with isolating children, but occasionally a case is found in which a child is raised in near-total isolation. Such a case was "Anna of the Attic." Anna was an illegitimate child whose unwed mother put her in an attic room in order to escape the violent disapproval of Anna's grandfather, who refused to acknowledge her existence. Anna remained in the attic for nearly six years, ignored by her mother, except for being fed just enough to keep her alive.

When social workers discovered Anna, she was little more than a skeleton and could not sit up, walk, or talk. She made progress once she was placed in a special school, but she never behaved normally in the four and a half years between the time she was discovered and her premature death. Sociologist Kingsley Davis concluded from his observations of Anna that very little human behavior arises spontaneously.

Parents

For most children, the first attachment is to the mother. Researchers believe that this vital connection begins before birth, and that after a baby is born, he or she wants to stay close to the mother. Psychologist Lee Salk found that if the rhythm of the mother's heartbeat is continued, the child seems more secure. When a recording of a mother's heartbeat (as heard in the womb) was played in a nursery of newborns, the babies cried less, breathed better, and rested more calmly. Of course, fathers play an early role in their children's development as they hold and care for them. Later, both parents serve as role models who shape children's perceptions of sex roles and family membership.

Influence of the Culture

Cultures shape the development of children's personalities. A society's cultural environment may determine which personality traits are emphasized. For example, modern U.S. culture encourages competitiveness and friendliness.

The Sense of Self

One of the most important results of early childhood socialization is the development of the sense of self. For the first month or two of life, babies don't know the difference between their own bodies and actions and the people and objects around them. They cry in reaction to such physical stimuli as hunger, wetness, or cold. At some point, babies realize that they make the noise and that they can control their voices and actions. The sense of self—the conscious perception of one's identity as distinct from others—develops gradually during childhood and changes throughout life.

Many sociologists and psychologists have studied the development of self. Each has a different point of view, but taken collectively, their theories help us understand how the socialization process shapes the sense of self.

Locke's Tabula Rasa

The 17th-century English philosopher John Locke believed that human babies are shaped by socialization to be good or bad, optimistic or pessimistic, generous or selfish. For Locke, each child is born a *tabula rasa* (Latin for "blank slate") that will accept just about any writing. Children have no personalities at birth, but acquire them through social experiences. Locke's view is generally *not* accepted today because most researchers believe that biology and such factors as birth order play some role in personality development.

Cooley's Looking-Glass Self

In the early 1900s, social psychologist Charles Horton Cooley proposed that we learn who we are by interacting with others. Our view of ourselves, then, comes from our impressions of how others perceive us. Cooley used the phrase **looking-glass self** to describe the self as developed by our social interactions with other people. According to Cooley, the development of a self-identity or self-concept is a **three**-step process:

1. You imagine how you appear to others—family members, friends, even strangers.

2. You then imagine how others judge you. Do they think you are friendly or aloof? Fat or skinny? Smart or not? Attractive or ugly?

3. You use these perceptions of others' judgments to develop feelings about yourself. You may develop a sense of self-respect or a sense of shame, a sense of confidence or a sense of inadequacy, depending on your idea of how others judge you.

This combination of feelings becomes your sense of self.

One thing to notice about Cooley's theory is that the sense of self results from how a person "imagines" he or she looks to others. That imagination may be incorrect, and so we may develop our self-concepts based on reactions that don't really exist. For example, you may believe your friends think that you are not very much fun to be around. Even if it is not true, you may come to see yourself as a boring person. However, you may adjust your self-view based on another set of interactions, so that you come to see yourself as boring to some people but not to others.

Mead's Role Taking

Like Cooley, American sociologist George Herbert Mead based his role-taking theory on how social interactions shape personality. According to Mead, the self emerges in **three** distinct phases:

1. **The Preparatory Stage,** in which children merely imitate the people around them, particularly family members. A child may sweep the floor with his or her own tiny broom, or may wheel a personal, pint-size suitcase through an airport, following Mom's or Dad's model.

2. **The Play Stage** (around the age of three), in which children develop skills in using symbols—gestures, objects, and language that form the basis of human communication. In this stage, the child develops the ability to pretend to be

other people, a process known as **role taking** . The child no longer just imitates, but actually pretends to be someone else—a parent, a cartoon character, or a fairy princess.

3. **The Game Stage** (around the age of eight or nine), in which children learn to respond to and understand the roles that others around them take. Not only do they play roles themselves, they understand that others around them take roles as well. For example, a child of eight or nine is able to play a game of baseball and understand that one person is playing the pitcher, another an umpire, and another the batter. In this stage, children respond to many people and are capable of understanding a wider social context.

Mead divides the sense of self into two parts, the "I" and the "me." The "I" is the unsocialized, self-interested part on which children under three rely almost totally.

"Oh, yes, indeed. We all keep a sharp eye out for those little clues that seem to whisper 'law' or 'medicine.'"

Did You Know?

"Significant Others"

The phrase "significant others," commonly used today to refer to important people in our lives, is derived from Mead's theory of role taking. Harry Stack Sullivan coined the term to refer to the first people a child imitates and eventually pretends to be, usually family members and close friends.

During the play stage, children begin to develop the "me," the part that is aware of other people's expectations and attitudes—the socialized self.

Freud's Unconscious and Conscious Minds

Have you ever commented that someone you know has a big "ego"? If so, you were borrowing from the theory of one of the most famous people in recent history: Sigmund Freud. Freud originated **psychoanalysis**, a theory holding that unconscious childhood experiences and instinct-based drives largely shape personality and behavior. Freud saw much less harmony between the individual and society than did Cooley and Mead.

Instead Freud believed that **three** parts of personality were continually at war:

1. **The Id** represents the most primitive and selfish part of human personality. Infants are born with an id that demands immediate fulfillment of biological needs. For example, the id controls hunger and physical discomfort, and a baby reacts to those stimuli almost instinctively.

2. **The Superego,** or conscience, develops as a child goes through the socialization process. The superego is the internalized voice of society that has the job of telling the id "no."

3. **The Ego,** according to Freud, develops last. It attempts to mediate between the selfish id and the societal demands of the superego. By trying to satisfy the id in a socially acceptable way, the ego becomes the heart of the personality, the acting self. Freud's writings reflect his belief that the ego's job is impossible, so constant conflict characterizes human personality.

Piaget's Stages of Cognitive Development

The changes over time in the way we think, learn, reason, and acquire language take place in a process known as **cognitive development**. Psychologist Jean Piaget recognized **four** stages through which children go as they mature:

1. **Stage 1.** This first stage involves acquiring *motor intelligence*. A child from birth to about two years old begins to develop motor and sensory skills, such as moving hands to reach an object, coordinating body parts to crawl and then walk, and developing taste preferences for food. In this stage, babies learn to distinguish hands, feet, and other body parts as part of themselves, distinct from all other objects.

RESEARCH

Moral Development

Suppose a boy is dying of a disease that can only be cured by medical procedures his parents cannot afford. In desperation, the child's father robs a store in order to save his son's life. Is his action right or wrong? Researcher Lawrence Kohlberg studied children's reactions to such moral dilemmas and concluded that a sense of morality develops in stages as children grow up.

At first, children do as they are told, mainly because they fear punishment. Next, they begin to realize that good behavior brings rewards. They become increasingly aware of the opinions of others and gradually develop ideas about right and wrong. Then, as children begin to listen to ideas that differ from their own, they start to recognize moral conflicts. For example, they might understand why the boy's father would steal, but they realize what a problem it would be if everybody decided to steal. Eventually, children become self-directed and develop universal principles of justice that may be applied to everyone.

2. **Stage 2.** During the second, or *preoperational*, stage, children begin to use words and symbols to describe objects or ideas. Between the ages of two and seven, children learn to communicate with other people, but they are still self-centered and unable to adopt the points of view of others. Children in this stage cannot yet understand volume, speed, or weight.

3. **Stage 3.** From seven to twelve, the intellect develops swiftly. Piaget called this the *concrete operational stage*. Abstract concepts such as love and death only have meaning in terms of specific "concrete" references, such as "Love is hugging Daddy and Mommy."

4. **Stage 4.** During the *formal operational stage* of adolescence, individuals begin to think abstractly and so are able to think about theories and questions of morality. In school, they are able to learn complex mathematical operations and understand the differences between two ideologies, such as capitalism and communism. They are able to reflect on their self-images and future hopes.

Agents of Childhood Socialization

A mother teaches her four-year-old son to dress himself. A father helps his daughter balance on a bicycle before setting her free to ride. These ordinary situations demonstrate the importance of **agents of socialization**—individuals or institutions that teach a society's culture.

Agents of Childhood Socialization			
	Main Task	**Level and Kind**	**Key Areas of Influence**
Family	Transmits attitudes, values, and norms.	*Strong, decisive* * verbal and nonverbal. * intentional and unintentional.	Gender roles. Love and affection. Political views. Religious practices. Marriage and parenthood.
Schools and Daycare Centers	Transmit knowledge and life skills.	*Significant* * intentional via curriculum. * unintentional via teacher behavior and attitudes.	Adult authority. Peer relationships. Workings of impersonal organizations.
Peer Groups	Transmit how to behave in voluntary relationships.	*Grows stronger with age* * indirect. * frequent.	Friendship. Playmates. Business relationships.
Mass Media	Transmit societal attitudes, values, and norms. Provide information of all kinds.	*Debated* * unintentional, but children spend more time in front of television than in school classes. * intentional in some programming, unintentional in others.	Attitudes about politics. Styles, fads, product brands. Social expectations regarding families and right and wrong behavior. Attitudes toward violence and vice.

The lifelong socialization process involves many different agents, as shown in the chart on page 76. The family is the principal agent of socialization for children.

Gender Roles in the South Pacific

Anthropologist Margaret Mead's study of three tribes in the South Pacific is a landmark analysis of cross-cultural gender roles. Mead lived with the Arapesh, the Mundugumor, and the Tchambuli. She found among the Arapesh that both men and women were loving, considerate, and cooperative. Both tended children and were responsible for food. The Mundugumor men and women, in contrast, were usually ruthless and violent toward each other. Among the Tchambuli, the women dominated the men, provided for their families, and were indifferent to their families. The men cared for the children and were more emotional. Mead concluded from her studies that masculine and feminine roles are taught by culture, not inherited.

Socialization Throughout Life

As we move through the different stages of life, we are socialized to new roles.

Adolescence

In preindustrial societies, children go right into adulthood through a ritual known as a *rite of passage*. For example, among the Kota people of the African Congo, adolescent boys paint themselves blue—the color of death—to symbolize the death of childhood. Among the Cheyenne Indians, marks are made on a girl's body to announce that she has become a woman. Fifteen- and sixteen-year-olds have children, take other responsibilities, and are fully accepted as adults.

Most teenagers in the United States, however, are not children anymore, but they are not yet adults. You are in a stage "in between" called **adolescence**, a status that exists only in industrial and postindustrial societies. The stage of adolescence exists primarily because complex societies need a highly trained and educated labor force. Education takes a long time, so we have a long period of adolescence that lasts through high school and college, and sometimes beyond.

Adolescents are physically adults, but they are not allowed to take on many adult roles, such as voting or going to war. This time "in between" is characterized by the heightened importance of peers, increasing levels of responsibility, a search for identity, and conflicting pressures and concerns.

Importance of Peers

The importance of peer groups increases as children grow older, reaching its peak when they become adolescents. While adults are eager to socialize a new generation to accept adult roles, adolescents are determined to gain independence from adults. Since adolescents realize that they must eventually become independent adults, they must shed the dependence characteristic of childhood. As adolescents begin the difficult process of gaining independence from their families, they turn to peers for guidance. The reactions of friends are more important to teenagers than those of parents, teachers, and other adults.

Adolescents tend to spend a great deal of time in tight-knit groups that provide strong emotional support. As they put distance between themselves and their families, they replace the old ties with ties to their new group of friends. Together

friends face the insecurity and uncertainty of being an "in between." They share secrets, listen to music together, and often annoy parents with long phone conversations. It's all a part of understanding their changing roles and finding new identities.

Increased Responsibility

The gradual transition from childhood to adulthood means that adolescents shoulder more adult responsibilities as they go through their teens. In U.S. society, most people learn to drive a car during adolescence. The day a teenager gets his or her driver's license is a watershed event in reaching adult independence. At home, parents may require their teens to baby-sit younger brothers and sisters, or they may help them set up their own bank accounts. As students, adolescents acquire knowledge and skills necessary for adulthood.

As high school graduation approaches, most teenagers make postgraduation plans for work or college. At the age of 18, they are able to vote, a major step toward civic maturity. Much socialization during adolescence is *anticipatory*—it prepares young people for the time to come when they are truly independent.

Search for Identity

As children, most of us get our sense of who we are from our families. We get a sense of place from our homes, and our dependence on our parents is almost complete. As we approach adolescence, we base more and more of our behavior on our peer groups. This dramatic shift understandably makes the question "Who am I?" a central one to teens. The redefinition of self often takes many turns during the teenage years, including changing dreams and aspirations. "What do I want to do when I grow up?" "How can I relate to peers in friendships and in love relationships?" The growing sense of identity defines how we feel about ourselves in adulthood.

Pressures and Concerns

Any transitional period in life is stressful, and adolescence is no exception. The fact that adolescence is spread over several years makes it especially difficult for many people. Peer pressure can encourage teenagers to make decisions about personal behavior that they later regret. Increasing responsibility brings new challenges and potential embarrassments. For example, a teenager may ask, "What if I fail my driver's test?" "What if I can't get into such and such a college?" Everyone will know!

Early and Middle Adulthood

All the socialization of childhood and adolescence pays off for people in many ways. For example, growing up in families prepares them to have families of their

U.S. Culture Connection

La Quinceañera: A Rite of Passage

Rites of passage are usually associated with simple or primitive societies, but modern societies have many rituals, such as graduations, debutante balls, or bar mitzvahs, that mark the end of childhood. In one example, Cuban-American girls mark the transition to womanhood at age 15 through a ceremony known as the *quinceañera*. Although ceremonies vary, the girls typically participate in a religious retreat, a church mass, and an elaborate dance or cotillion. In Miami, the popularity of the *quinceañera* supports a network of party planners, caterers, and dress shops and the Miss Quinceañera Latina pageant.

own. Learning to read and write, to be law-abiding citizens, and to follow basic societal norms certainly helps adults cope with their lives.

However, no early socialization pattern can fully prepare a person for adulthood, partly because anticipating adult roles is not the same as actually taking them on. Parents may provide models for marriage relationships, but the experience of actually being married is different from what most young people ever imagine. Also, times change. Much adult socialization takes the form of **resocialization**—altering what we have learned earlier and learning new kinds of appropriate behavior.

Male and Female Life Patterns

As 21st-century Americans, we are taught to equally value the roles and statuses of men and women. Young women today have many of the same opportunities at work as men, and many fathers have taken more and more responsibilities at home. Nonetheless, men and women have somewhat different experiences as they go through early and middle adulthood. Psychologists Daniel Levinson and Irene Frieze point out some of those differences in their studies of the stages of adult development.

Daniel Levinson outlines **three** developmental stages for males in early and mid-adulthood:

1. **The Novice Phase.** From 17 to 32, men go through the ups and downs of first experiences with the adult world. They must leave home and achieve psycho-logical and economic independence. Next, they deal with the contradictory expectations to explore new options—both in personal relationships and in the workplace—and to "settle down" to become responsible members of society. Finally, they must take stock of early decisions that they made and gear themselves up to "make it" in the adult world. This process often involves marriage, becoming a parent, and deciding on a career direction.

2. **The Settling Down Period.** The settling down period lasts from about age 33 to 39 and focuses on establishing oneself in society, usually by advancing in an occupation. During this period, men form commitments to work, family, friendship, and/or community.

3. **The Midlife Transition.** This period, from about age 40 to 44, is the bridge between early and middle adulthood. Many men take stock of the likelihood that they

"Your mother and I are feeling overwhelmed, so you'll have to bring yourselves up."

will realize their earlier dreams. Often they revise their dreams to be more realistic and achievable, and sometimes they become **mentors**, or close advisors, to younger people. By helping someone younger achieve his or her dreams, mentors may find that they can extend their influence beyond their own careers.

Irene Frieze focused her study on adult female development and found both similarities with and differences from the development of males. She suggests women go through **three** phases in early and middle adulthood:

1. **Leaving the Family.** Like men, women must leave home and establish their own adult identities. For many women, emphasis is placed on the influence of marriage in shaping their development. For women who combine marriage with career, marriage usually plays the dominant role, even in modern society.

2. **Entering the Adult World.** The dual roles of career and marriage—particularly including motherhood—place a strain on young women. They often feel they should be in two places at once and are not able to do both jobs as well as they would like. Many women have a break in employment when children are young, an experience that distinguishes female development from male.

3. **Entering the Adult World Again.** Many women find that their children's growing independence allows them to reenter the workforce by the time they reach their early to middle 30s. Women then face many of the challenges men faced in their 20s. Ironically, women develop commitments to their careers right about the time their husbands are beginning to have serious doubts about their own careers.

Jobs and the Workplace

Increasingly, both men and women are expected to work for pay during most of their adult lives, which can mean working for 50 years or so. By definition, the labor force consists of all people 16 and older who have paid jobs or are seeking employment.

Occupations may be broken down into several categories:

* *Managerial and Professional Specialty*—business executives, office and sales managers, store supervisors, doctors, lawyers, computer specialists, editors, and engineers.
* *Technical, Sales, and Administrative Support*—laboratory technicians, X-ray and imaging technicians, retail salespeople, and secretaries.
* *Service Occupations*—teachers, social workers, and nurses.
* *Precision Production, Craft, and Repair Occupations*—skilled workers such as carpenters, electricians, and plumbers.

* **Operators and Laborers**—unskilled workers in jobs requiring manual, often repetitive, skills, most of which involve operating some type of machinery.
* **Farming, Forestry, and Fishing**—only a small percentage of Americans hold these jobs today.

Old Age

What is "old age"? Part of the definition seems to depend on how old you are. To young people, it may mean anyone over 30, but to people in their 50s, old age may refer to anyone over 70. The definition also changes as life expectancies increase. Many people today expect to live well into their 80s and 90s. Generally, we define old age by decreasing activity, retirement from work, and increasing problems with health.

Myth and Reality

A common misconception is that people over the age of 65 are all the same. People go through different stages as they grow older. Life at age 65 is very different from life at 85.

EXAMPLE: Among people in their late 60s, adjusting to retirement is a major developmental issue. For many people, by the time they reach their 80s, health issues take precedence over other issues.

Work and Retirement

Because U.S. society places a great deal of emphasis on work, for most adults an occupation is a master status. When retirement time comes, the transition may be very difficult. Adjustment to retirement depends on many factors: feelings of achievement of work-related goals, financial security, health concerns, and type of profession.

EXAMPLE: Some researchers have found that professionals and executives seem to adapt most easily to retirement. Their level of education may have prepared them to enjoy activities beyond the world of work. Their level of income may also be a factor.

New Expectations

As more and more people live well beyond retirement, they will socialize to a new set of expectations about the roles of seniors. Many will observe their peers taking up new interests, doing those things they had always wanted to do but had no time for when they were working and raising children. Some become active in voluntary service at youth centers or in hospitals. They find that giving of oneself in this way brings increased rewards.

Death and Dying

The last stage of life for all of us is the period that immediately precedes death. For most of us, this period comes at the end of old age, and it may include a prolonged period of illness. As we complete our life cycles, we often lose the hard-earned independence of adulthood and again rely on others for physical or financial assistance.

Many studies show that whereas the elderly fear dependence, many do not have an equal fear of death. Almost certainly this feeling comes from the sense that death is natural, and that one has lived as long as can be expected. Religious beliefs also influence an individual's reaction to death.

Did You Know?

Dying "On Our Own Terms"

According to a 2000 poll conducted by *Time* magazine and CNN, seven out of ten Americans say they want to die at home; instead, three-fourths die in medical institutions. Many die in pain, and in the presence of hospital personnel, not surrounded by family and friends. Research by Bill and Judith Moyers led them to argue that dying people should be allowed more freedom to choose how and when they die, and that we should all die "On Our Own Terms."

In a classic study, researcher Elisabeth Kübler-Ross outlined **five** stages of dying:

1. **Denial,** in which people ignore the truth that they are dying.
2. **Anger,** the reaction "Why me?"
3. **Bargaining** for the future, perhaps promising better behavior if allowed to live.
4. **Depression,** feeling hopeless about the future.
5. **Acceptance** of the sum total of one's life experiences and the inevitability of death.

The socialization process for human beings lasts a lifetime. Humans use their ability to learn in constantly readjusting to the ever-changing demands of society. Personality development is influenced by both heredity and culture, and a sense of self develops as we age.

Children, adolescents, and adults have much to learn and relearn—values, beliefs, and norms as well as physical, mental, and social skills. Agents of socialization such as the family, schools, peers, and the media convey information and skills both intentionally and unintentionally. Individual variations abound, but experiencing a socialization process is one thing humans all have in common. Socialization continues throughout life, with each stage facing its own challenges.

Sociology

adolescence—period between childhood and adulthood in industrial and post-industrial societies; the teenage years. *p. 77*

agents of socialization—individuals or institutions that teach the culture of a society. *p. 76*

birth order—position of an individual among his or her siblings on the basis of the order of their birth; first born, middle child, and so forth. *p. 69*

cognitive development—process of changes over time in the way an individual thinks, learns, reasons, and acquires language. *p. 74*

instinct—inherited behavior pattern. *p. 69*

looking-glass self—Charles Horton Cooley's description of the development of self through social interactions with other people. *p. 71*

mentor—close advisor; usually an older person who takes an active interest in the career development of a younger person. *p. 81*

personality—all the relatively stable patterns of thinking, feeling, and acting that distinguish one individual from another. *p. 68*

psychoanalysis—Freud's theory that unconscious childhood experiences and instinct-based drives largely shape personality and behavior. *p. 73*

resocialization—process of altering what was learned earlier in life and learning new kinds of appropriate behavior. *p. 80*

role taking—activity in social development in which a child pretends to be other people. *p. 73*

socialization—process by which individuals learn to become members of society. It involves internalizing the rules and norms of society and learning to perform expected social roles. *p. 68*

sociobiology—study of the biological bases of social behavior. *p.69*

Deviance and Crime

In this chapter, you will learn about:

- deviant behavior
- criminal behavior and the justice system

Winston Churchill, the great British prime minister who lead the country during the difficult years of the second world war, was known to hold meetings with his advisors in his bathroom while he was soaking in the tub. Simon Rodilla, an American, built a series of towers in the Watts area of Los Angeles out of bits of stone, steel, cement, and found objects like bottle caps, bits of broken china, and seashells. The writer Henry David Thoreau built himself a cabin of sticks and mud and lived for two years on what he could get from the woods. Such eccentric behavior—behavior that violates social norms—is called deviance.

Deviant behavior may serve both positive and negative social functions. Sociologists have offered explanations from biological, psychological, and sociological perspectives. If deviant behavior also breaks a law, it is called a crime, and the person who commits it is labeled a criminal. The criminal justice system is one of society's ways of dealing with criminal, deviant behavior.

What Is Deviance?

Sociologist Emile Durkheim once observed that behaviors that qualify one person for sainthood may condemn another to prison, a mental asylum, or the stake. Behavior that violates norms is called **deviance**. Durkheim was suggesting that no behavior is consistently considered to be deviant across circumstances, time, and cultures.

Social norms determine deviance, and because norms vary widely, the cultural definition of deviance differs, too. Also, to understand why a certain act is considered deviant, we must always know the context in which it occurred.

Deviance in Perspective

Some norms—such as crossing the street at the corner, writing thank-you notes for gifts received, or waiting your turn in lines—are often violated. Yet people who break them are not usually labeled "deviant."

When a behavior is deviant, it brings about social disapproval from many members of a society. Deviant behavior is usually condemned and often punished. The punishment can be as simple as ignoring or isolating an offender, or it may be as strong as a fine, imprisonment, or death. In other words, deviance is a matter of degree.

Deviance is decided by **two** things:

1. **Extent of Disapproval.** The number of people who condemn an act must be considerable.
2. **Degree of Societal Outrage.** The hostility or outrage set off by the act must be intense.

If most people in a society strongly disapprove of and wish to punish an action, it almost certainly will be labeled deviant.

Social Controls and Conformity

Society employs **social controls** to prevent deviance. These are techniques and strategies for punishing wrongdoing and rewarding appropriate behavior. Social control occurs on all levels of society. Parents punish and reward their children, peer groups encourage adherence to dress codes and friendship norms, and the workplace requires adults to follow standards and rules. On the broadest societal level, all of us are subject to laws and government regulations that control deviant behavior.

Social controls are of **two** main types:

1. **Internal social controls** exist within the individual.
   EXAMPLE: You experience a feeling of discomfort when you say something that is not true. Your conscience represents social controls working actively within you.

We all have internalized the norms of our society. That is the outcome of our socialization. Conformity, or going along with acceptable behavior to please others, provides predictable internal social controls on many actions.

2. **External social controls** go into effect when internal social controls don't work. Most people don't seriously think about committing murder or arson, but those who do pose a big threat to a society's well being. Laws provide external social controls to prevent and punish those who commit certain deviant acts. The severity of external social controls depends on the seriousness of the violation. **EXAMPLES:** A student who skips class may be subject to a detention. A member of a sports team may have to sit out a game because he or she violated the rules. A murderer may be sentenced to spend the remainder of life in jail.

U.S. Culture Connection

The Homeboy Graffiti Removal Crew

Gangs use graffiti to mark turf and to show disrespect for enemies, which has often spilled over into violence. In Los Angeles, "tagging"—drawing graffiti in public places—is not just an eyesore. It has led to gang warfare.

Recently, a ten-year-old girl was killed in the crossfire between two gangs arguing over their graffiti. In response, a Jesuit priest who had been working with gang members for years devised some external social controls to help improve the neighborhood and prevent future violence. He started the "Homeboy Graffiti Removal Crew" by convincing former gang members to work for nine dollars an hour traveling around in a truck full of different colors of paint and stopping to paint over graffiti. According to one of the crew, who had done his share of "tagging" in the past, "I'm doing some good, and I love it. It's the first job I ever had."

The Effects of Deviance

At the very least, deviant behavior is annoying and, in the extreme, it is dangerous. Yet good motives can impel people to break with social norms, and sometimes positive social change results from deviant activity.

Positive Social Functions

Although deviance is by definition behavior that poses a threat to the social order, it may actually have some positive effects as well.

* **It Can Promote Unity.** A community that faces a common threat often unites to stop it.
  EXAMPLE: A Midwestern community mainly ambivalent about problems of racial discrimination became mobilized in defense of an African-American family when their home was repeatedly attacked by racists who burned crosses on the lawn and left threatening messages on their telephone answering machine.

* **It Can Relieve Tension.** Sometimes people who are frustrated with their social and economic situations express their unhappiness through deviant behavior. If the deviance is minor, such as playing pranks on neighbors, it may allow an individual to avoid more serious violations.

  EXAMPLE: Opening fire hydrants on a hot summer day, while illegal, is preferable to more serious expressions of frustration, such as rioting.

* **It Can Clarify Norms.** Defining what is deviant can help clarify existing norms.
  EXAMPLE: A high school has a policy that students arrive on time to class, but due to a lax administration, students who come to class late are not penalized. A new principal comes in who first reminds everyone of the existence of the policy and then enforces it by giving out detentions to tardy students. This punishment resolves any uncertainty about the existing norms.

* **It Can Identify Problems.** The difference between normal behavior and deviance may be blurred, especially when many people are breaking the rules. When a particular norm is frequently violated, it may be a signal that the norm doesn't make sense anymore. People leading social movements are often seen as deviant, but they can bring about positive changes in society.
  EXAMPLE: During the 1950s and '60s, the people who first refused to follow segregation laws were deviants of their time, but now they are seen as brave reformers.

Anne Hutchinson: A Deviant Puritan

Anne Hutchinson made many people in colonial Boston uncomfortable when she criticized the exclusive rights of ministers to interpret the Bible. She began drawing audiences, and Puritan ministers feared that she was undermining church authority. Yet she was an upright citizen, and she was breaking no laws. How could they define her as a deviant? To solve their problem, they wrote a law that made what she was doing illegal, found her guilty, and banished her from the colony. Without

realizing it, Anne Hutchinson helped the Massachusetts Bay Colony redefine the norms that bound the community together.

Negative Social Functions

Minor deviations from social norms may actually be good for a society, but high levels of deviance are dangerous and seriously disrupt the social fabric.

* *Deviance Disrupts Norms.* When people break social norms, they call them into question. Others respond with anger, feeling their basic values are being threatened.

    EXAMPLES: Artists who depicted religious figures in unholy situations or attitudes, people who wanted to fund abortions with public money and those who threatened and attacked doctors who performed abortions, students who protested the Vietnam War by burning

American flags—all threatened some people's sense of social order by disrupting norms.

* *Deviance Makes Life Unpredictable.* Norms help assure citizens that life is predictable. Chaos results when people cannot expect each other to observe the norms.

    EXAMPLE: Sexual offenders violate the basic trust that children have for adults. When a convicted child molester freed from jail moves into some communities, laws have been passed saying this information must be public. Residents feel they must know that someone among them does not observe a basic norm, so they can take extra precautions.

"We teach them that the world can be an unpredictable, dangerous, and sometimes frightening place, while being careful not to spoil their lovely innocence. It's tricky."

Ways of Explaining Deviance

What causes a person to be deviant? We all exhibit minor forms of deviant behavior. To be labeled a "deviant," a person either has to repeatedly violate norms or commit a single serious crime. Are deviants biologically different from other people? Do the answers lie deep in their personalities? Or does something in the social environment make them react negatively? These questions have intrigued people for centuries, and many explanations have been offered.

Biological Explanations

Some of the early scholars who attempted to explain deviant behavior looked at the physical nature of criminals.

Early Theorists

Three theorists whose ideas may seem strange today include:

1. **Cesare Lombroso,** a 19th-century Italian physician, who suggested that criminals were biologically less advanced than law-abiding citizens.
2. **Ernest Hooten,** a U.S. anthropologist, who concluded in 1939 that criminals were genetically and physically "degenerate" human beings.
3. **William Sheldon,** a U.S. psychologist, who stated in 1949 that body type could be linked to criminal behavior, and that the same genes that produce a stocky body type (the mesomorph) also produce an inclination to break social rules.

Chromosomes

In the 1960s, Menachem Amir and Yitzchak Berman suggested there was a link between criminal behavior and genetics. They reported that a high percentage of men who had committed violent crimes were found to have a combination of chromosomes that rarely occurs—XYY instead of the normal XY for males. A later investigation revealed that Richard Speck, a Chicago man who was convicted of killing seven nurses in one night, had this abnormality.

It is important to note that the XYY pattern is very rare. The overwhelming majority of those who commit crimes have a normal arrangement of chromosomes.

Psychological Explanations

Psychologists and sociologists have both suggested that some types of personality are more often associated with deviant behavior than others. One hypothesis is that while everyone has inner impulses to deviate from the norm, some people are less able to control them.

Freud's Explanation

Sigmund Freud argued that children, through identification with their parents, acquire a *superego*, or conscience, that forbids deviant behavior. Freud's psychoanalytic theory suggests that criminal behavior may indicate an underdeveloped superego. Other psychologists have argued that an overdeveloped superego may also lead to deviance. They suggest that people who are ashamed of their urges may commit deviant acts to receive the punishment they feel they deserve.

Frustration-Aggression Theory

The **frustration-aggression theory** suggests that deviance is a form of aggression toward others and society produced by an individual's frustration. When a person has a need that is not fulfilled, he or she becomes frustrated and vents frustration in aggression. The degree of frustration is based on the strength of the needs that are not met, and the degree of aggression is related to the amount of frustration.
EXAMPLE: Poor living conditions may frustrate a person. Suppose a tenant has her electricity cut off because she didn't pay the bill. Her frustration with her poor housing and her inability to pay bills or make life better would grow. She may be more likely to behave aggressively—slam doors, break something, yell at or harm her children.

Sociological Explanations

While biological and psychological explanations may help us understand something about an *individual's* deviance, only sociological explanations help us understand why *groups* of people deviate from social norms. Sociological explanations shed light on why rates of deviance vary from country to country, group to group, or neighborhood to neighborhood. The different sociological perspectives each offer explanations.

Functionalist Perspective

According to functionalists, deviance is a common part of human society. It has both positive and negative consequences for social stability. On the positive side, deviance helps define the limits of proper behavior. To explain the negative consequences, functionalists talk in terms of **structural strain.** When people cannot reach goals the society admires, the structure of society is strained. Deviance becomes a way of life for many.

The most famous structural strain theory is the **anomie theory of deviance** devised by sociologist Robert K. Merton. *Anomie* is a state in which there are either no rules for behavior or there are so many that people don't know which to follow. The norms have broken down.

Emile Durkheim's Legacy

Emile Durkheim used the term *anomie* to describe the loss of direction felt in a society when social control had become ineffective. He saw anomie as a breakdown of norms, or "normlessness." It often occurs during or after a time of great change and disorder. In 1789 when revolution toppled France's government, chaos followed. Different factions fought for political and economic control. Since the country's rules and laws were overturned, citizens were in a state of anomie. Without the old structure, people lost their direction, and many resorted to rioting, looting, and murder.

Merton focuses on the high value U.S. society places on the goal of economic success and the means of achieving it. The socially approved means are getting a good education, acquiring the necessary skills for a good job, and working hard. Yet not all Americans have an equal opportunity to get a good education and acquire the skills for a good job. Poverty, poor schools, a culture that does not value study—all these things may pose impossible hurdles.

Merton argues that when people cannot achieve the goals that society values by legitimate means, they fall victim to anomie and will pursue their goals in deviant ways.

Merton identifies five ways in which individuals respond to culturally approved goals and ways of reaching them: conformity, innovation, ritualism, retreatism, or rebellion. Conformers work hard to achieve economic success, and their behavior is not deviant. The **four** deviant behavior patterns are:

1. **Innovation.** Deviant innovators accept society's goals, but they find alternative ways of reaching them.
   EXAMPLE: Trading in drugs or stolen merchandise is against the law. Those who engage in these activities are pursuing the goal of economic success, but not by following socially accepted rules.

2. **Ritualism.** Instead of violating the norms for achievement, ritualists observe rules of behavior. However, they don't believe that they can achieve their goals, so they experience anomie. They feel their behavior is pointless and hopeless. Their outward behavior is a sham.
   EXAMPLE: A middle manager in business continues to go through the paces of the "rat race" in corporate life, though he knows he will never be promoted.

3. **Retreatism.** Retreatists reject both the cultural goals and socially acceptable means of reaching them. They "retreat" from society to become loners or drifters.

   EXAMPLES: Drug addicts, alcoholics, and "bums."

4. **Rebellion.** Finally, people who are alienated from both the goals and the standards of their culture may come up with new ideals and new rules for pursuing them.

   EXAMPLES: Idealists who believe that the goal of economic success should be replaced with a general sharing of wealth; members of right-wing militia groups that make freedom from government control their main goal and use their guns and rifles to threaten social stability.

Conflict Perspective

Sociologists with a conflict perspective see deviance as the result of competition and social inequality. Deviant people with power break norms in an effort to maintain their power. Deviant people without power act either to obtain a slice of the economic pie or to compensate for low self-esteem and feelings of powerlessness.

Why are most of the people arrested for crimes from the lower classes? A conflict theorist might argue that it is the result of a power struggle (conflict) between the people in power and those who threaten their power base. Business leaders and others in power promote law-enforcement efforts that are directed toward the types of crimes committed by the working and lower classes—drug traffic, shoplifting,

U.S. Culture Connection

Racial Profiling

Social observers point out that a disproportionate number of people of color are stopped and arrested by police for all types of suspected criminal activity, from murder and assault to traffic infractions. The practice of "racial profiling" has been an issue in many communities, and public mores are beginning to reject it. Evidence of discrimination in a police department can become a major news story, as the public demands the retraining of police officers and changes in official policy.

holdups. Upper-class crimes such as bribery and misuse of funds are pursued less vigorously and with much less public attention.

Interactionist Perspective

Interactionists focus on everyday interactions among people and how these interactions influence people to commit deviant acts. They also are interested in why crime occurs on some occasions and not on others. The interactionist perspective is emphasized in **two** theories:

1. **Cultural transmission theory** holds that deviance is learned through interactions with others. In the 1930s, sociologist Edwin Sutherland pioneered a theory of delinquency and deviance. He said criminal behavior was not biologically determined but was learned. Sutherland said that if most of a person's interactions are with deviant individuals, the person is likely to be deviant. On the other hand, if most of a person's associates conform to social norms, the individual will also conform. Through a socialization process called **differential association**, individuals acquire the behavior patterns of the group of people with whom they associate the most.

   EXAMPLE: The culture within a gang teaches the members to be deviant.

   Differential association helps us understand why some neighborhoods have high crime rates and others do not.

2. **Labeling theory** says deviant behavior is not the result of biology or of individual psychology, but is the result of social control. It explains that deviance is what we call it. Not just the violation of a norm, but the behavior that gets its perpetrator *labeled* as deviant is what defines deviance.

   Sociologists Edwin Lemert and Howard Becker note that, once a person is labeled as a deviant, he or she becomes more deviant. The deviant comes to see himself or herself that way.
   EXAMPLE: When a person is labeled "insane," that can become a step in the development of his or her mental illness.

   Labeling does not cause the original deviant act or acts, but it can cause further deviance. Deviance becomes a master status.

   Lemert and Becker identify two types of deviance. **Primary deviance** is the original nonconforming act or acts, which occur before a person gets labeled as deviant. **Secondary deviance**, in contrast, is the result of labeling. Secondary deviance can start a spiral of **stigma**—outward symbols that set a deviant apart from the rest of society.
   EXAMPLES: Arrest records, jail time, bad publicity, and other marks of disgrace.

Criminal Behavior

Criminals pose such a serious threat to social order that we separate them from the rest of society and put them under lock and key. Their behavior is not only deviant, but dangerous. The justice system serves to find and apprehend suspected criminals, judge their guilt or innocence, and punish, or possibly correct, their behavior.

What Is Crime?

Crime is deviant behavior that is prohibited by law and is punishable by the government. Laws divide crimes into categories depending on the seriousness of the offense, the age of the offender, the potential punishment that can be administered, and the court that holds jurisdiction over the case.

EXAMPLES: Murder is treated differently from disorderly conduct; teenage offenders generally are not punished as severely as older criminals; and some crimes violate state laws, whereas others violate federal laws.

Statistics and Trends

The Uniform Crime Report, published every year by the Federal Bureau of Investigation (FBI), compiles data from local police departments into national statistics. More than 1.6 million violent crimes are reported each year in the United States, including more than 19,000 homicides.

Although Americans continue to regard crime as a major social problem, violent crime rates declined significantly in the

Did You Know?

How Accurate Are Crime Reports?

Social scientist Donald Black cautions us that formal crime statistics may not be as accurate as we think. Why? Sometimes victims don't report crimes. People are less likely to report a crime if family or friends are involved. Victims of sexual assault often don't report the crime, perhaps out of fear that the authorities won't believe them.

According to Black, police are more likely to file formal reports on serious crimes when the victims are from the higher social classes. An officer is also more likely to file a formal complaint if the person making the complaint shows courtesy and respect.

late 1990s. Why? Many explanations were offered, including:

* A booming economy and falling unemployment rates.
* Local and national crime-prevention programs.
* A large increase in the prison population, which keeps inmates from committing crimes in the community at large.

In spite of this trend, the numbers of reported crimes in the United States remain well above those of other nations. The "crime clock" shown below can give you an idea of how often crimes occur in the United States.

International Crime

Comparing crime data from the United States with statistics from other countries is difficult because information is not gathered in uniform ways. However, some differences seem clear.

* Rates of violent crime such as murder, rape, and robbery are much higher in the United States than in Western Europe.
* England, Italy, Australia, and New Zealand all have higher rates of motor vehicle theft than the United States.
* Overall, Japan's crime rate is consistently low. Tokyo has the lowest rates of murder, rape, robbery, and theft of any major city in the world.
* Crime in Russia has skyrocketed since the overthrow of Communist party rule in 1991.

U.S. Crime Time

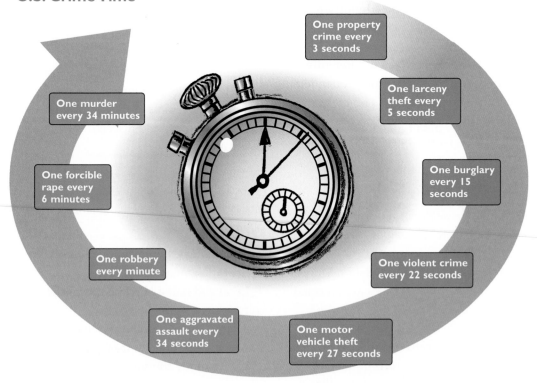

One property crime every 3 seconds

One larceny theft every 5 seconds

One murder every 34 minutes

One forcible rape every 6 minutes

One burglary every 15 seconds

One robbery every minute

One violent crime every 22 seconds

One aggravated assault every 34 seconds

One motor vehicle theft every 27 seconds

Source: Federal Bureau of Investigation, Uniform Crime Reports (1999)

The Gun Myth

Why is the U.S. rate of violent crime so much higher than that in other modern democracies? One common idea is that citizens have tolerated many forms of violence since the country was settled. Guns have come to symbolize individual independence, and the right to bear arms is a tradition as old as our country.

Historian Michael A. Bellesiles refutes this argument in what he calls the "Gun Myth." According to his research, guns were rare in the United States before the Civil War. The early guns and muskets were too clumsy, inaccurate, and dangerous for the ordinary person to handle. The murder rate in early America was very low outside Indian warfare, and murders that did occur were committed with knives. Guns became more common only after the 1840s invention of Samuel Colt's pistol and the Minie ball of the Civil War.

Today, guns are a major ingredient of modern U.S. street crime. According to the FBI, in 2000, 70 percent of reported murders, 40 percent of reported robberies, and 20 percent of all reported aggravated assaults involved a firearm.

Types of Crime

The FBI tabulates data for **seven** index crimes:

1. Murder.
2. Rape.
3. Robbery.
4. Assault.
5. Burglary.
6. Larceny theft.
7. Motor vehicle theft.

The first four are violent crimes against people, and the last three are property crimes. Arson is often included as an additional property crime. The chart on page 98 shows the relative proportion of the seven index crimes in 1999. **Three** kinds of crimes are not indexed:

1. Organized crime.
2. White-collar crime.
3. Victimless crime.

Violent Crime

Murder, forcible rape, robbery, and aggravated assault make up a small percentage of all crimes, but by their very nature, even at low rates these crimes are considered to be a great threat to society. African-American males are much more likely to be victims of violent crimes than

U.S. Index Crime Offenses	
Percent Distribution	
Forcible rape	0.8%
Murder	0.1%
Robbery	3.5%
Aggravated assault	7.9%
Motor vehicle theft	9.9%
Burglary	18.0%
Larceny theft	59.8%

Source: Federal Bureau of Investigation,
Uniform Crime Reports (1999)

anyone else. Their victim rate is about 5 times that of African-American females, over 7 times that of white males, and about 22 times that of white females.

Crimes against Property

Burglary, larceny (theft other than auto), motor vehicle theft, and arson are about ten times more common than crimes of violence. Crimes against property involve no violence and no force or threat of force against individuals. Most people who commit property crimes do not wish to confront their victims or hurt them physically, nor do they wish to get hurt themselves.

Organized Crime

Networks of criminal groups make up the large-scale, professional, criminal syndicates known as organized crime. They control such illegal businesses as drug

trafficking and prostitution and are also major stockholders in such legitimate businesses as hotels and restaurants. They look to invest their illegally earned profits in businesses in which it is relatively easy to keep fraudulent accounts.

While they employ violent acts such as beatings, kidnappings, murder, and arson, organized crime most often works carefully to avoid public attention.

Organized crime is rarely prosecuted because of public apathy and the close connections crime figures have to people in power positions in society.

White-Collar Crime

The label **white collar** refers to people in management, politics, the professions, and office workers. It is distinguished from **blue collar**, which refers to factory workers and manual laborers, such as miners or workers on road repair crews. These terms are status labels. A crime committed by a person of high social status in the course of his or her professional life is called **white-collar crime.** Business owners, corporate officers and managers, and politicians often have access to large sums of money that do not belong to them. For some, the temptation to illegally manipulate those resources is irresistible.

EXAMPLES of white-collar crime include:

* Tax evasion.
* Fraud.
* Embezzlement.
* Price fixing.
* Stock manipulation.
* Political corruption.

These actions are often concealed, so white-collar crime rates are difficult to determine. However, investigative reporting and government supervision have revealed many high-profile cases of insider trading on Wall Street, political corruption, and computer crimes.

Victimless Crime

These activities are outlawed, but the only victims are the participants themselves.

EXAMPLES:

* Gambling.
* Public drunkenness.
* Prostitution.
* Drug possession and sale.

Not A Crime

These crimes are not included in the FBI's index crimes. To apprehend the offenders, the police often must rely on undercover work, informants, and luck to gather evidence and make arrests. Only a small fraction of offenders is actually arrested.

White-Collar Crime: "The Love Bug"

Highly skilled computer experts from around the world have made news in recent years by "hacking" into supposedly secure web sites. Sometimes the motivation is economic—to "fix" books, transfer funds, conceal embezzlement, or gain advantage over business competitors. However, more often the motivation is unclear. In early 2000, some computer hackers in the Philippines intentionally placed a Valentine's Day "love bug" message in e-mail attachments that corrupted computers all over the world.

The "virus" was traced to the hackers, who had no apparent economic motive for their actions.

The Criminal Justice System

The U.S. criminal justice system has the responsibility of protecting society from dangerous crime. In **four** steps, the justice system performs its function:

1. Apprehending suspected offenders.
2. Determining their innocence or guilt.
3. Deciding their punishment.
4. Keeping the guilty separated from other citizens.

There are **three** major elements of the criminal justice system:

❶ Police

In the United States, state and local police generally have control over who is arrested for committing a crime. Although we might expect the police to arrest everyone who is accused of a crime, in reality the police have to make a lot of choices. Police must make decisions about whom to arrest, who is merely warned, and who will not be pursued.

Several factors determine a police officer's decision to arrest an offender:

* Seriousness of the offense.
* Wishes of the victim.
* Attitude of the suspect.
* Presence of bystanders.

A crime victim sometimes tells police not to pursue an offender, especially if that person is a relative.

EXAMPLE: A victim of domestic abuse may be primarily interested in having the police stop the immediate attack. He or she may be unwilling later to press charges.

Offenders are more likely to be arrested if they are aggressive or if bystanders witness the crime. Police are more likely to arrest members of minority groups than whites, a common accusation backed by research.

❷ Courts

Once the police make an arrest, the courts take responsibility for:

* Determining guilt or innocence.
* Assigning some form of punishment.

In reality, most cases don't go through this formal process. To save time and money, cases are often settled by **plea bargaining**. In a plea bargain, the accused person pleads guilty to a crime less serious than the crime of which he or she is accused. In return for the guilty plea, the accused person receives a lighter sentence than would have been recommended for the original offense. Research shows that offenders who plea bargain often get lighter sentences than those who plead innocent but are found guilty.

❸ The Correctional System

If an accused person is found guilty, the courts assign a punishment called a correction. The punishment may be a fine, but for more serious crimes it is often imprisonment. Corrections serve **four** major functions for society:

1. **Retribution.** Punishing an offender is a way for the victim and society to "get even."

2. **Deterrence.** Corrections are meant to discourage offenders from committing crimes again and provide a warning to others not to pursue a life of crime. How well deterrence works is open to question. For example, a *New York Times* study showed that 10 of the 12 states that in the year 2000 did not allow the death penalty actually had lower homicide rates than the states that did allow it. Proponents of harsh penalties would argue that other factors may explain this difference.

3. **Rehabilitation.** Some prison authorities and criminologists believe that criminals should be reformed so that they may return to society as law-abiding citizens. Efforts at rehabilitation in prisons are not very successful, in part because in prisons criminals associate with other criminals like themselves. Deviant behavior is reinforced by association with other deviants. Rehabilitation requires major change in the prison culture. However, when rehabilitation works, it can be the beginning of a new way of life for some individuals.

4. **Social Protection.** Whether criminals are locked in a prison or put to death, one major function of corrections is served— the criminals cannot commit additional crimes. In this way, law-abiding citizens are protected from the threat of future criminal activity.

One way to judge how effective corrections are is the rate of **recidivism**— the tendency to return to previous, that is, criminal, behavior. In the United States, around half of all persons released from prison are later arrested for another offense.

Chapter 5 Wrap-up
DEVIANCE AND CRIME

Deviant behavior violates a society's norms. One person's deviance affects other members of society, sometimes positively, but more often negatively. Societies exercise both internal and external social controls to reward positive behavior and punish wrongdoing.

The sociological perspectives differ in their outlook on deviant behavior. A functionalist might view it in terms of the anomie theory of deviance. A sociologist using the conflict perspective will focus on competition and social inequality as explanations for deviance. An interactionist may look at differential association and labeling theory.

When deviance takes the form of lawbreaking, it is criminal behavior. There are a range of types of crime. For the most serious, deviance can have major consequences for the deviant individual, such as the death penalty. Society responds to criminal behavior through the attentions and resources of a criminal justice system.

anomie theory of deviance—sociological view that deviance is the result of a breakdown in the norms of society (anomie). *p. 91*

blue collar—status label that refers to factory workers and manual laborers, such as miners or workers on road repair crews. *p. 98*

crime—deviant behavior that is prohibited by law and is punishable by the government. *p. 95*

cultural transmission theory—sociological view that deviance is a behavior learned through interaction with others. *p. 94*

deviance—behavior that violates social norms and brings social disapproval and intense hostility from many members of a society. *p. 86*

differential association—socialization process in which individuals acquire the behavior patterns of the group of people they associate with the most. *p. 94*

external social controls—checks on an individual's behavior that come from others and from society at large. *p. 87*

frustration-aggression theory—psychological explanation of deviance that suggests deviance is a form of aggression toward society produced by an individual's frustration. *p. 91*

internal social controls—checks on behavior that exist within a person as a result of having internalized society's norms through the socialization process. *p. 86*

labeling theory—view that identifying an individual as a deviant causes deviance to become a master status. *p. 94*

plea bargaining—negotiation process that allows an accused person to plead guilty to a lesser charge in return for a lighter sentence. *p. 100*

primary deviance—original nonconforming act or acts that occur before a person gets labeled as deviant. *p. 94*

recidivism—tendency to return to previous (criminal) behavior. *p. 101*

secondary deviance—nonconformity that results from an individual's being labeled a deviant. *p. 94*

social controls—techniques and strategies for punishing wrongdoing and rewarding appropriate behavior. *p. 86*

stigma—outward symbols that set a deviant apart from the rest of society. *p. 94*

structural strain—stress on the social structure when individuals cannot achieve the goals society values; structural strain invites deviant behavior. *p. 91*

white collar—status label that refers to people in management, politics, the professions and to office workers. *p. 98*

white-collar crime—illegal acts committed by persons of high social status in the course of their professional lives, such as embezzlement. *p. 98*

CHAPTER 6

Social Stratification and Class

In this chapter, you will learn about:

- **social stratification and social mobility**
- **class structure in the United States**
- **poverty**

Ask your classmates if they believe in equality, and most will answer "of course." However, question them a bit further, and you may hear something else. Could it be fair for some people to have more wealth, respect, or power than others? Don't hard work and special talents deserve reward and recognition?

    Inequalities exist to some extent in every society. When we look at the people in a society from the top to the bottom, we are looking at how the society is stratified, or layered. Societies include different classes of people who have different levels of power, privilege, and resources. In some societies, people can move from one class to another. In other societies, they are stuck in the class to which they were born. In this chapter we will look at the class structure in the United States and at the characteristics of people of the lowest class, who have so few economic resources that they live in poverty.

Social Stratification and Social Status

Sociologists use the term **social stratification** to describe a structured ranking of entire groups of people in which some have more power, prestige, and wealth than others. When people are "stratified" into ranked groups, some hold higher positions and others hold lower ones.

The concept of social **class** is useful in discussing stratification. It refers to the group of people who share economic and social position in society. People in the same social class have common values and norms and recognize each other as members of their own class.

Three Dimensions of Stratification

About a century ago, German sociologist Max Weber observed that the nobility sometimes lacked wealth, but had enormous power. Similarly, some people with great wealth had less power and a lower position.

EXAMPLES: In the German society of Weber's day, only nobles could be officers in the army. On the other hand, some citizens who owned factories or large companies lacked power and social standing because they were Jewish.

Weber proposed **three** independent dimensions on which people could be ranked in a stratification system:

1. **Wealth and Property.** Wealth, because it can be expressed in numbers, is the most easily measured dimension.

Weber used the term *class* to group people with similar "life chances" to earn income and gain property. Individuals identified as "lower class" have less opportunity to gain wealth and property than those in the "upper class." In most societies, large assets and high income are concentrated in the hands of a small percentage of the population.

2. **Power.** Even though people with wealth often have power, Weber argued that power stands independently. He defined *power* as the ability to get one's way despite the resistance of others.

A person's power may be based on almost anything, from special talents, to personality characteristics, or even the use of force. A powerful person isn't necessarily wealthy, but power often increases an individual's wealth.

EXAMPLE: Former U.S. presidents and influential members of Congress often write books that sell well because of their fame. Or they may be offered high-paying consulting positions because of the powerful positions they once held and the influence they have with others in power.

3. **Prestige.** People may also be ranked by *prestige*, the respect or recognition they receive from other members of society. Weber referred to prestige as social status that people express through their lifestyles. People of similar prestige form communities, invite one another to dinner, go to the same places, and marry one another.

In some countries, such as Weber's early 20th-century Germany, prestige was often ascribed: One was born into the nobility or the peasant class. In many modern societies, prestige is often linked to occupation. Weber noted that prestige can be independent from wealth, separating its owners from those who "just" have money.

Explaining Social Stratification

Sociologists who attempt to explain unequal distributions of wealth, power, and prestige in human societies tend to take two opposite sides. On one side are the functionalists, who argue that stratification is necessary for societies to function efficiently. On the other side, conflict theorists maintain that stratification is the result of the selfish struggle among individuals for scarce rewards and resources.

Functionalist Theory

In the mid-20th century, sociologists Kingsley Davis and Wilbert E. Moore first proposed that in all societies people in some positions perform functions that are, by any objective measurement, more important to the society than others—generals, judges, lawmakers. Davis and Moore reasoned that stratification would

U.S. Culture Connection

Status Symbols

People often communicate their high social status through outward symbols. Status symbols, such as expensive cars, homes, or clothing, show off wealth. Some status symbols reflect an individual's membership in a prestigious group. In the United States, college students often wear tee-shirts with the names of their university, identifying themselves as members of a higher education community. Class rings and bumper stickers perform the same function. Credit card companies try to sell social status symbols with their platinum, gold, and silver levels.

not be necessary if all the necessary tasks were equally important and pleasant, and if they all required equal skills and capabilities. In reality, positions are unequal. Society offers higher rewards as incentives to ensure that people will acquire the skills to do the more important tasks. The size of the rewards must be proportional to **three** factors:

1. **The importance of the task.** The more important the task, the higher the rewards must be to guarantee that the most competent people can be encouraged to do it.

2. **The pleasantness of the task.** If the task is enjoyable, there will be plenty of volunteers, so high rewards aren't necessary.

3. **The scarcity of the talent and ability necessary to perform the task.** When relatively few people have the ability to perform an important task (such as dentistry or legal work), high rewards are necessary to compensate practitioners for the time and expense of acquiring the skill.

Occupational Prestige Rankings

Sociological studies have asked respondents to rank occupations according to their prestige. Probably the best-known measure of occupational prestige was designed for the National Opinion Research Center (NORC) in the 1940s. Follow-up studies from the 1960s and in 1989 found that relative rankings have remained fairly stable over time.

High Prestige	Average Prestige	Low Prestige
U.S. Supreme Court justice	Reporters for daily newspapers	Clothes pressers in laundries
Physicians	Farm owners	Garbage collectors
Scientists	Bookkeepers	Street sweepers
College professors	Carpenters	Shoe shiners
	Mail carriers	

Two Theories of Social Stratification	
Functionalist Theory	**Conflict Theory**
1. It is universal, necessary, and inevitable.	1. It may be universal, but it is not necessary or inevitable.
2. It is based on the need to motivate and reward people to do the most important work of society.	2. It is based on group competition for limited resources, and conflict is the natural result.
3. It is widely accepted by most members of society.	3. It is accepted by controlling groups and resented by the working class.
4. The people who have power and wealth usually deserve what they have.	4. People who have power and wealth don't deserve as much as they have because they exploit the "have-nots."

Conflict Theory

The old saying "The rich get richer, and the poor get poorer" describes the conflict theorists' view of social stratification. They start with the principle that there are only so many resources and rewards to go around. They do not see stratification as the result of some orderly process to encourage leadership and skill development. To them, it is the result of competition for limited economic resources. Inevitably, there are winners and losers. The winners take all and remain firmly determined not to surrender any advantage. Because winners have the upper hand, the poor have few chances to advance, and the rich remain on top. To conflict theorists, this situation is inherently unfair.

In modern America, conflict theorists believe that "elites," such as CEOs of big corporations and political leaders, control their companies and the government to protect their self-interests. Members of the working class harbor deep resentments that have inspired them to form labor unions and begin social movements that call for more equality.

"It appears you're a bit overqualified to be exploited but somewhat underqualified to exploit others."

Systems of Stratification

Very little stratification exists in most hunter-gatherer and horticultural societies. There, status differences are based mainly on gender and age. Of course, people have little opportunity to change their stations in life.

Now think of phrases such as "Rags to riches" and "Log cabin to White House."

In the United States, we believe in **social mobility**, the ability of individuals to change their social status during their lifetimes. Our system of stratification is relatively open. Think of a line with "closed systems" at one end and "open systems" at the other. The social systems of the world could be placed along such a line. We would call this line a *social mobility* **continuum**. (See the diagram below.)

Closed Systems

Once humans develop agricultural skills, they settle into permanent groups and begin to stratify labor, with different amounts of status attached to each layer, or **stratum** (plural *strata*). Most nonindustrial societies have developed **closed systems** in which little social mobility exists. Individuals have no opportunity to change their social status during their lifetimes. **Three** examples of closed systems are:

1. **Slavery.** In a slave system, slaves are treated as property. Usually, the people who own slaves have complete control over them and profit from their forced labor.

2. **Caste Systems.** **Castes** are lifelong statuses determined by the status of one's parents. Castes are rigidly stratified, and the order of superiority is clear. Individual effort and talent can affect a person's position within a caste, but they cannot help that person move to a higher stratum. Closely governed norms define the roles of caste members and their interactions with people of other castes. Usually, *endogamy*—marriage within one's own caste—is required. Otherwise, the social status of children would be unclear.

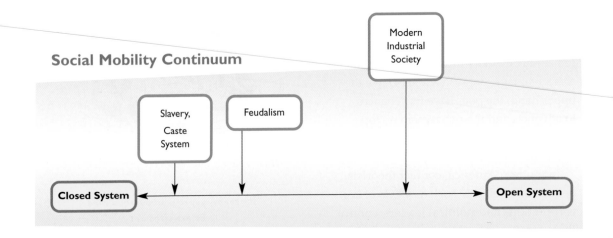

Social Mobility Continuum

Modern Industrial Society

Slavery, Caste System

Feudalism

Closed System ⟷ **Open System**

Castes in India

The world's best-known caste system has its roots in ancient India. According to traditional beliefs, four original castes—the Brahmins, Kshatriyas, Vaishyas, and Sudras—have subdivided in India over the years into thousands of subcastes based on specific occupations. Below these four castes are a class of "outcastes," or untouchables, who are shunned by others and given only the most undesirable work to do.

In the past half-century many Indians, especially in urban areas, have abandoned the caste system. India's legislature has abolished the caste system as the basis for legal rights, such as property ownership and access to public facilities. In many rural areas, however, the caste system continues its role in organizing daily life.

3. **Feudalism.** The feudal estate system is almost as restricted as the caste system in limiting the social mobility of its members. Most people spend their lives as serfs (peasants) working the land of the lord, who controls their livelihood. A few people occupy middle layers as teachers, healers, or merchants. People may occasionally change their "estates" by doing a favor for a lord or king, by

joining the priesthood, or by marrying someone of a higher position. The feudal estate system has existed in many parts of the world, including Japan, Europe, and Latin America.

Open Systems

Modern industrialized societies depend on people with special skills and extensive education to fill various jobs. These societies tend to have **open systems** of stratification, in which people have a significant chance of moving from one level to another. Statuses are more likely to be achieved rather than ascribed, and social mobility is based on ambition, skill, and talent. However, few systems are totally open, and significantly different opportunities are available at different levels of society.

Sociologists use the concept of class to analyze stratification systems in countries with a great deal of social mobility. Members of the same social class have similar opportunities, values, goals, and ways of behaving. They share economic and social position in the society. People can be members of a given class depending on their incomes, education levels, and occupations. Usually, a society has a very small "upper class." Most citizens are divided into a "middle class" (owners of small businesses, professionals, managers, and civil servants), a "working class" (manual workers in industries such as manufacturing, mining, and construction), and a "lower class" (unskilled laborers, those in low-paying service jobs, and the permanently unemployed).

Karl Marx: *Bourgeoisie* and *Proletariat*

The writings of Karl Marx are the foundation of modern conflict theory. Marx believed that throughout history, social stratification has been based on economic factors. Whoever has controlled the means of production (land, factories, equipment, and money) has controlled everything else.

Marx identified two social classes: those who control and those who are controlled.

In modern capitalist societies the *bourgeoisie* control businesses and factories, and the *proletariat* provide the necessary labor. Marx believed that the bourgeoisie take advantage of the proletariat, exploiting their labor and forcing them into poverty. He urged the proletariat to use their greatest strength—their large numbers—to overthrow the bourgeoisie.

Class Divisions and Class Consciousness

Class consciousness—personal identification with one's status group—can be complex in modern societies. Middle-class people have different interests, behaviors, child-rearing habits, and goals from those in the working class. Those who have steady, dependable jobs see themselves as different from those who don't. In the United States, social mobility tends to blur the distinctions created by class consciousness.

Types and Patterns of Social Mobility

Social mobility may take different forms:

* **Upward mobility** and **downward mobility** occur when an individual moves up or down the ranks of social strata during his or her lifetime.

EXAMPLES: A son or daughter of a skilled factory worker who becomes a doctor experiences upward mobility. A child born into a prosperous upper-middle-class family who is chronically underemployed as an adult experiences downward mobility.

* **Intergenerational mobility** and **Intragenerational mobility** occur between (*inter-*) or within (*intra-*) generations. If a child's status as an adult is significantly different from that of his or her parent, the mobility is intergenerational.

EXAMPLE: A lawyer who is the child of a truck driver.

If an individual's status changes significantly as he or she ages, intragenerational mobility has taken place.

EXAMPLE: A person who drops out of high school and later becomes a noted author.

* **Horizontal mobility** happens when an individual moves from one comparably ranked status to another. A person's social status may change, or may differ from that of a parent, but not be necessarily higher or lower.

   EXAMPLE: A lawyer's son or daughter becomes a college professor (the prestige level of the two occupations is about the same).

Mobility in the United States

The belief that "anyone can get ahead" is a traditional American value, so social mobil-ity is not only possible but encouraged. Yet how much social mobility really exists?

In one study of how Americans view equal opportunity, researchers found significant differences in opinion according to race and social class. In response to the question, "Do you think America is a land of opportunity?" about 80 percent of whites interviewed agreed with the statement, but only about 60 percent of blacks agreed. Even further disparities were found in answer to the question, "Does a poor boy have the same chances as a rich boy to make a given amount of money?" Almost 60 percent of the wealthy white

U.S. Culture Connection

White, Pink, and Blue Collars

The terms *white collar* and *blue collar* describe jobs that reflect social class membership. Sociologists originally coined the terms, with "white-collar" jobs referring to middle-class occupations in which jobholders wear white dress shirts to work. "Blue-collar workers," such as plumbers, electricians, and other manual laborers, gained their name from the open-collar, casual blue shirts they wore. Fashions and gender roles have transformed the original distinctions, but the terms have become a part of popular culture. In recent years, a new term, *pink collar,* has been coined to refer to some jobs held by women.

people in the study said yes. Among middle-income people, however, only 21 percent said yes, and just 11 percent of poor blacks answered the question affirmatively. Are these perceptions accurate?

Studies that concentrate on intergenerational mobility show that father-to-son mobility steps are usually quite small. (The few studies on social mobility of women indicate that their patterns are similar to those of men.) Rarely does a son get a job with prestige or pay much higher or lower than that of his father. Vertical movements between the bottom and the top of the occupational structure are also rare. In other words, few sons of garbage collectors rise to become Supreme Court justices. Still, exceptions to this pattern exist, and the United States maintains a comparatively open class system.

Class Structure in the United States

Most Americans like to think of themselves as "middle class," no matter what their occupation, level of education, or income. When asked about their social class, very few people label themselves as "upper class" or "lower class." After all, American culture values the ability of average people to govern their own affairs. Most of all, we value equal opportunity, the potential individuals have to change their status in life. Yet social inequality exists in the United States, and even children understand that some people have more wealth, prestige, and power than others.

Social Classes in the United States

	Lower Class	Working Class
Main Feature	Poverty, underprivilege.	Irregular employment.
Economic Factors: Employment	Unemployed, underemployed, and the "working poor."	Blue-collar or manual labor (repair technicians, dog groomers).
Income	Lowest.	Low.
Social Factor: Education	Minimal school or job skills.	At least high school, some college attendance but no degree.
Lifestyle Issues, Challenges	Powerless; barely able to provide for their needs.	Insecure at work; only able to receive education at a personal sacrifice.

Social Classes

How many social classes are there in the United States? Most people think of three: upper, middle, and lower classes. However, sociological analysis is more complex. Sociologists usually break socioeconomic status into several layers based on social factors, such as levels of education and lifestyles, and economic factors, such as income and occupation. Most researchers refer to at least five classes in U.S. society. Each class shares a cluster of status characteristics that distinguishes it from others. The **five** socioeconomic classes in U.S. society, described in the chart below:

* Lower class.
* Working class.
* Lower-middle class.

* Upper-middle class.
* Upper class.

Effects of Class Differences

Class differences have profound effects on *life chances*, such as a person's access to health care, education, and housing, as well as on one's relationship with the law.

Health and Longevity

While almost all industrial societies have some way of providing health care for everyone, the level of that care can vary enormously based on an individual's income. Good health care of the mother during pregnancy, regular checkups with doctors and dentists during the growing years, access to expensive screening tests for various forms of cancer, quality nursing care in old age—all these extend an

Lower-Middle Class	Upper-Middle Class	Upper Class
Steady employment.	Professional occupations with stability and prestige.	Wealth, high social status.
"Lower-white collar" jobs (police, small business owners).	"Upper-white collar" jobs in professions and businesses.	Prestigious occupations, often professional.
Enough to own a home.	High, enough to save and accumulate assets.	Highest combination of income and assets.
Training beyond high school, with or without college.	Most have college education, many have advanced degrees.	College and above; may attend prestigious schools.
Concerned about saving enough for retirement and health care.	Pressured by career demands that threaten the quality of family life.	Challenged to find ways to be socially responsible.

U.S. Culture Connection

The New "Ultra" Middle Class

In 2000, *Money* Magazine identified a new and growing class in the United States. Families in this "ultra" middle class were headed by adults between the ages of 35 and 55 who lived in metropolitan areas and had at least a bachelor's degree. Family income was more than $100,000 a year; many families had investment portfolios.

When family income increased to a "confidence zone" of $150,000, members experienced a lifestyle change that allowed them to afford homes in the top 10 percent of the market, send 2 children to a private college without financial aid, own a high-end luxury car, and establish savings for retirement.

individual's life. They are more readily available to those who can pay for them.

One of the most powerful influences on life expectancy in developed countries is the level of socioeconomic inequality. The greater the gap between the rich and poor within a population, the lower the country stands when ranked with other countries. This helps explain why the United States, the richest and most powerful country in the world (spending more than any other on health care), ranks below 25th in the list of countries ordered by life expectancy. Income differences between rich and poor are bigger in the United States than in any other developed nation.

Changes in a population's income distribution appear to be associated with changes in health. Studies have shown that reducing income disparity decreases death rates; increasing income disparity raises them.

Education

Social class affects an individual's level of education in two ways, through the socialization process and through the ability to pay for good education. Affluent, well-educated parents are likely to socialize their children into values compatible with future success. Their expectations and values encourage children to work hard in school and aspire to professional occupations.

Access to education is crucial to socioeconomic success because it strongly influences a person's ability to qualify for high-paying jobs and fit into more affluent lifestyles. Children from poor families are

114   **Introduction to Sociology**

significantly less likely to attend college than children from prosperous families and thus are less likely to acquire the skills, knowledge, and associations that lead to higher-level positions.

Housing

The quality of housing affects many aspects of an individual's life. In poor areas, apartments and houses are small. Sanitation is often inadequate and poses health hazards. Few poor people own their homes, so they depend on a landlord's ability or willingness to maintain adequate living conditions. The neighborhoods of the poor lack safe places for children to play or for others to walk in.

The rich enjoy comfortable neighborhoods with access to better hospitals, more efficient transportation, and more effective police protection. The poor are more likely to live in areas where streets are littered with trash, shopping centers are inadequate or nonexistent, and crime rates are dangerously high.

The Law

The poor are often the losers in the criminal justice system. They include more victims as well as more perpetrators. Residents of low-income neighborhoods are frequently arrested for the victimless crimes of drunkenness, vagrancy, and gambling, which together account for about 60 percent of all arrests. For crimes that carry jail sentences, the poor are more likely to be sent to jail if convicted than are the wealthier members of society.

Class and Language

According to researcher Paul Fussell, people often betray their social class in their speech. Each class uses different words to describe the same objects. For example, working-class people say "tux," middles say "tuxedo," and uppers say "dinner jacket" or "black tie." With some humor, Fussell observes that middle-class people try to achieve high status by multiplying syllables, substituting complex words for simple ones. They say "individuals" instead of "people," "position" instead of "job," "purchase" instead of "buy," and "proceed" instead of "go."

Persons in Poverty by Race/Ethnicity

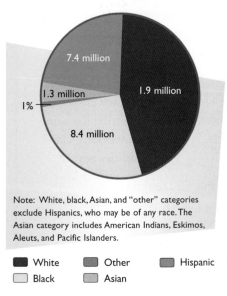

7.4 million

1.3 million

1%

1.9 million

8.4 million

Note: White, black, Asian, and "other" categories exclude Hispanics, who may be of any race. The Asian category includes American Indians, Eskimos, Aleuts, and Pacific Islanders.

■ White ■ Other ▨ Hispanic
▢ Black ▨ Asian

Source: U.S. Bureau of the Census (1998)

Poverty

What causes poverty? Many answers have been given. Karl Marx believed that the poor were the victims of the greedy rich. Believers in the American philosophy of "rugged individualism" argued that poor people were responsible for their own poverty because they were lazy, unmotivated, and uninspired. Such answers do little to produce solutions. Sociologists analyze the components of poverty: How would we define poverty? What groups live in poverty? Over time, how do these groups change?

Defining Poverty

To start understanding poverty, we must establish a standard for identifying who we are talking about. Who are the poor?

Measuring poverty is a complex matter that must take into account many influences on costs of living. The U.S. Census Bureau uses a **poverty line** based on income and the number of members in a family. All who fall below the line are defined as "poor." The statistic is used in many ways, including determining who is eligible for public welfare and who is not.

The Census Bureau adjusts the poverty line every year for inflation. In 2001, the poverty line was defined as a household income of $17,650 for a family of four.

The graph opposite shows how all people in poverty are distributed by race. It shows, for instance, that 45 percent of all people in poverty are white—not that 45 percent of all white people in the United States are in poverty.

Poverty Rates and the Poor

The *poverty rate* is a measure of how many people in a particular population fall below the poverty line. It is used to look at group membership in poverty. We could compare the percent of musicians living in poverty to that of other occupations, or children living in poverty to that of other age groups. The poverty rate can reveal much about our society.

Studies of poverty rates have shown that **five** factors are strongly related to poverty levels:

1. **Race and ethnicity.** Most of the poor are white, however, Latinos and African Americans are *more likely* to be poor than whites.
2. **Female head-of-household.** Of all population categories, female-headed households produce the greatest number of poor people. Especially hard-hit are women living without husbands and with one or more children.
3. **Region.** Some areas of the country present fewer economic opportunities than others and, as a result, have a higher percent of impoverished people.
4. **Age.** Older people are an unusual economic group because they include such a range of income and wealth. But even though some older people have accumulated wealth, overall the aged are more likely to live in poverty than the rest of the population.
5. **Disabilities.** Disabilities often mean that people cannot be employed full-time, and as a result, about a fifth of all disabled people live below the poverty line.

Sociologist's Perspective

Income Disparity

According to an analysis by the Center on Budget and Policy Priorities, the gap between rich and poor in the United States grew much wider between 1977 and 1999. In 1999, the richest 2.7 million citizens (the top one percent) collectively had as many after-tax dollars to spend as the bottom 100 million. The ratio has more than doubled since 1977. The data show that income disparity has grown so much that four out of five households—about 217 million people—took home a thinner slice of the economic pie in 1999 than in 1977. It should be pointed out, however, that the "pie" had become much larger. The poorer families had more buying power in 1990 than in 1977.

Declining Poverty Rates

According to research by the Census Bureau, the percentage of households living in poverty in 2000 dropped to the lowest point in more than two decades. The bureau noted that 11.8 percent of the population lived below the poverty line in 2000, down from 12.7 percent the year before. The bureau also reported sharp gains for those far down the income scale:

* Median income for African-American, Hispanic, and non-Hispanic white households reached the highest levels ever recorded.
* Households in the bottom fifth of the income scale saw their household earnings rise by 5.4 percent, the largest increase of any income group.
* While several states and the District of Columbia saw an overall decrease in poverty rates, no state saw a statistically significant rise in poverty.

Chapter 6 Wrap-up
SOCIAL STRATIFICATION AND CLASS

Social stratification appears in every society. The strata are made up of social classes, each with a different degree of power, wealth, and prestige. A person is born into a social class. Societies can be ranked on a continuum between open and closed systems. The more open societies permit people to move from one class to another.

In the United States, sociologists recognize five social classes: the lower class, the working class, the lower-middle class, the upper-middle class, and the upper class. Economic and social factors differentiate these classes. Class differences influence people's life chances in such areas as health care, housing, education, and treatment under the law.

Poverty is related to low incomes and inadequate living conditions. The poverty line defines the combination of income and family size that makes people "poor." The poverty rate indicates what percentage of a given population lives in poverty. One's risk of living in poverty is influenced by race and ethnicity, household composition, region of the country, age, and level of disability.

castes—lifelong statuses determined by the status of one's parents. *p.108*

class—group of people who share economic and social position in society. *p.104*

closed system—stratification system that allows little or no social mobility. *p.108*

continuum—continuous, uninterrupted extent, like a line, that has opposite concepts at either end of it, used to show relative position of institutions to each other with respect to the ideas conveyed at the ends. *p.108*

downward mobility—movement from a higher to a lower rank of the social strata. *p.110*

horizontal mobility—movement from one level of society to another of the same rank. *p.111*

intergenerational mobility—movement of a son or daughter up or down the social strata from the position of the parents. *p.110*

intragenerational mobility—movement up or down the social strata within one's lifetime. *p.110*

open system—stratification system that allows some significant degree of social mobility. *p.109*

poverty line—measure by the United States Census that divides people into poor and non-poor groups on the basis of income. *p.116*

social mobility—ability of individuals to change their social status during their lifetimes. *p.108*

social stratification—structured ranking of entire groups of people within a society based on differences in power, prestige, and wealth. *p.104*

stratum (plural *strata*)—layer; in sociology, a level of society comprised of people with similar social, cultural, or economic status. *p.108*

upward mobility—movement from a lower to a higher rank of the social strata. *p.110*

CHAPTER 7

Race and Ethnicity

In this chapter, you will learn about:

- racial and ethnic minorities
- prejudice and discrimination
- minority groups in the United States

Two middle-aged women are ahead of you in line at the post office. One says, "We were stuck in traffic next to a bus full of ethnics." What does she mean about the people on the bus?

One way people understand their world is by creating categories. We couldn't make sense of all the information flooding our senses if we didn't. We categorize almost everything we encounter. One kind of category is based on the racial or ethnic group into which people are born. Racial and ethnic groupings include much cultural information. The differences among groups of people have enriched human lives in countless ways, but have also spawned some of the biggest conflicts in history. The woman in line is not just acknowledging the different culture groups of the people she saw, she is also making a judgment about them. It is an unfavorable judgment. Prejudice and discrimination in the United States can be illustrated by examining the experiences of minority groups.

Racial and Ethnic Minorities

The oldest human records speak of minorities and raise the question of how they should be treated. There were minorities in ancient Egypt and Babylon, and the Hebrew scriptures furnish complete descriptions of numerous minority groups. How do sociologists view this aspect of human society?

Dominant Groups

In a society, the group of people that has the power—whose members include the rulers, lawgivers, and religious, military, and educational leaders—is the dominant group. A nation's history identifies its **dominant group**.

EXAMPLE: In Spain, the dominant group is the group whose power dates from the time of Ferdinand and Isabella and their European ancestors. These 15th-century rulers expelled and persecuted Jews and Muslims and established a white, Roman Catholic nation with Castilian Spanish as its official language.

Groups in a society that have been overpowered by the dominant group—such as American Indians in the United States—or have come in after the dominant group's power is established—immigrants in the United States other than the English—make up minority groups.

The dominant group establishes the values and norms of the society. It creates a social structure that operates in its favor. Minority groups have to live by the rules set by the dominant group, which usually means they don't have the same privileges and must accept inferior housing and jobs and are often treated differently by the justice system.

Minority Groups

A common misconception about minority groups is that they are always numerically smaller than the majority group in a society. That may be true, but a **minority group** is better defined as any recognizable group in a society that suffers some disadvantage due to prejudice or discrimination by the dominant group. In some nations of the world, religion distinguishes a minority group. Major minority groups in the United States are identified by race and ethnicity.

Racial Groups

The concept of **race** is based on observable physical differences among people resulting from inherited biological traits. It divides people into groups based on skin color and ancestral origin. Traditionally, English-speaking people have talked in terms of three races with their origins from **three** of the world's continents:

1. Africa.
2. Asia.
3. Europe.

Centuries of racial mixing— through migration, exploration, and invasion— have resulted in a great intermingling of races. We cannot accurately categorize individuals as "black" or "white." Sociologists are not interested in the biology of race. They are interested in race as it relates to the social structure.

In order to make the gathering of data uniform, sociologists rely on the categories of race that the Census Bureau uses or on the definition of race that individuals give themselves or others.

If you read a U.S. Census Bureau report, you might find data divided among the following **five** groups:

1. White, not Hispanic.
2. Black.
3. Hispanic.
4. Asian and Pacific Islander.
5. American Indian, Eskimo, and Aleut.

In actual practice, the Census Bureau invites people to check one of dozens of categories to identify their race. In the 2000 census, there were about 60 different racial combinations recognized for non-Hispanics and another 60 for Hispanics. Census forms were available in English, Spanish, Chinese, Korean, Vietnamese, and Tagalog, the language of the Philippines. Guides for the census takers were written in 49 languages. As you can see, race in the United States is a matter of culture, and is not easy to define.

In the United States, about 30 percent of the population is non-white. African Americans make up the largest racial minority group. However, by around 2005 the Hispanic population is expected to outnumber the black population. If current trends continue, by 2050 almost half of the U.S. population will be non-white.

Across **Cultures**

Skin Color and Race

Variations in skin color are used to categorize minority groups in many societies. But variations in skin color take on different meanings across cultures. When observing skin color, historically Americans have lumped people broadly into black, white, and Asian categories. In contrast, many nations of Central and South America distinguish many shades of color. In Brazil, for example, people recognize approximately 40 color groups. Terms in other countries, such as Mestizo Hondurans and Mulatto Colombians, recognize the cultural heritage of the hemisphere.

Ethnic Groups

While racial groups are based on physical characteristics, **ethnic groups** are based on such cultural factors as national origin, religion, language, norms, and values. As with the concept of racial groups, there is great variety within broad ethnic categories.

EXAMPLES: Asian Americans comprise a minority group that includes many different national groups. Japanese Americans not only speak a different language from Korean Americans, but they have different customs and political and social beliefs as well.

Jews, although they are racially diverse and live in many countries around the world, are bound together by their common religious beliefs, customs, and values.

Within the United States, nationality groups often settle in the same neighborhoods and retain separate identities. Poles, Ukrainians, Mexicans, Puerto Ricans, Italians, and Germans who live in the United States may vary in the strength of their ethnic identities, but national heritage often sets such groups apart.

Ethnic groups retain their separate identities as long as they pass their cultural beliefs and practices from generation to generation. A common ancestry is usually—but not necessarily—shared by group members. In groups with strong ethnic identities, members are encouraged to form friendships with and to marry only others of the same ethnicity. In fact, the term *ethnic* comes from the Greek word *ethnos*, meaning "people" or "nation." The special feeling of "my people" sets the group apart from others and discourages members from forming close ties with "outsiders."

Characteristics of Minority Groups

Sociologists identify minority groups by **four** characteristics, in addition to their receiving unequal treatment in society:

1. **Shared Physical or Cultural Characteristics.** Members of a minority group are identified by a wide array of physical and/or cultural differences, including race, religion, ancestry, language, and customs. The foods served, the celebrations observed, the ways in which people choose their spouses—these are often similar among members of an ethnic group.

2. **Ascribed Statuses.** Membership in a minority (or dominant) group is not voluntary. People are born into the group; race and ethnicity are ascribed statuses.

3. **Group Solidarity.** When a group is the object of long-term prejudice or discrimination, the feeling of "us *versus* them" often becomes intense. Members of ethnic groups stick together when they feel under attack from the dominant group or from other minority groups.

4. **Endogamy.** Members of a minority generally marry others from the same group, a practice known as **endogamy**. Two factors account for this: (1) the unwillingness of members of the dominant group to marry into, and thus in some way join, a lower level of society; and (2) a minority group's sense of solidarity, which encourages marriages within the group.

Patterns of Repression and Response

Societies vary in the degree to which racial and ethnic minority groups participate in mainstream society. Minorities respond to their situation with behaviors ranging from submission and acceptance to agitation and violence.

In history, repression of minorities by the dominant group has taken **four** forms:

1. **Forced Removal**—in which a minority population is transferred to a separate geographic location.
   EXAMPLE: The Trail of Tears removal of the Cherokee from Georgia to Oklahoma in 1838.

2. **Segregation**—in which a minority group is kept separate from the dominant population in the same location. It can be *de jure*, based on laws, or *de facto*, based on informal norms.
   EXAMPLES: Earlier laws in the South that kept blacks and whites from attending the same schools (*de jure*); the discriminatory practice of sellers, real estate agents, and mortgage lenders in the North that kept African Americans from living in neighborhoods with whites (*de facto*).

3. **Subjugation**—maintaining control over the minority population by force.
   EXAMPLE: The Israeli use of curfew laws and troops with guns and tanks to punish the Palestinian minority following acts of terrorism by militant individuals.

4. **Annihilation**—the destruction of a targeted minority population. Also called *genocide*.
   EXAMPLE: In Rwanda, the efforts of the Hutu rebels against the Tutsis.

Did You Know?

The Holocaust

The most extreme form of unequal treatment of a group is genocide, the systematic, wide-scale killing of people merely because they are members of a particular group. During World War II the German Nazis exterminated millions of minorities, including Jews, Slavs, gypsies, and homosexuals. The Nazi actions were based on the belief that the Germans were a "master race," which was mentally and physically superior to all others. Nazis argued that an end to their problems would come only after they had exterminated people who might "pollute" their greatness. The horror that came from this ghastly idea was on a scale unknown in the world. This massive slaughter has been named the Holocaust, after a Greek word that means "burned whole" and was used to describe religious sacrifices.

Minority groups have often responded to these negative forms of treatment in **three** ways:

1. **Submission and Acceptance**—deferring to members of the dominant culture and learning ways of "getting along."

2. **Withdrawal**—avoiding contact with the dominant culture through self-segregation.

3. **Agitation and Violence**—protesting minority status and unequal treatment or organizing a revolt against the dominant group.

Melting Pot or Cultural Salad

Society in the United States has tried to encourage most of its immigrant minority groups, particularly those that are white, to join mainstream society. Historically, it has done this in **two** ways, described by figures of speech:

1. **The Melting Pot** (from the container in which metals are melted to make such

U.S. Culture Connection

"Uncle Toms" and "Oreos"

Minorities sometimes disdain members of the group who accept their status. This feeling may be expressed through insulting nicknames. For example, African Americans have used the name "Uncle Tom" (from the hero of Harriet Beecher Stowe's novel *Uncle Tom's Cabin*) to refer to someone who seems overly anxious to win white people's approval. A late-20th-century insult was "Oreo," because the cookie is "black on the outside but white in the middle." This term indicates one who doesn't accept one's own people.

alloys as steel) is a term for American society that suggests the people of different nations have given up their distinctive ways to become members of the dominant culture through **assimilation**, the process by which people become like others around them, taking their norms on as their own.

2. **The Salad Bowl** refers to the idea of **cultural pluralism** in which mainstream society acknowledges there is value in preserving the uniqueness of the subcultures that comprise it. Minority groups are encouraged to maintain unique identities within the larger culture, and society accepts diversity as part of its own definition.

Prejudice and Discrimination

We often think that prejudice and discrimination are pretty much the same thing, or that one always accompanies the other. Actually, they are two related but separate phenomena, and one can occur without the other.

Prejudice is a negative attitude toward an entire category of people, often an ethnic or racial minority. **Discrimination** is the denial of opportunities and equal rights to people based on their group membership. Prejudice is an *attitude,* whereas discrimination is an *action* that

The Authoritarian Personality

In the late 1940s, sociologist T. W. Adorno researched the question of whether some personality types were more likely to be prejudiced than others. He concluded that hostile attitudes toward minority groups are characteristic of an "authoritarian personality." Authoritarians, as described by Adorno, hold a rigid, hierarchical view of human relations, and have a tendency to view reality in simple, black-or-white terms, ignoring shades of gray. They are preoccupied by rules and regulations, with who gives orders and who takes them, and with different levels of power and status. Since they see life as a competition between winners and losers, authoritarians are uncomfortable with "democratic" situations and strive to dominate others. Authoritarians are suspicious and fearful of anything that is different, so they tend to reject anyone who is a member of a minority group.

deprives someone of equality. Both are aimed at a person's group membership, without regard for the individual.

The Roots of Prejudice

The Latin roots of the word *prejudice* mean prejudging, or judging before knowing. A prejudice may be either positive, such as the belief that one's school is the best in the country, or negative, such as the belief that all people on welfare are lazy.

A certain amount of prejudice comes from our tendency to generalize. Prejudging may even be functional. If, for example, you are in trouble and need someone to run as fast as she can for help, you may turn to your softball teammate rather than to your book-loving friend.

Prejudice becomes a problem when the preformed judgment remains unchanged even after facts show it to be inaccurate. So, if your reading friend has won many track races and you still don't recognize her running talent, you probably are prejudiced against the athletic abilities of studious people.

What causes people to develop hostile attitudes toward other groups? Prejudice has psychological, cultural, and social roots.

Psychological Roots

Prejudice may serve a psychological function for dominant-group members who feel frustrated, insecure, or inferior. These people may take satisfaction in **scapegoating**—placing the blame for troubles on an innocent individual or group.

"Is it OK to discriminate against bigots?"

People who scapegoat seem to get psychological satisfaction from knowing that no matter how low they sink, there are still some people—a whole race or group—who are lower. Once they identify a scapegoat, people justify their irrational feelings and behavior by "discovering" evidence that the group is indeed "wicked" and "inferior."

Cultural and Social Roots

Sociologists seek to identify cultural and social factors that shape prejudice. In some societies, prejudice is explicitly encouraged. In others, economic or political conflict may cause groups to be hostile toward one another. Socialization can reinforce prejudices. **Two** roots of prejudice include:

1. **Ethnocentrism.** Ethnocentrism is the belief in the superiority of one's own culture group. This attitude may lead to **racism**, the belief that one race is superior to others. When racism is common in a society, most members of the dominant group are prejudiced against minorities. Racism may reflect a group's desire to have power over others, or it

may come from a wish to keep one's culture as it is. Minority groups may be perceived as bringing unwanted change.

2. **Economic and Political Conflict.** When culturally separate groups live in the same geographical area, they have often had a history of competing for scarce resources. Warfare that erupts between them from time to time leaves deep scars. Sometimes it seems these will never heal, as each generation passes on the stories of old grievances and the hatred born of

U.S. Culture Connection

Hate Crimes

Hate crimes, fueled by prejudice, are directed toward individuals solely because they are members of a minority group. In 1990, the U.S. Congress passed the Hate Crimes Statistics Act. This law requires the Department of Justice to gather data on victims of hate crime by their race, religion, ethnicity, or sexual orientation. By 1998, 537 active hate groups were identified in the United States. The Southern Poverty Law Center reported in 1999 that hate crimes were directed at minority individuals every day.

Daily Hate Crime Victims	
8 African Americans	3 Caucasian Americans
3 homosexuals	3 Jewish persons
1 Latino	

violence. This situation exists in many places, including the Balkan Peninsula and the Middle East.

Discrimination

It makes sense to assume that discrimination is always the result of prejudice. However, prejudiced people do not always act on their biases. Sometimes people go to great lengths to keep from acting on their prejudices.

EXAMPLE: A white supervisor realizes that he is prejudiced toward blacks and works hard to treat his employees equally, despite his bias.

Discrimination can also occur without a direct connection to prejudice.

EXAMPLE: A supervisor without bias refuses to hire African Americans because her biased clients would take their business elsewhere.

Bias-motivated Incidents
Race 4,321
Religion 1,390
Sexual orientation 1,260
Ethnicity/national origin 754
Disability 25
Multiple biases 5

Source: Federal Bureau of Investigation (1999)

In the first case, the supervisor is prejudiced without discrimination, and in the second, discrimination occurs even though the prejudice is not "first-hand."

We can identify **three** types of discrimination:

1. **Legal Discrimination.** Discrimination that is supported by law is less common than it was even a few decades ago. Both constitutional interpretation and federal laws have thrown out state and local segregation laws in the United States. Apartheid (separation of the races) in South Africa is now illegal. However, historical examples of legal discrimination are plentiful. In Germany during the 1930s, Jews were barred from government and professional jobs and their property was confiscated. During World War II, the United States placed Japanese immigrants and Japanese Americans into internment camps.

2. **Nonlegal Discrimination.** Discrimination that is not supported by law but results from actions by individuals is far more common than legal discrimination. In the United States, minorities have been barred from good neighborhoods by discriminatory real estate practices. They have been kept from promotion to the best jobs. No laws support either behavior.

3. **Institutional Discrimination.** Institutional discrimination refers to the denial of opportunities and equal rights that results from the normal operations of a society. Some examples are:

* Rules that only English be spoken at a place of work.

Election 2000

The Fifteenth Amendment of the United States Constitution guarantees black Americans the right to vote, but for years after the amendment was passed, Jim Crow laws—demanding that voters pay poll taxes and pass literacy tests—made black voting almost impossible in many Southern states. In a controversy surrounding the 2000 general election, some African Americans in Florida claimed they experienced systematic problems in trying to cast their votes. Civil rights leaders from such groups as the NAACP and the Rainbow Coalition charged that African Americans were intimidated by police sweeps and roadblocks and victimized by widespread confusion. The groups sent hundreds of sworn statements to the Justice Department, and representatives were sent to investigate the charges.

* Preferences shown by schools in the admission of children of wealthy and influential alumni.
* Restrictive employment leave-taking policies that make it difficult for a parent to take time off.
* Lack of computer access at home and in school.

In each of these examples, minority group members are disadvantaged. Those who cannot speak English, who lack influential parents, who do not have a spouse to share childcare when children at home need someone to stay with them, or who lack sufficient resources to get the tools they need to perform work are discriminated against in the job market. Institutional discrimination becomes part of a vicious circle that makes it very difficult for minorities to get ahead.

Across Cultures

Koreans in Japan

Legal discrimination toward Koreans is increasingly controversial in contemporary Japan. About 96 percent of the population is Japanese; only about 700,000 Koreans live in Japan. It is not easy for Koreans to obtain citizenship, and without citizenship, they cannot vote and they cannot work as teachers or government officials. In 1995 Japan's Supreme Court ruled that local governments could permit resident Koreans the right to vote, but there was little movement to make this a national policy.

Minority Groups in the United States

American society is enriched by the various racial and ethnic groups that make up its minorities. Members of minority groups can be found in all the classes of society. While membership in a minority group affects an individual's status, it does not prevent social mobility.

African Americans

The 34 million African Americans in the United States make up one of the nation's largest minorities, about 12.1 percent of the total population. According to projections by the U.S. Census Bureau, the African-American population is expected to grow more than twice as fast as the white population between 1995 and 2050.

This population is not distributed evenly throughout the country. Although African Americans have been migrating out of Southern states for more than a century, in 1996, 53 percent of African Americans still lived in the South. There, they made up about 19 percent of the region's population. Nationwide, 55 percent of African Americans resided in the central cities of metropolitan areas.

African Americans in the United States date back to 1619, when the first African immigrants settled in Virginia as indentured servants. By the end of the 1600s, nearly all U.S. blacks and their descendants were either indentured servants or slaves. It took a civil war and the Thirteenth Amendment in 1865 for African Americans to gain freedom and citizenship. Another 100 years went by before members of this group won the rights of full participation in the benefits of U.S. society. The Civil Rights movement of the 1950s and 1960s resulted in significant gains for African Americans.

Today, the percentages of African Americans and white Americans completing high school are nearly identical. African Americans hold managerial and professional jobs, and their percentages in these jobs has been growing significantly for more than 40 years. As a result of better job opportunities, there is a major group of middle-class African Americans. In business, there are African American multimillionaires. In the leadership ranks of government, there are African American mayors, Supreme Court justices, and members of the President's Cabinet.

Thus, we can see that class and race are two different concepts. African Americans occupy all classes in our society. Yet statistics reflect continuing inequalities:

* The percentage of African Americans completing four or more years of college is about half that of whites, and the percentages are decreasing.
* In 1999, the mean income for African American families was $27,900, as compared to $44,400 for white families.
* The unemployment rate for African Americans in 2000 was 7.7 percent, compared to 3.9 percent for whites.
* The percentage of African Americans below the poverty line in 1999 was 23.6, compared to 7.7 for whites.

U.S. Race and Ethnic Composition, 1999 and 2025

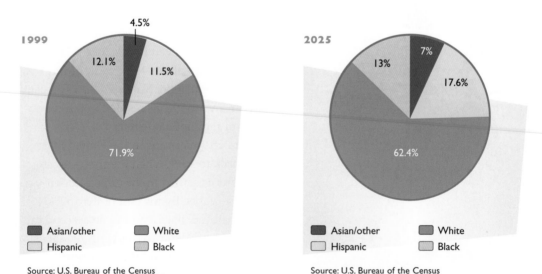

1999

4.5%
12.1%
11.5%
71.9%

Asian/other   White
Hispanic   Black

Source: U.S. Bureau of the Census

2025

7%
13%
17.6%
62.4%

Asian/other   White
Hispanic   Black

Source: U.S. Bureau of the Census

African Americans and the Justice System

Recent studies, including one conducted by Eric Lotke in the District of Columbia, reveal that growing numbers of young black men are in trouble with the law. According to Lotke, the number of African Americans in prison nationwide grew from 146,900 in 1980 to 541,900 in 1995, and the number on probation and parole grew from 410,000 to 1,395,000. In 1997, one in three young black men nationwide was under the control of the justice system on any given day.

Lotke believes that these increases were sparked by the decision to use law enforcement to manage social problems, such as mental health, drug abuse, or disorderly teens, problems previously handled by

other means. He asserts that those caught in the justice net are often the poor or minority group members. Often they lack the community and personal resources to handle their problems differently.

Latinos

The many groups included under the general terms *Latinos* and *Hispanics* represent the second largest minority in the United States. They are soon to become the largest. In 2000, 12 percent of the population, or 32.8 million, were Hispanic. More than 21.6 million, or 66 percent, were of Mexican origin. Nearly 2 million were Puerto Rican, and smaller numbers were Cuban Americans and people of Central or South-American origin. The numbers of

Latinos are increasing rapidly. According to Census Bureau data, Latinos make up the majority of residents in such cities as Miami, Florida; Santa Ana, California; and El Paso, Texas.

Latino groups share a common language and some cultural characteristics, although cultural customs vary widely among the different nationalities. The increasing number of Spanish-speaking populations in the United States has created a demand for bilingual education programs in some public schools.

Sociologist's Perspective

Cultural Identity of Latinos

Many Latinos clearly identify themselves as an ethnic group apart from other whites in the United States. Geographer Daniel L. Roy provides evidence for the importance of being Latino in a recent survey of ethnic attitudes from more than 1,000 Latino respondents. Ethnicity was deemed "very important" in defining identity by 755 respondents (72 percent), "somewhat important" by 222 respondents (21 percent), and "not important" by 58 respondents (six percent).

Some inequities between Latinos and the white majority are reflected in the following statistics from 2000:

* 10.6 percent of Latino adults had completed college, compared with 28.1 percent of non-Hispanic whites.
* The median household income of Latinos was 76 percent that of whites.
* 22.8 percent of all Latinos living in the United States lived below the poverty line.

The **three** largest Latino groups are:

1. **Mexican Americans.** Members of the largest Latino population trace their roots to Mexico. Some are descendants of the residents of territories annexed by the United States in the mid-1800s. Many others have migrated over the years into the Southwestern states. Today the highest concentrations of Mexican Americans are in California and Texas, although many have migrated to other areas of the country. Many Mexican Americans have strong family ties in both Mexico and the United States; most are devout Roman Catholics. Politically, Mexican Americans tend to be more liberal than most other Latinos.

2. **Puerto Ricans.** This second-largest group of Latinos in the United States is concentrated in large eastern cities. Since 1917, residents of Puerto Rico have held the status of U.S. citizens. The easy access between the island and the mainland has kept family ties and loyalties strong. Puerto Ricans living in the continental United States have barely half the

family income of whites, so a reverse migration has occurred for the past three decades: More Puerto Ricans have been going back to the island than coming to the mainland.

3. **Cuban Americans.** Cuban immigration dates back as far as 1831, but the numbers increased dramatically after Fidel Castro assumed control of Cuba in 1959. Throughout the various waves of immigration since then, most Cuban Americans have settled in southern Florida, particularly around Miami, where today they make up a majority of the population. Many Cuban Americans, especially those who came in the first round of immigration after the 1959 revolution, are successful professionals. Politically, Cuban Americans tend to be more conservative than other Latino groups. As a group, Cuban Americans have the highest rate of income, rate of employment, and proportion of professionals of all Hispanic Americans.

Asian Americans

Asian Americans come from many ancestral and national backgrounds. The **six** largest groups are from:

1. China.
2. Japan.
3. The Philippines.
4. India.
5. Korea.
6. Vietnam.

Until the 1960s, the United States severely limited the numbers of Asians who could immigrate to this country, so Asian Americans make up a smaller percentage of the total population than African Americans and Latinos, just 4 percent. However, their numbers are increasing rapidly, from 3.5 million in 1980 to 10 million in 2000. Some experts predict that by 2040, Asian Americans will make up about 10 percent of the U.S. population.

Asian Americans have been called a "model" minority group because they have succeeded economically, socially, and educationally. This label ignores the fact that Asian Americans are very diverse. For example, Southeast Asians living in the United States have the highest welfare dependency of any racial or ethnic group. For every Asian American family with an annual income of $75,000, there is another earning less than $10,000.

Asian Americans trace their roots to at least 25 different countries. However, most Asian Americans belong to one of the **two** largest groups:

1. **Chinese Americans.** The largest numbers of Asians in the United States are Chinese Americans. In the mid-1800s, about 200,000 Chinese people immigrated to this country, attracted by job opportunities created by the discovery of gold in the West. So many came that Congress enacted the Chinese Exclusion Act in 1882, effectively halting further immigration until the 1960s. During that time Chinese Americans suffered from economic, political, and social discrimination.

2. **Japanese Americans.** As an immigrant group, Japanese Americans are relatively recent arrivals to the United States. Many came during the early 20th century to escape political and social upheavals in Japan. When Japan attacked the U.S. Navy at Pearl Harbor in 1941, the government reacted by sending Japanese Americans to "evacuation" camps, uprooting them from their homes and communities on the West Coast. This mass detention branded them as "disloyal" to the country and cost Japanese Americans billions of dollars. Not until 1988 did the U.S. government formally apologize and set up a $1.25 billion trust fund to compensate victims of this discrimination.

Asian Americans: Discrimination in College Admissions?

Since the mid-1960s affirmative action programs have encouraged colleges and universities to ensure that minorities have equal access to higher education. However, in recent years many colleges and universities have been accused of "reverse discrimination" toward Asian Americans. According to critics, Asians do so well on admissions exams and make such good high school grades that selective schools worry that the percentages of Asian students will be too high. These schools have been criticized for creating higher admission standards for Asians than for other students—an accusation they have strongly denied.

Native Americans

Native Americans probably numbered in the millions before Europeans arrived on this continent. By the end of the 1800s, the Native American population had been reduced to only about 250,000 as a result of diseases introduced by the Europeans and the warfare and relocation visited on them by the dominant culture group.

By 2000 nearly 2.5 million citizens identified themselves as Native American. Native Americans are the nation's most poverty-stricken minority.

* About 14 percent are unemployed.
* About 32 percent live below the poverty line. On reservations, the numbers are probably higher.

* Less than 10 percent have graduated from college.
* The suicide rate among Native Americans is almost twice as high as in the general population.
* About one-third of Native American deaths are alcohol related.

In recent years Native Americans have formed political groups that actively lobby for equal rights and improved living conditions. These groups have also encouraged renewal of tribal identities and development of Native American businesses.

White Ethnics

"Give me your tired, your poor,/Your huddled masses yearning to breathe free,/The wretched refuse of your teeming shore./Send these, the homeless, tempest-tossed to me./I lift my lamp beside the golden door."

This verse is from Emma Lazarus's poem inscribed on the Statue of Liberty, which welcomed the huge numbers of European immigrants who came through New York's harbor in the 19th and 20th centuries. Each group faced difficulties as its members struggled to learn the language and customs of their new home. As they competed for jobs with American-born workers, they faced prejudice and open hostility, often violence. Those who were from Ireland, Italy, and the countries of Eastern Europe were Roman Catholic or Eastern Orthodox—religions that were feared and despised in the largely Protestant nation.

These "white ethnics," like members of other immigrant groups, tended to live near each other in the large cities. They helped each other find work, often dominating certain occupations. They formed close-knit societies. However, their children found it easier than other immigrants to move out of the lower class. For some, English was their first language. They learned in school the ways of the dominant culture. As they grew up, they moved away from the "old neighborhood."

Today, some white ethnics live in close-knit ethnic neighborhoods, but many have been assimilated into American culture, leaving the "old ways" behind. Although white ethnics in general don't face the same kinds of discrimination today as other minority groups, some research indicates that they are still underrepresented among the rich and the powerful. White Anglo-Saxon Protestants are still more likely to be CEOs of large corporations and major political leaders. We have had only one Roman Catholic President, John F. Kennedy (1961–1963).

Throughout history, societies have been composed of a dominant group and minority groups. The dominant group establishes the norms of the society and establishes a social structure that favors its members. Minority groups, therefore, generally have fewer privileges and suffer disadvantages.

Treatment of minority groups by the dominant group may involve assimilation, cultural pluralism, forced removal, segregation, subjugation, and, in extreme cases, annihilation. Reactions to such treatment by members of minority groups may include acceptance, submission, withdrawal, protest, or revolt.

Prejudice and discrimination are characteristic behaviors of the dominant group. Prejudice is an attitude and discrimination is a behavior. They have psychological, cultural, and social roots. Discrimination can be legal, nonlegal, and institutional.

Major minority groups in U.S. society include African Americans, Latinos, Asian Americans, and Native Americans. Members of these groups occupy all levels of the social hierarchy. Minority group membership does not predetermine class. White ethnics, the last of the minority groups discussed, include European immigrants who have not assimilated into mainstream society.

assimilation—process of becoming absorbed into the dominant group, taking on its norms and values. *p. 126*

cultural pluralism—condition of society in which different ethnic and racial groups coexist while maintaining separate identities; the enriching influence of their differences is valued. *p. 126*

discrimination—denial of opportunities and equal rights to people based on their group membership. *p. 126*

dominant group—group in a society that sets the values and norms and creates a social structure that operates in its favor. *p. 121*

endogamy—custom of marriage within a particular group. *p. 123*

ethnic group—group of people identified by their common cultural background; national origin, religion, and language distinguish ethnic groups. *p. 123*

institutional discrimination—denial of opportunities and equal rights to

individuals and groups that results from the normal operations of a society. *p. 129*

minority group—recognizable group of people who suffer disadvantages due to prejudice or discrimination by the dominant group. *p. 121*

prejudice—negative attitude toward an entire category of people, often an ethnic or racial minority. *p. 126*

race—major division of the world's population based on biologically inherited physical characteristics. *p. 121*

racism—belief that one race is supreme and all others are inferior; discrimination or prejudice based on race. *p. 128*

scapegoating—placing the blame for troubles on an innocent individual or group. *p. 127*

segregation—physical separation of racial and/or ethnic groups within a culture. *p. 124*

CHAPTER 8

Gender, Age, and Health

In this chapter, you will learn about:

- **gender and society**
- **age and society**
- **health and society**

If you could choose to be born male or female, which would you choose? If you could be any age, which would you choose? Your answers to those questions probably reflect your socialization into our society. Gender and age are ascribed statuses. We cannot do anything about them, and they carry social position. We have expectations of how individuals will behave based on their age or gender. We say, "How like a man!" or "Girls shouldn't do that." Descriptive terms like young, middle-aged, *and* senior citizen *are loaded with meaning. Societies vary widely in their attitudes toward the young and the old, and toward women and men.*

Health care is a topic that spans our lifetime. From the care of the pregnant mother through the sickness and wellness of life until the moment of death, we need it. We can get a more informed picture of the different groups in our society as we look at how access to and quality of health care differ.

Gender and Society

What kind of work do men do? What is "women's work"? Are men's and women's interests different? Most societies label some activities and behaviors as more masculine than feminine and vice versa.

Let's look at words for a moment. One's *sex* is determined by biology. Sex is either male or female. The term **gender** is used by sociologists to describe the cultural, psychological, and social traits associated with a biological sex. These traits are called either *masculine* or *feminine*.

The ways societies organize gender roles vary widely. In many times and places, men's roles have been in the public arena, and women's roles have been in the domestic arena, or home. Men were the recorders, the historians, and thus activities associated with women were often undocumented. They came to be seen as less important than those associated with men. Even when a culture's gender norms are informal, they can be very powerful.

Differences Between the Sexes

How much of the differentiation between gender roles is based on biology, and how much is determined by society? Some researchers believe that biological differences determine many societal expectations of men and women. Others believe that differences in behavior between males and females are learned, not inborn. The truth probably lies somewhere in between and is almost certainly a complex combination of both.

Biological Differences

For centuries most people assumed that biology dictated different interests and abilities for women and men. Men were thought to be naturally aggressive, and women were believed to possess a "maternal instinct" fulfilled only by bearing and caring for a child. We now know that a person's sexual characteristics are influenced mainly by **two** physical factors:

1. **Chromosomes.** Every human being has 23 pairs of chromosomes, thread-like bodies in each cell that determine hereditary characteristics. Each pair is alike except one—the pair of sex chromosomes. Females have two X chromosomes; males have an X chromosome and a Y chromosome.

   It is the father who determines the sex of a baby, because sperm cells carry either an X chromosome or a Y chromosome. An ovum, the mother's egg, always has an X chromosome. If the ovum is fertilized by a sperm with an X chromosome, the baby will be a female (XX). An ovum fertilized by a sperm with the Y chromosome will result in a boy (XY).

2. **Hormones.** Hormones are chemical substances in the body that stimulate or inhibit chemical processes, such as those that contribute to growth. The major female sex hormones are *estrogen* and *progesterone*. The major male hormones are *testosterone* and *androgen*. Hormones are active throughout life, and their effects are especially noticeable when a person reaches puberty. Do sex

hormones influence behavior? The answer is yes, they certainly do. But a caution lies in the word *influence*. Hormones can influence behavior. Most scientists do not believe that hormones *determine* behavior.

Cultural and Psychological Differences

Most sociologists believe that social influences on gender behavior are far greater than the influence of chromosomes and hormones. All societies have norms governing how males and females should act. Individuals are socialized in accordance with these norms. **Gender roles** are the particular behaviors and attitudes a society establishes for men and women.

Margaret Mead's study of three New Guinea societies in the 1930s found that gender roles vary widely from culture to culture. (See page 77.) Further evidence that culture shapes gender roles has been found in some **matrilineal societies**, which base status and inheritance on the female's kinship descent.

EXAMPLE: Among the Iroquois Confederation of Native Americans in the 1700s, the women's political and ritual influence rivaled that of the men. Women owned the land, which they inherited from mothers and aunts, and they controlled the production and distribution of food. Although the governing council was composed of male chiefs, the women controlled which men became leaders, and the senior women, or matrons, constantly monitored the chiefs and could impeach them.

Across Cultures

"Gender Power Ratio"

In 1995, the United Nations developed a scale to measure the proportional power of women to men in various countries. They called the measure a "gender power ratio," with the higher percentages indicating more equality. They found the highest power ratios in Scandinavian countries, and the lowest in developing countries in Africa and Asia.

Women's Power			
Sweden	.76	Brazil	.36
Norway	.75	Ghana	.31
Canada	.68	India	.22
United States	.62	Nigeria	.20
Great Britain	.48	Pakistan	.15
China	.47	Afghanistan	.11
Japan	.44		

Marketing to Teenage Girls

The Census Bureau tells us that the U.S. teen population is expected to grow to 30 million in 2010, up about 18 percent from 1990. This group has considerable spending money, and so designers and stores that cater to it have become a major business. Interest in clothes and fashion appears to be much higher for girls than boys. According to a 2000 Rand Youth Poll, the average income of girls 16 to 19 was $131 a week in 1999, up from $103 in 1997. The *New York Times* reported that marketers expected the girls to spend a great deal of their money on clothes and cosmetics.

These businesses invest in a gender expectation. Are they reinforcing a stereotype? Are they helping create one? What do you think?

Socialization and Gender Roles

Imagine a world with absolutely no social differences between the sexes. Families would have identical expectations of sons and daughters; men and women would act and dress the same. In reality, no matter how much equal opportunity exists in a society, the socialization experiences of men and women differ.

Stereotypes are conventional, oversimplified, often exaggerated images. Nevertheless, they point to general attitudes. Some in contemporary U.S. society include:

* Differing expectations of boys and girls begin at birth and continue as children go through school. Boys are expected to engage in rough-and-tumble play, to excel in math, to love sports. Girls are expected to be talkative, to like pretty clothes, to be good at reading.
* While a woman who chooses to marry and raise children rather than pursue a career is considered to be acting within normal expectations, a man who does the same is often treated as odd.

Gender Inequality and the Economy

Anthropologist Patricia Draper observed in her field work among the !Kung people of Botswana in Africa that only when they settled in one place—herding, growing crops, and working for wages—did the !Kung begin to see men as ranking higher than women. When the !Kung were foragers, their gender roles were interdependent. When women discovered information about game animals while they were gathering food, they passed it on to the men. Men and women spent about the same amount of time away from camp. Once the !Kung settled and had less food gathering to do, women were confined more to the home, boys gained mobility through herding, and girls' movements were limited.

* Gender expectations of women and girls are less rigid than for men and boys. Girls can wear dresses or pants. They can dress in many colors, fabrics, and styles. Men's business wear is restricted to long pants in a narrow range of colors and styles. Many bright colors are "forbidden" for men, except in such specialized garments as swimming trunks. Most people don't disapprove of girls playing with trucks or action video games. Boys may play with action figures, but not with baby dolls.

Much gender socialization takes place within the family, where parents, siblings, and other relatives serve as role models. Later, as a child grows older, peer influence increases. In the teen years, gender expectations are dominated by the views of other teenagers.

Gender expectations are continually provided by the media, especially advertising, movies, and television. What examples can you recall?

Roots of Gender Role Inequalities

As a broad historical trend, women seldom have equaled men in terms of power. Current trends show a narrowing of the traditional inequality between men and women, but full equality of the sexes remains to be accomplished. Why? Some explanations are based on physical size and strength differences, others on women's biologically based responsibilities for childbearing and early care of infants. What might be the social roots of gender roles?

Because the most ancient human societies were based on hunting and gathering, social scientists have thought that modern hunting and gathering societies might shed some light on gender roles. In studying them, anthropologists have observed that gender statuses are fairly equal.

Some social scientists have suggested that inequality between genders is related to a society's economic system. Researchers M. Kay Martin and Barbara Voorhies suggested that with the development of agricultural communities, women's status fell. They hypothesized that this inequality occurred as new agricultural tasks, particularly plowing, were assigned to men because of their greater average size and strength.

Others have pointed out that industrialization reinforced inequality, particularly for the middle and upper classes, as work became more clearly separated from the home. Is it possible that in postindustrial societies, where education is the primary determiner of an individual's role, gender inequalities will diminish? Or are they merely changing?

The Economy and Gender Roles

Economic variations in a society influence gender roles. Wartime brings the expectation that young, able-bodied men will become soldiers. In the 1940s, when World War II took huge numbers of men out of the workplace, women took their place making the materials that society and the war effort required. When men returned after the war, women who could afford to resume their customary roles at home did so.

During the great economic expansion that began in the 1980s, women again returned to the workplace. Social expectations of material goods and higher education were out of the range of families in which only one adult was employed. Also, increasing numbers of women wanted to pursue careers outside the home as an expression of self-fulfillment. As economic needs and social attitudes changed, so did expectations about women's work.

Mothers Employed Outside the Home

The U.S. Department of Labor gathers statistics about women in its Women's Bureau. In 2000, it reported that the likelihood that women with children would be in the labor force depended on the children's ages, using statistics from the previous year.

Working Mothers	
Age of Children	**Mothers in the Workforce**
14–17, none younger	78.9%
6–13, none younger	78.3%
Under 6	64.4%
Under 3	60.7%

Expressions of Inequality

Many sociologists believe that at least part of the trend in changing gender roles in the United States is due to increasing life expectancies. Women today spend much of adulthood free from the responsibilities of child care.

But gender inequalities still exist. Two expressions of this inequality are sexism and feminism.

* **Sexism** is the belief that one sex is superior to the other, and sexist behavior involves discriminating against people solely because of their gender. The long history of male economic and political dominance in the United States has led many people to believe that men are superior to women. This belief is self-perpetuating. When men oppose women's entry into certain jobs, women are reluctant to pursue those jobs. This in turn reinforces the stereotype that women are not capable of doing the jobs.

* **Feminism** is the corrective response to sexism. It is both the belief in the social, political, and economic equality of the sexes and also the movement organized around this belief.

Change and Conflict

Over the years, many people in the United States have actively resisted the idea that women have been systematically denied equal opportunity in our society.

* *The Suffrage Movement.* The fight to obtain voting rights for women began in the 1840s but did not achieve its goal until 1920.
* *The ERA.* A major feminist movement of the 1970s led to the proposal of an Equal Rights Amendment to the

U.S. Constitution (the ERA). It stated that "equality of rights under the law shall not be denied or abridged by the United States or any State on account of sex." The proposed amendment did not receive enough support to be enacted into law. Strong opposition came from people who viewed the amendment as a threat to "traditional family values." They felt the proposed amendment undermined their fundamental social norms. Though the amendment failed, discrimination on the basis of gender did become illegal. Numerous state and federal laws were passed to assure equality in school programs, in employment, and in most areas of public life.

Americans value equal opportunity. There have been many changes since the days in the 1950s when "Father Knows Best" was a popular sitcom and a major florist made ads showing a wife looking up lovingly at her flower-bearing husband from her position on her hands and knees scrubbing the kitchen floor. Where lingering gender inequalities exist, there will be people who will address them. We can expect that we will continue to grapple with issues of difference and power between the sexes.

Marriage

Marriage customs often reinforce inequality between the sexes. This is so true that some early feminists swore they would never marry. Marriage is the institution that societies create to provide a secure place for their next generation, the children. In marriage, women are provided for during the time when pregnancy and nursing make them less able to care for themselves. This view of marriage emphasizes the weakness of the female partner and the strength of the male. It underlies many of the world's customs.

Marriage also provides a stable environment for children to grow and learn the ways of their society. When children arrive, society often expects women to take care of them in the home while men go out into "the world" to provide for their families. Of course the mother has a biological connection to the child, but the mother-father role differences are not in themselves natural. Many couples today feel free to work out the balance of work and home life for themselves.

Women in the Workplace

Women's participation in the paid labor force of the United States increased steadily throughout the 20th century. In 1999, 60 percent of women aged 16 and over held jobs outside the home, as compared with 38 percent in 1960. These women made up over 46 percent of the labor force. Of the 62 million working women, 75 percent were employed full time.

While women occupy jobs at all levels from Supreme Court justice, Cabinet member, and senator on down, most women work in technical, sales, and administrative support occupations. These "service" jobs have features in common with tradi-

Babies on the Job

A growing shortage of U.S. workers has led some companies to allow new parents to bring their babies to work. Daycare centers are provided by some companies, and a few even allow workers to bring babies to their desks and care for them while doing their jobs. In December 2000, the *New York Times* reported that Dr. Mary Secret, a professor of social work, surveyed 5,000 Ohio companies and found 85 (1.7 percent) that allowed babies at work.

She believes this is because many jobs today revolve around computers, not factories or other places unsuitable for infants. However, most companies withdraw the welcome mat for babies over six months old.

tional home-based roles. "Women's jobs" are those of teachers, secretaries, office managers, librarians, medical assistants, and cashiers.

Women are underrepresented in occupations historically defined as "men's jobs," which often carry better salaries and more prestige. In 1997, women accounted for only 10 percent of all engineers, 26 percent of all physicians, and 29 percent of all computer systems analysts.

Women continue to earn less than men. In 1999, the median weekly income for year-round male workers was $618, compared to $473 for women. As a group, women were earning 76 percent of what men were.

Women in Politics

Men have traditionally dominated the U.S. political arena, but women are increasingly taking positions of power. Franklin Roosevelt appointed the first female Cabinet member in the 1930s—Frances Perkins as Secretary of Labor. In 1981 Ronald Reagan appointed Sandra Day O'Connor as the first woman Supreme Court justice. Bill Clinton appointed Madeline Albright as the first female Secretary of State and always had at least three women in Cabinet positions, and George W. Bush named three women to Cabinet positions heading the departments of Agriculture, the Interior, and Labor during his first months in office. By 2001 growing numbers of judges, governors, and mayors were women, and a record 12 women were serving in the U.S. Senate.

Age and Society

Age is a master status. When we interact with people in another age category, we usually are acutely aware of the status difference, and we alter our behavior accordingly. Societies place varying values on both old age and youth.

Birth Rates and Death Rates

Scientists who study human populations are called *demographers*. Among the measures of a society they consider are its birth and death rates. The **birth rate** is the relationship of the number of live births in a year to the total population. It is usually expressed as a number of births for every 1,000 people.

EXAMPLE: The birth rate in the United States in 1999 was 14.2 per 1,000 total population.

The **death rate** is the relationship of the number of deaths to the total population.

EXAMPLE: That same year, the nation's death rate was 9.4 per 1,000 population.

These rates are not understandable by themselves, but are used as a way of looking at changes within or among societies. A changing rate can demonstrate progress in health care, or it can cause concern. When the death rate decreases faster than the birth rate, a society may face challenges. High birth rates and low death rates can lead to overpopulation and decreasing standards of living for a nation's people.

Life Expectancy

Life expectancy—the average number of years a person can be expected to live—is a general measure of health. Usually the figure is reported as life expectancy at birth. In almost every country, female life expectancies are higher than those for males. Currently, life expectancies vary widely from country to country. Generally, people who live in Africa have the lowest life expectancies, and people in Europe, Australia, and Japan have the highest.

Life Expectancy at Birth	
Afghanistan	45.88 years
Australia	79.75 years
Burma	54.91 years
Central African Republic	44.02 years
France	78.76 years
Japan	80.70 years
Russia	67.19 years
Rwanda	39.34 years
United States	77.12 years
Vietnam	69.27 years

Source: Central Intelligence Agency, The World Factbook 2000

Age Groups

In very general terms, people belong to one of **three** age groups in their lifetimes:

1. **The Training Years.** From birth until sometime in the late teens, earlier in less well developed countries, people are learning the skills they will need to be productive members of society. In these years, their status is relatively low.

2. **The Productive Years.** From the late teens until about age 65, people are working members of society. They are raising families and doing the work their society needs. They hold the highest status they can achieve during these years.

3. **The Retirement Years.** The age of retirement varies with individual and social circumstances. For statistical purposes, it is generally regarded as 65. After this age, people are often very active. However, once past retirement, their contribution to society is not seen to be as "useful" as it was during their productive years, and their status consequently declines. This is not true in all societies. In some societies, older individuals are greatly valued for their years of experience.

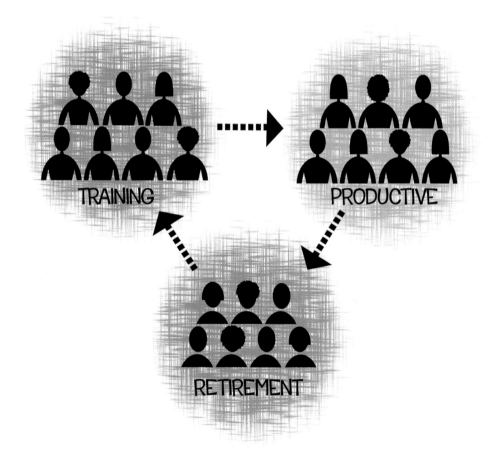

Population Patterns

It can be very interesting to look at how populations are distributed across the age spectrum. Look first at the population graphs (for the year 2000 from the U.S. Census Bureau) to analyze **three** societies:

1. **Kenya.** What does it mean when most of the people are 14 or younger? For one thing, it means the childhood mortality rate is very high. Many do not survive to adulthood. For another, it says that the working individuals are supporting a great many young people. It could mean that children "grow up" fast because their society needs them to be productive.

2. **Mexico.** Look at what happens to this chart after the age of 30. What do you think it means? How does life expectancy in Mexico compare with that in Kenya?

3. **United States.** You can see huge differences between the age distribution in the United States and that in the other two countries. Life expectancy at both ends of the graph is higher. A substantial percentage of the population is in its retirement years.

Now look at the three graphs that reflect the projections of the Census Bureau for the year 2025. Projections, are of course, just estimates. They are very good, scientific guesses. These are based on trends in birth control and health care—both in discoveries that lead to the eradication of diseases and in access to health care.

In Kenya, you can see a significant increase in the numbers of people who live into their 80s, and, as in Mexico and the

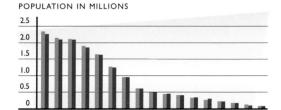

Kenya: 2000

POPULATION IN MILLIONS

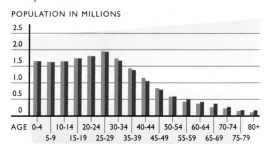

Kenya: 2025

POPULATION IN MILLIONS

Mexico: 2000

POPULATION IN MILLIONS

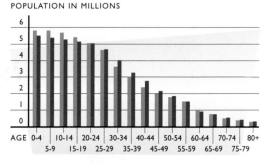

Mexico: 2025

POPULATION IN MILLIONS

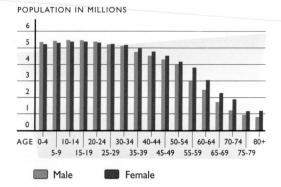

■ Male   ■ Female

Source: U.S. Bureau of the Census (2000)

United States: 2000

POPULATION IN MILLIONS

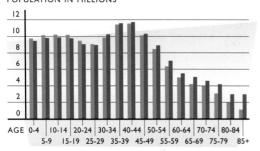

```
AGE 0-4  10-14 20-24 30-34 40-44 50-54 60-64 70-74 80-84
      5-9  15-19 25-29 35-39 45-49 55-59 65-69 75-79 85+
```

United States: 2025

POPULATION IN MILLIONS

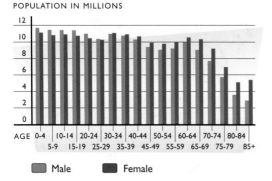

```
AGE 0-4  10-14 20-24 30-34 40-44 50-54 60-64 70-74 80-84
      5-9  15-19 25-29 35-39 45-49 55-59 65-69 75-79 85+
```

■ Male   ■ Female

Source: U.S. Bureau of the Census

United States, more women are in this group than men. You also see a reduction in the birth rate, and more of the babies born live to adulthood. Look at the population bulge among 25- to 29-year-olds. What might explain it?

In Mexico, the graph has a completely different shape. What has changed? Which groups of people have increased in number? What expectations about Mexico could lead to this projection?

How does the U.S. population projection for 2025 differ from the 2000 graph? What could cause this to become true? What might it mean for society?

A Global Aging Crisis

The world held an estimated 426 million people aged 65 or over in 2000. Industrialized countries such as the United States, Japan, and the European nations particularly have benefited from reduced incidence of

Across   Cultures

Worldwide Problems of the Elderly

In 1996, the United Nations cosponsored an international conference to examine social and economic policies dealing with the "oldest old"—people 80 and over. The conference identified **three** major issues:

1. In both industrialized and developing countries, this growing group is depending for their security on a

declining proportion of the population that is of working age.

2. In their search for support systems from family and/or government, those 80 and over may be forced to migrate, affecting the immigration policies of many nations.

3. The needs of the oldest old may intensify the pressures on their children to postpone retirement for five to ten years.

diseases and better health care. The overall population of Europe is older than that of any other continent, with the median age of such countries as Sweden, Germany, and Switzerland in the high 30s. Japan lags behind the other industrialized nations, but by 2020, one quarter of Japan's population will be over 65.

Though the aging of the world was one of the great triumphs of the 20th century, it has brought new problems. Many countries find they can't offer extensive financial support to the elderly. Many that can, including the United States, are raising the age at which retirees will qualify for pensions. In addition to retirement costs, the large number of elderly puts pressure on health care systems.

The "Graying of America"

Sociologists call the aging of the U.S. population the "graying of America."

In addition to advances in health care and better living conditions, another reason for the rapidly increasing number of older Americans is the change in the birth rates that occurred between 1946 and 1964. Members of the **baby boom generation**, who were born in the years after World War II, are beginning to reach retirement age. They had fewer children than their parents did, and the birth rate began to fall in 1964 and has remained relatively low ever since.

Did You Know?

How the U.S. Has Viewed the Elderly

Modern U.S. society is often described as being obsessed with youth, but it has not always been so. In colonial days, the few people who survived into old age were regarded as special. Elders organized and ran the churches and made decisions in local governments. Among the well-to-do, land was usually owned by the oldest male, so younger relatives often treated him with great respect.

As Americans built their fortunes during the 19th century, wealth replaced age and inherited social position as the basis for leadership, and people began to poke fun at older people.

By the late 20th century, a "cult of youth" had developed, propelled by businesses that found new markets in the disposable cash of baby boomer teenagers and those in their 20s. Advertisers and people in the entertainment business delivered a constant message as they sought customers for their products. It was "cool" to be young.

It will be interesting to see whether the rapidly growing population over 60 will not have a similar effect on business. In the United States, the business message often drives what society "thinks."

Social Attitudes and Old Age

Attitudes about old age vary from culture to culture. Some cultures revere old age. **EXAMPLES:** Almost all elderly members of the Sherpa culture in Nepal own their homes and most are in relatively good physical condition. Most value their independence and prefer not to live with their children. In Japan, elderly people enjoy a high degree of respect, even though the aging of the population has strained the tradition of receiving support from one's extended family. Respect for the old is partly based on Japan's ancient tradition of Shinto, which defines the elderly as wiser than, and thus superior to, the young.

The norm in other cultures, however, is to disdain the elderly. **EXAMPLES:** The Fulani of Africa expect older men and women to move to the edge of the family homestead where they sleep over their own graves. They are viewed as already socially dead. During the 1960s, the Ik of northern Uganda were forced off their game-rich plains into the arid mountains above the plains. Threatened with starvation, people took food from the mouths of the old, for whom they had little regard.

Attitudes in the United States are not anywhere near as negative, but a stigma is generally attached to old age.

The Elderly in the United States

When does a person in U.S. society become "elderly"? Officially, the age has been 65, the age that the Social Security Administration has set for eligibility for retirement benefits. Many U.S. companies have policies that require people to retire from their jobs at that age as well. However, the definition is changing. To keep the costs from being unsupportable, a new Social Security scale slowly raises the age for benefits toward 70.

Improved health care has led to many people over 65 being able, and eager, to continue working. On the other hand, many people retire early, in their 50s, in order to actively pursue leisure, travel, and/or a second career.

Ageism

One social problem that confronts older Americans is **ageism**, which is prejudice and discrimination directed against people because they are old. Ageism relies on a stereotype of the aged as ill, helpless, mentally slow, forgetful, isolated, and self-pitying. This stereotype of old age assigns the elderly to an inferior social status and can make younger people dread old age. While declining health is a part of the physical process of aging, for most people it is not a major aspect of life until close to their death. The vast majority of the population over 65 is not suffering from any of the characteristics described by the stereotype.

In U.S. society, ageism is reinforced by the media. Few television characters are age 65 or older, with older women particularly underrepresented. This is especially ironic, as there are significantly more women than men over the age of 65. The men and women seen in the pages of magazines and in television advertisements are mostly under 40. Older people are largely invisible.

Ageism

The term *ageism* was popularized in the early 1970s by the Gray Panthers, a national organization dedicated to fighting age discrimination. Today the American Association of Retired Persons (AARP) is one of the largest, most influential interest groups in U.S. politics. The AARP sponsors group health insurance and offers travel and prescription drug discounts. It has effectively lobbied Congress for Social Security benefits and favorable legislation on health care and prescription drugs. The AARP magazine *Modern Maturity* has one of the largest circulations in the nation and features the lives of active, healthy older people, including celebrities. AARP promotes a new image to compete with the old stereotypes of ageism.

It is not attractive, this suggests, to be old. As the population ages, this trend may well change. The baby boom generation may continue to dominate styles and tastes as its large numbers bubble up the age structure.

The Elderly as a Subculture

The elderly as a group have certain social characteristics:

* **They live on fixed incomes.** This means they cannot expect earnings to increase as working people do, through raises or job transfers. The incomes of retired people come from Social Security and company pensions and from the return on their investments. These do increase somewhat, but not enough to keep up with a sudden increase in the cost of energy or gasoline, or a new need for expensive prescription drugs or medical procedures.

* **There are more women than men.** The longer life expectancy of women is not always a blessing. Many find themselves living alone, without the emotional support and helpfulness of a partner as they outlive their husbands. Elderly women are more than twice as likely to live alone or with nonrelatives as elderly men.

* **They cluster in several areas of the country.** Many elderly people prefer to live in a warm climate, where the difficulties of getting around in winter snows and ice are not a problem. As the numbers of retired people grow, their migrations have affected population distribution in the United States. The classic retirement haven is Florida, but communities for people 50 and over are popular all over the country.

    Choice is not the only reason for population clusters of elderly residents. In some areas, younger people have left to seek better job opportunities. Rural states tend to have concentrations of older people who are less prosperous. The map below shows the percent of people age 65 and over living in each state.

Where the Elderly Live

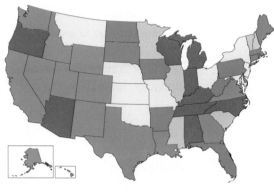

■ 13.9%–18.2% (11)	▨ 11.6%–12.4% (6)
☐ 13.2%–13.9% (10)	■ 5.6%–11.6% (14)
■ 12.4%–13.2% (10)	

Source: U.S. Bureau of the Census (1999)

Age-based Inequality

Ageism has often led to unequal treatment of older Americans in **two** areas:

1. **Employment.** While firing people because they are old violates federal laws, courts have upheld an employer's right to lay off older workers for economic reasons. When someone over 50 seeks a job, he or she is at a distinct disadvantage. Employers concerned that an older worker's experience may be the "wrong" experience for their company prefer younger workers whom they can socialize to their company's norms.

2. **Health Care.** It is more expensive to provide health care for older people than younger ones. The Medicare program provides medical benefits for those 65 and over. However, Medicare does not cover many health expenses, such as prescriptions, dental care, and eyeglasses. It also does not cover long-term nursing care or the assisted-living help that many older people find they need.

Age Discrimination in Employment

A controlled experiment conducted in 1993 by AARP confirmed that older people often face discrimination when applying for jobs. Comparable resumes for two applicants—one 57 years old and the other 32 years old—were sent to 775 large companies and employment agencies around the United States. The younger applicant received a favorable response more than twice as often as the older applicant.

Health and Society

During the 20th century, great global progress was made in combating disease. Vaccinations for killers such as smallpox, polio, rubella, tetanus, diphtheria, mumps, and measles lengthened life expectancies around the world. Great scientific strides were made in fighting heart disease, cancer, and AIDS. Health conditions were improved by more efficient methods of food production and distribution and by better sanitation in many countries.

Disease Control

Infectious diseases are a leading cause of death around the world, accounting for a quarter to a third of the estimated 56 million deaths worldwide in 1999. The spread of infectious disease is influenced by new strains of infectious organisms as well as by changes in human behavior, including changing lifestyles and land use patterns, increased trade and travel, and inappropriate use of antibiotic drugs. Recent changes include:

* Twenty well-known diseases, including tuberculosis (TB), malaria, and cholera, have reemerged or spread geographically since 1973, often in more dangerous and drug-resistant forms.
* At least 30 previously unknown disease agents have been identified since 1973, including HIV, Ebola virus, hepatitis C virus, and Nipah virus, for which no vaccines are presently available.
* Of the seven biggest killers worldwide, the incidence of TB, malaria, hepatitis, and HIV/AIDS continues to grow.

HIV/AIDS and TB are projected to account for most deaths from infectious diseases in developing countries by 2020.
* Governments try to control the spread of disease by restricting immigration, setting up trade inspections and restrictions, and monitoring new cases as they occur.

The World Health Organization of the United Nations has studied the effects of disease and has promoted and financed prevention programs and treatments. However, we are a long way from a consistent worldwide plan to control the spread of infectious disease.

Health Care Access

Social class can be associated with differences in death and illness rates in countries around the world. Differences exist not only between rich and poor countries, but also within the population of

Did You Know?

AIDS in Africa

One of the deadliest epidemics of modern times is the spread of AIDS, which is caused by the human immunodeficiency virus, or HIV. While progress has been made in treating HIV-infected people in many developed countries, in Africa, AIDS is still out of control. Infection rates run as high as 35 percent of the entire population in some regions.

each country. Studies consistently show that people in the lower classes have higher rates of death and disability.

Crowded living conditions, substandard housing, poor diet, and stress all contribute to the ill health of many low-income people. So can a lack of knowledge of how to maintain good health. A key reason for ill health among the poor is lack of access to health care.

Many developed countries offer national, government-funded health care that makes some medical assistance available to all.

In the United States, a variety of institutions help make health care accessible. State and local municipalities operate hospitals and clinics for those who cannot afford private institutions. Churches and other charitable organizations do so as well. Health insurance is provided for a large portion of the population through employers. But many are left without insurance, because the cost to small businesses and individuals is high.

Those least able to pay for health services often don't go to the doctor when they need to. As a result, they don't get the benefits of disease prevention, and they may end up in emergency rooms with diseases far advanced and more expensive to treat.

Rights of the Disabled

There are more than 43 million people with disabilities in the United States. Their infirmities include physical disabilities, serious health impairments, mental retardation, mental illness, and visual, hearing, or speech impairments. Although most Americans with disabilities would like to work, most are unemployed. A disproportionate number live in poverty.

The passage of the Americans with Disabilities Act of 1990 (ADA) demonstrated a social norm: We believe we have a responsibility to help all members of society participate to the best of their abilities. The ADA made it illegal for employers to discriminate against people with disabilities, and it required companies to provide job training and other support to improve employment opportunities. Since its passage, public services, programs, and activities have included wheelchair-accessible facilities and used sign language interpreters and Braille to improve communication. Transportation facilities, hotels, restaurants, and theaters—all have been affected.

The U.S. Health Care Industry

The United States is one of the few industrialized nations without a national health care program. In the United States, health care is largely in private hands. The health care industry is made up of:

1. Individual physicians.
2. Groups of doctors.
3. Hospitals.
4. Nursing homes.
5. Pharmaceutical companies.
6. Insurance providers.

While public and charitable hospitals are not operated for profit, most of the other parts of the industry are. Health care is a business in many ways like any other.

Health Costs

The cost of providing health care in the United States has risen dramatically. **Six** factors that have been suggested to explain the high cost include:

1. New, expensive, tools for diagnosing illness, such as magnetic resonance imaging (MRI).
2. Major breakthroughs in the effectiveness of surgical procedures and transplants.
3. Fear of malpractice lawsuits.
4. Patients and doctors with an "insurance will pay for it" attitude.
5. Health service charges patients don't understand.
6. Unreasonable profit expectations.

Partly in reaction to rising health care costs, health maintenance organizations (HMOs) began appearing across the United States during the 1980s. Their original purpose was to pool doctors and clinics in an effort to promote prevention of disease and to reduce costs for patients and insurance companies. While they have met many of their goals, they are criticized for delivering an impersonal level of health care (because patients do not choose their own doctors) and for delaying patients' access to specialists.

Health Insurance

Health insurance in the United States comes one of **three** ways:

1. Employee-funded plans.
2. Individual plans.
3. Government-funded plans.

Health insurance in the United States is provided primarily through employers. For many years the bills were paid by a handful of private insurance companies. As health care costs increased, more employers offered insurance plans provided by HMOs. Private insurance is still available, but employees increasingly are expected to pick up part of the cost.

Individuals who do not belong to group plans may buy insurance on their own.

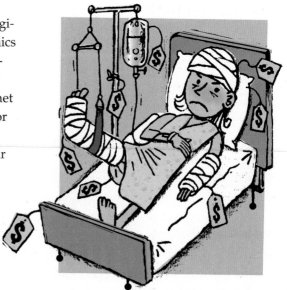

However, it is very expensive. The health insurance industry bases its rates on the incidence of claims of people within a given group. The rates go up as more and more people make claims to pay for their care. As the rates go up, younger people or healthier people drop out, seeking cheaper plans. Those who remain find themselves paying even higher rates as the costs are spread over an increasingly smaller number. Over time, many find they cannot afford insurance at all.

The U.S. government provides health insurance free to the families of the 9 million federal employees. It also insures citizens 65 and older through Medicare. The government-sponsored Medicaid program provides medical care for the poor through grants to the states. States each determine who's eligible, for what services, and what the services will cost. The states then run their own programs. As a result, care varies widely among the states, and many people in poverty receive only partial or no benefits.

U.S. Health Care Inequality

The United States has often been criticized for having both the best and the worst patient care in the world. We have fine hospitals, well-trained doctors, and some of the most sophisticated medical research centers in the world.

Much of the controversy surrounding health care in the United States focuses on issues of access and cost. Research shows that health care access is less available to many African Americans, Latinos, and Native Americans than it is to whites. Not surprisingly, illness and death rates for these groups are significantly higher than for white Americans.

One indication of inequalities among racial and ethnic groups are differences in **infant mortality rates**—expressed as the annual number of children per 1,000 who die before they reach the age of one. In 1999, the overall infant mortality rate in the United States was 7.1 infant deaths per 1,000 live births. According to the National Center for Health Statistics, the infant mortality rate is twice as high among African Americans as whites. Latinos and Native Americans have infant mortality rates lower than African Americans but still higher than whites.

The issues of health care costs and inequality have led to many suggestions for reform. These include:

* Expanding government-sponsored programs.
* Instituting more prevention programs to encourage healthy living.
* Increasing the use of hospice programs. Hospice programs help people who are dying live their last months in dignity outside of hospitals. Medicare allows patients to enter hospice care if their doctors expect them to live less than six months.

Reform efforts represent the numerous controversial and complex issues surrounding the issue of health care.

Gender and age describe major groups in all societies. Gender roles are developed through socialization, and their expectations operate in all arenas of society—in families, the workplace, and politics. Age differentiates the less productive from the more productive members of society. Status is associated with age, as it is with gender. Older people may be victims of ageism. In the United States, people over age 65 form a large subculture.

Health care is a strong indicator of social position. Birth and death rates and infant mortality rates distinguish the nations of the world as well as the different groups within a national society. Worldwide, major diseases have been eliminated and improvements are projected to continue. However, social inequalities remain and are reflected in health issues. In the United States, much progress has been made in medicine, but issues of health care costs and access to insurance plague the poor and are disproportionately felt by minorities.

Sociology

ageism—prejudice and discrimination against people because they are old. *p. 155*

baby boom generation—large number of Americans born between 1946 and 1964. *p. 154*

birth rate—relationship of live births in a year to total population. *p. 150*

chromosomes—threadlike bodies in each cell that determine hereditary characteristics. *p. 142*

death rate—relationship of number of deaths in a year to the total population. *p. 150*

feminism—belief in the social, political, and economic equality of the sexes. *p. 147*

gender—cultural, psychological, and social traits associated with a biological sex. *p. 142*

gender roles—specific behaviors and attitudes that a society establishes for men and women. *p. 143*

hormones—chemical substances in the body that stimulate or inhibit chemical processes, such as growth. *p. 142*

infant mortality rate—annual number of children per 1,000 who die before they reach the age of one. *p. 161*

life expectancy—average number of years a person can be expected to live under current conditions. *p. 150*

matrilineal societies—groups that base status and inheritance on the female's kinship descent. *p. 143*

sexism—belief that one sex is by nature superior to the other. *p. 147*

stereotypes—conventional, oversimplified, often exaggerated images. *p. 144*

The Family

In this chapter, you will learn about:

- the structure and function of families
- problems and trends in the American family
- how families are changing

Few families resemble those on television. Most family members aren't running off to exotic places or tracking down murderers. Neither is conversation around the dinner table a series of one-liners. What is a family? Is there such a thing as a "typical" family? In this chapter, you will learn about the most important social institution, the family.

Throughout their lifetimes, individuals belong to different families. Different societies as well as groups within a society hold quite different values and beliefs about families. These can affect how children are raised, how mates are selected, and how descent is traced. Sociologists are interested in what functions families play in society, how power is distributed, and what interactions govern family members' negotiations.

Over the past several decades, there has been an increase in the types of families accepted as "normal" by society. These include families where divorced parents with children marry, creating stepfamilies, and single-parent families.

Family Organization

The **family** is the most basic social institution in all societies. It is a relatively permanent group of people connected by ancestral lineage, marriage, or adoption. It is a very sturdy social unit that has survived and adapted through time. A variety of different types of family organization can be found throughout the world.

Nuclear and Extended Families

Although the concept of family seems fairly simple, it is really quite complex. Siblings, cousins, grandparents, and step-parents describe just some of the statuses family members hold.

The Nuclear Family

The **nuclear family** consists of parents and their children who live together but apart from other family members. People in nuclear families actually belong to **two** families.

1. **Family of Orientation**—the family to which a person belongs as a child, where he or she receives the initial orientation to society.
2. **Family of Procreation**—(also called the family of marriage)—the family people form as adults when they marry.

When sociologists study the nuclear family, they look at its relationship to other family members. They have examined how its values may differ from those of a wider family network and are interested in how the nuclear family prepares children for certain lines of work.

The Extended Family

The **extended family** is composed of family members of several generations who share a household and are economically and emotionally bound to one another. The extended family may include grandparents, cousins, aunts, and uncles in addition to parents and children.

EXAMPLE: In rural America, it wasn't uncommon for siblings to stay on the farm after they were married. They sometimes built homes on the same land and worked together to make their living from the farm. This can be called a *joint* extended family.

EXAMPLE: Today, aging parents often live with their adult children and their families—three generations living in the same residence. This is a *vertical* extended family.

Modern Families

Most U.S. families today are **modified extended families**. Different generations do not necessarily live under the same roof, but very important contacts are maintained. The telephone and e-mail make it easy for people to stay in touch, even when they live very far apart geographically. Family members provide practical assistance with a whole range of daily concerns from how to manage a sick member's fever to how to get a college loan.

Kinship Groups

A **kinship group** is a complex network of people whose social relationships are based on common ancestry, marriage, and adoption. Affiliates such as godparents may also be included.

Kinship groups differ from extended families in that they include all one's relatives, including those who may live far apart or rarely see one another. People speak of "close kin"—those with whom they frequently interact—and "distant kin" —those they may see only at weddings, at family reunions, or on holidays. The chart below defines types of family relationships.

Family Relationships	
Consanguineal	People related by biological ties, such as siblings, parents, or grandparents.
Affinal	People related by marriage, such as in-laws and step-relatives.
Adopted	People related through the adoption process.
Fictive	People related through special ties of ritual or friendship, such as godparents.

Patterns of Descent

If you were to do genealogical research, would you start with your father's name, your mother's name, or both? The way people trace their descent is based largely on culture.

EXAMPLE: Navajo children describe their lineage in terms of their mother's kinship group, rather than that of their father.

In some cultures, lineage is a very important part of the social structure. It can determine the control of property and the eligibility of marriage partners.

Unilineal Descent

Unilineal descent traces ancestry through only one parent. Property and names are passed from father to son or mother to daughter. It takes **two** forms:

1. **Patrilineal descent** traces lineage through the male line—your father, your father's father (your grandfather), his father, and so forth. Patrilineal descent is common in cultures where the men provide most of the necessary resources for the family.

2. **Matrilineal descent** traces heritage through the female line—your mother, your mother's mother (your grandmother), her mother, and so forth. Matrilineal descent is less common. It can be found in cultures where women grow the crops and are therefore more responsible for maintaining the family.

Changing Surnames

Some American women choose to combine their maiden name with their husband's surname to create a new last name for themselves and their children. What happens when those children marry? If Esther Woo-Jones marries Joe Avila-Lee, what surname will they use?

One answer is for male children to take the father's surname and female children the mother's surname. In that way, both family names are carried on, provided that the marriage produces children of both sexes.

Nonlineal Descent

Nonlineal descent traces ancestry through both parents. It also has **two** forms:

1. **Bilateral descent** traces heritage equally through both the men and women on both the mother's and father's sides of the family.
2. **Double descent** traces heritage through the male ancestors of the father's side and the female ancestors of the mother's side.

Patterns of Authority

Gender differences can define the power base in families. The more powerful gender holds the purse strings, makes the major decisions, and often has the laws of society to support his or her power base:

* *In a* **patriarchy**, the father or grandfather holds the authoritative position in the family. It is common in many societies.
* *In a* **matriarchy**, the female has the legal and moral authority. This pattern is prevalent in some cultures and in many single-parent families in the United States.

* *In* **egalitarian families,** authority is shared equally between spouses. In families where both parents earn income, this sharing of authority has become common.

Residence

In some societies, living patterns reveal which family line is the more powerful. There are **four** patterns:

1. **Patrilocal residence,** in which married couples live with or near the husband's family. One study of more than 550 world societies showed that more than two-thirds practiced patrilocal residence. In most of these societies, women had little authority or control.

2. **Matrilocal residence,** in which families live with or near the wife's family. This pattern is found in societies organized around matrilineal descent.

3. **Bilocal residence,** in which the husband and wife have equal say in choosing which family to be near. It is associated with egalitarian authority.

4. **Neolocal residence,** in which families establish their own homes without regard for where their families of orientation live. This is common in industrialized societies.

One important consequence of residence patterns is that they determine which family of orientation will have the greatest influence on the new family of procreation, particularly in the area of child rearing. Children in families living far from either the mother's or father's parents experience less multigenerational influence.

When grandchildren live near grandparents, that family has the opportunity to pass on its values. ▶

Marriage

Societies differ in their norms for the number of spouses you may have at one time and also in their rules about whom you can and cannot marry.

Types of Marriage

The most common and, in many industrial societies, the only socially and legally accepted form of marriage is **monogamy**—the practice of being married to only one person at a time. Custom in monogamous societies is for the marriage to be for a lifetime. With divorce and remarriage increasing, people are sometimes said to practice "serial monogamy."

While people in most societies are monogamous, some of the world's societies allow or prefer **polygamy**—a form of marriage where a person has more than one spouse. (Polygamy is illegal in the United States.) There are **two** types of polygamy:

1. **Polyandry**—in which a woman marries two or more men. Few societies practice this form of marriage.
2. **Polygyny**—in which a man marries two or more women. While this form is more common, few men in most polygynous societies have the wealth or social status to support multiple wives and their children. Even here, monogamous marriages are more often the rule.

Selecting a Partner

The way families are formed differs in various societies, but **two** sets of rules define which partners are socially acceptable.

1. **Exogamy** specifies which individuals are *not* acceptable as marriage partners. Relationships among close family members (incest) are almost universally prohibited, both legally and socially. Marriage outside the family encourages biological and social diversity and limits the genetic defects that accompany inbreeding.
2. **Endogamy** specifies the class of persons with whom marriage is both legal and socially encouraged. In large, complex societies, endogamous rules are often related to race, religion, ethnicity, or social class. While there may be no prohibition against marrying outside of these groups, family expectations often limit the selection process.

Exogamy and endogamy together define the pool of socially acceptable potential marriage partners. The rules governing this vary from culture to culture. Although incest is unacceptable in most cultures, marriage between members of different races or religions is no longer uncommon in Western society. Many traditional cultures, however, maintain very rigid rules of eligibility.

Courtship among the Hausa

The Hausa people live in northwestern Nigeria and southwestern Niger in Africa. Among the Hausa, marriage is considered a union between two families, not between individuals. Potential marriage partners must undergo a thorough background check.

Couples must follow a strict set of rules during courtship:

* The boy introduces himself to the girl and tells her who his parents and ancestors are. If she is interested, she smiles or nods.
* The couple dates. If the boy touches the girl in any way, he is considered to have a bad character. Eventually, the boy asks the girl to marry him. She arranges a formal meeting with her father and elder relatives.
* At the meeting, the oldest member of the girl's family questions the boy about his ancestors. Later, the girl's family discusses what they know about the boy's family and investigates that family thoroughly.
* The boy's family carries out a similar investigation of the girl's ancestors. Only when both families are satisfied is the marriage approved.
* Before marrying, the boy's family must pay a bride price to the girl's family. This compensates them for the loss of their daughter's work. Only then does the marriage take place.

Sociological Views of the Family

Sociologists bring their different perspectives to their study of families. Each looks at the family in somewhat different ways.

Functionalist View

According to functionalist theory, the family forms the foundation of social order because it performs the following basic functions for society:

* *Socialization.* Families shape the attitudes, values, and beliefs of children. They pass along society's norms and assure continuation of the social structure.
* *Regulation of Sexual Activity.* Marriage provides an approved outlet for the sexual drive, and, in addition to assuring continuation of the society, it protects the community from disease and weaknesses in the gene pool.
* *Replacement of Societal Members.* Through childbearing, families replace members who die. Families also encourage the continuation of the work within the society that its members perform.
* *Protection and Economic Security.* Families take care of their members who cannot, because of age, disability, or disease, take care of themselves. Family members help each other in times of trouble.
* *Emotional Support.* Families meet the emotional needs of their members with love, affection, and a sense of belonging. They are "there for them" no matter what happens.

* *Social Placement.* Families stabilize society by providing individuals with an initial social identity and standing in the community.

Functionalists of the mid-20th century argued that the nuclear family met important needs of an industrial society. That idea, however, has been rejected as further research has shown modern American families are not really nuclear, but are modified extended families.

Conflict View

Those who hold a conflict perspective are interested in the areas of family that some might call dysfunctional. Conflict theorists describe families as arenas of conflict where family members compete for power, wealth, and prestige. They point to the following **four** ways in which family life encourages the exploitation of society's weaker members by its stronger ones.

1. **Family life diminishes women and children.** The word *family* comes from the Latin word meaning "servant," and, in the ancient Roman world, women and children served the father in the family. Just as the Latin word is found in our language, so do the ancient ideas underpin many of our traditions. Until very recently, most women accepted the traditional role of homemaker and nurturer assigned them by a patriarchal society. They had little influence or power either within the home or outside of it. Children have even less.

Functions of Families

Social Placement

Regulation of Sexual Activity

Emotional Support

Replacement of Societal Members

Protection and Economic Security

Did You Know?

Domestic Violence

* Although women and children are the most frequent victims of domestic violence, about 5 percent of reported cases involve battered men. The number may be higher because many men fail to report such incidents.

* The American Medical Association estimates that more than 4 million women are victims of severe assaults by boyfriends and husbands each year.

* In more than 50 percent of all domestic violence situations, children are also abused.

* Domestic violence is not limited to certain levels of society. Approximately one-third of the men counseled for battering are professionals who are well respected in their workplaces and communities. These persons accused of domestic violence have included doctors, psychologists, lawyers, ministers, and business executives.

2. **Family life permits violence.** In many societies, it is acceptable for husbands and wives to beat children and for husbands to beat wives. About one-third of female murder victims in the United States are killed by current or former partners. Wife-against-husband abuse, while much less acknowledged, occurs as well.

3. **Families perpetuate social stratification.** Functionalists say that the family serves to stabilize society by perpetuating social placement. In the conflict view of sociology, that stability is seen as undesirable because it reduces social mobility and limits a person's opportunities. Conflict theorists see the advantages of children raised in upper- or middle-class families as evidence that families serve to perpetuate inequalities in society.

4. **Families limit lifestyle choices.** The predominance of the traditional image of the family makes other lifestyles unacceptable. A family wages an uphill battle against community norms when it chooses that the wife be the breadwinner and that decisions be shared among both spouses and with reasoning children. In general, conflict theorists argue that the traditional family should not be a model for everyone because it limits choices for women and men, stifles creativity and productive change, and prevents individuals from moving through society to improve their lot in life.

Interactionist View

Interactionists see family life as a series of ongoing negotiations. They are interested in what those interactions are and how they change.

Husbands and Wives

What expectations does each partner have about the other's role in the family? Jesse Bernard wrote in *The Future of Marriage* that husbands and wives often bring different understandings to the relationship depending on the dynamics in the family in which they were raised. Those differences include:

* Who makes the decisions.
* What responsibilities each has in support of the family.
* Child-rearing practices.

These differences require negotiation if the marriage is to succeed.

EXAMPLE: In a little over four percent of U.S. families, couples decide the husband will stay home with the children while the wife will earn the family income.

Answers to questions about the dynamics of family interactions are important to people who are trying to form social policy. **EXAMPLE:** Does improving access to child care improve family economic strength? Or does it merely increase the pressure on mothers to give up a fulfilling mothering role to join the "rat race"? Sociologists research such questions.

Interactions and Happiness

In 1994, John Gottman identified **three** main types of interactions that occur in families. These include:

1. **Validating interactions,** in which participants compromise, show mutual respect, and accept their differences.
2. **Conflict-avoiding interactions,** in which participants make light of their differences rather than confronting and resolving them.
3. **Volatile interactions,** in which conflict erupts, resulting in loud, emotional disputes.

Family interactions
▼

Gottman found that in families where validating interactions predominate, there is a greater sense of "happiness" as reported by family members. Volatile interactions produce the lowest sense of happiness.

Interactions that influence happiness can also be described as:

* **Positive.** Interactions that demonstrate thoughtfulness and friendliness are positive interactions.
  EXAMPLES: Touching, smiling, paying sincere compliments.

* **Negative.** Interactions that demonstrate thoughtlessness and nastiness are negative.
  EXAMPLES: Ignoring, criticizing, or name-calling.

Gottman found that families in which there are at least five positive interactions for every one negative interaction are generally happy. The degree of happiness decreases as this ratio decreases.

Patterns in Family Life

Family life encompasses several stages: the newlywed or pre-parental stage, the parental stage, the post-parental or "empty nest" stage, and the retirement stage. Changes in modern families have influenced these stages:

* More than 20 percent of people 18 years or older have never married.
* Many people are delaying marriage into their late 20s, their 30s, and even longer.
* Mothers are having children at an older age than they used to.
* Some couples choose to remain childless.
* Two-income families are common.
* High divorce rates and remarriage have added to the complexity of family life.
* With improved health care, people remain employed and active longer.

Theories of Mate Selection

Social Exchange Theory	Each person brings certain assets to a relationship. Partners choose each other depending on what one has to offer and what the other offers in return.
Equity Theory	People choose partners with whom there is a fair exchange of assets. If a person feels he or she brings more to the partnership than the other person, the relationship may not last or the weaker partner becomes the other's victim.
Complementary Needs Theory	A person chooses a mate who provides for his or her individual needs.
Psychodynamic Theory	Individuals choose partners who satisfy emotional needs arising from earlier life experiences.

Courtship and Marriage

Most Americans seek out "romantic love" as they search for a mate. It remains a central theme of books, television, movies, and music. Intimacy in marriage is a fairly new phenomenon, as sociologist Philippe Aries pointed out in his book *Centuries of Childhood.* Love for a potential mate often makes "leaving the nest" easier.

Physical attractiveness is a factor in choosing a mate, but it is not nearly as important as the media make it appear.

Sociologists look at mate selection as a series of "trade-offs" or social exchanges. The chart above summarizes four theories of mate selection.

Two kinds of mate selection have been prevalent in many of the world's societies:

1. **Homogamy,** in which individuals or their families select a mate from the same group as their own—someone with similar education, race, religion, age, and social class. This practice has been the norm throughout the world.

2. **Heterogamy,** in which a mate is chosen without regard for such characteristics. In postindustrial societies, this practice has been on the rise. In cities, in the workplace, and in social groups with mixed populations, unmarried people are meeting potential mates who are outside their usual group.

The social stigma of interracial marriages and, especially, of marriages between people of different faiths has lessened considerably.

EXAMPLE: In only 30 years, from 1960 to 1990, the number of Jewish people in the United States married to non-Jews rose from 6 percent to more than 50 percent.

Challenges of Parenthood and Work

Few events produce such a total change in social roles as parenthood. The addition of children turns a couple into a family. Being a parent necessarily broadens interests and brings people into contact with other social institutions such as schools or clubs.

Two-Career Couples

In many families, women enter marriage with a career. The cost of living also encourages both partners in a marriage to seek employment. By 2000, both parents worked in more than 64 percent of U.S. families with children.

This dictates certain roles for parents and introduces new challenges.

"I've finally managed to balance work and family. I hired my wife and kids."

* Responsibilities of parenthood become more evenly divided between mother and father. If the woman's income exceeds that of the man, the father may remain home and raise the children.
* Schedules must be juggled to suit the needs of both parents and children, particularly as children begin to engage in activities outside the home.
* In some cases, the family must maintain two different households in different parts of the country. These commuter marriages increase the challenges of child rearing and care.

Parenthood appears to affect the decision in some families for parents to work from home. In a 1997 study, researchers found nearly 18 percent of the non-agricultural workforce worked at home as all or part of their primary employment. More than 70 percent of these people were members of married-couple families. While the researchers did not investigate why these people worked from home, they did record that the numbers rise several percentage points among couples who have children.

Child Care

The increasing availability of nursery schools, daycare centers, and preschools has helped working parents to some extent. The pie chart at the top of the next page shows the distribution of care for preschoolers whose mothers are employed.

Who Cares for Preschoolers When Mother Works?

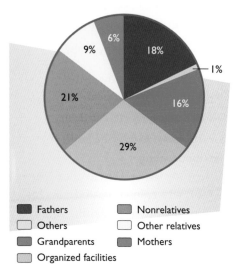

- 6%
- 9%
- 18%
- 1%
- 21%
- 16%
- 29%

- Fathers
- Nonrelatives
- Others
- Other relatives
- Grandparents
- Mothers
- Organized facilities

Source: U.S. Bureau of the Census (1998)

The downside is that the expense of daycare programs may negate the benefit of having both parents work. Often parents find they have little choice because relatives or suitable programs are simply not available.

Once children enter school, the situation changes. Some parents for whom childcare is unavailable or unaffordable opt to have the child stay alone in the home before and after school. Statistics indicate that between 5 million and 12 million school-children between the ages of 5 and 13 are "latchkey" children.

Did You Know?

Latchkey Children

The term *latchkey children* originated in the 1800s when children wore the keys to their homes around their necks. Some people feel that allowing children to take care of themselves improves their self-esteem and confidence. Others point to problems that can occur, such as:

* Risk of injury, accident, or victimization.
* Increased fear, boredom, or loneliness.
* Increase in delinquent behavior.

* Increased responsibility placed on the child before he or she is mature enough.

Obviously, the maturity of the child has much to do with the effect of these issues on latchkey children.

Some parents have looked to public libraries to provide a safe place for children after school. Although librarians have concerns over legal liability, medical emergencies, staffing, and security, many have begun programs specifically for latchkey children.

Divorce

Divorce rates have been declining in the United States. Nonetheless, about 11 percent of the adult population is currently divorced. Twenty-five percent of adults have been divorced at least once in their lifetime. Among people 35 to 54 years of age, about 30 percent have been divorced. Factors that contribute to a high divorce rate include:

* *Teenage Marriages.* People who marry in their teen years are much more likely to divorce than other people. Divorce rates are two-thirds lower among women married after age 25 than among those married as teenagers. Teens who marry because they are pregnant are at even greater risk of divorce.

* *Dissimilar Social Background.* Differences in values or lifestyles prior to marriage can magnify problems and lead to divorce.

* *Increased Emphasis on Personal Happiness and Fulfillment.* Traditionally, people were willing to sacrifice some of their own needs to meet the needs of other family members. This has become less common in modern America.

* *Ease of Obtaining a Divorce.* Changing divorce laws and availability of "no-fault" divorce have made it easier for some couples to dissolve a marriage than to work things out. Social stigma attached to divorce has lessened.

* *Dual-earner Families.* When both partners are able to support themselves, it becomes economically possible for women or men to leave unhappy or abusive relationships. Also, spouses in two-income families may grow apart from each other as each becomes devoted to the active pursuit of a career.

Problems associated with divorce include:

1. **Feelings of personal failure.**
2. **Loneliness and financial hardship.**
3. **Children's feelings of grief, guilt, and abandonment.**
4. **Child custody issues.** Where once women were routinely granted custody of children, joint custody is becoming more common. It allows children to maintain a relationship with both parents, but the parents may find it a strain to maintain a relationship with a divorced spouse. Working out schedules can be difficult. The need of one parent to move away can pose another problem.

"You caught me at a bad time. Call back after my kids grow up and leave home."

The Changing U.S. Family

Recent years have seen many changes in the makeup of families. Two types are increasingly common.

Single-Parent Families

In 1998, 28 percent of all children under 18 lived with a single parent. Of those, 84 percent lived with their mother. The number of single fathers grew 25 percent from 1995 to 1998.

Types of Single Parents

* *Divorced Mother or Father.*
* *Widow or Widower.*
* *Unmarried Mother.* In 1997, nearly a third of all births were to unmarried women. Many of these mothers were teenage girls, and their pregnancies were unplanned. In addition, some women choose to remain unmarried yet have children. Increased economic independence and reduced stigma attached to single motherhood have contributed to this trend.
* *Adopting Single Parent.* Of more than 42,000 adoptions in 1998, 30 percent were to single females and 2 percent were to single males.

Problems of Single-Parent Families

While life in a single-parent household can be very rich emotionally, there are social problems associated with such families.

* The problems in providing adequate childcare are magnified in a single-parent family where the parent is almost always employed.
* Single-parent families generally have more financial problems, particularly when there is no financial support from another parent.
* Single-parent children are three to four times more likely than children with two parents to have emotional or behavioral problems. Eighty-four percent of teens hospitalized for psychiatric care come from single-parent homes. Children living without a father's influence were 11 times more likely to exhibit violent misbehavior in school.

Blended Families

A blended family is one in which at least one of the adults is a stepparent. A little more than one in six U.S. families is a blended family. With the number of divorces and remarriages on the rise, some sociologists have estimated that in the 21st century, between one-half and one-third of today's young people will become stepsons and stepdaughters, as well as stepsiblings.

Each parent and his or her children have a shared history that persists after the new family forms. It takes time for the new family to build a similar base of experience that leads to a true feeling of "family" rather than "us versus them."

Depending on their ages and relationships to their other parent, children may experience resentment or anger, necessitating great patience and flexibility among the new family's members. It takes time for children to get used to the idea of having three and sometimes four "parents" and a whole host of new relatives.

In the interests of children, programs are being developed to help adults in stepfamily relationships develop a "parenting coalition" in which all involved parents work cooperatively.

Families of the Future

Sociologists suggest that there may no longer be a "typical" U.S. family. If the trends of the past several decades continue:

* Families will continue to grow smaller.
* Families will continue to get more socially diverse.
* More people will choose to remain single.

New Babies in Blended Families

What happens when the parents in a blended family have a new child? Kay Pasley, Director of Research for the Stepfamily Association of America, has researched this question.

In any marriage, children decrease the likelihood of divorce because the parents consider the effects the divorce may have on the child. Yet along with the joy they bring, children complicate married life, increasing demands on time and money and pitting parenting needs against other needs of the married couple.

In addition, while young stepsiblings often accept the new baby as they would any new family addition, older children sometimes see the baby as "extra baggage" or as having special status.

The main reason parents in a blended family give for having a child together is the hope that it will "cement the bond" of marriage.

Another reason for having a child together is real or perceived social pressure to be more like "a normal family."

Partners who have children from a previous marriage recognize potential problems and are more likely to weigh the consequences before deciding to have a mutual child.

* The number of single-parent families and unmarried couples living together will increase.
* Patriarchal marriages will decline, replaced by more egalitarian relationships.

Government may play a larger role in the future of the family in terms of:

* Tax relief or support for families where both parents work.
* Support for poor families.
* Childcare and other children's programs.

Other factors will almost certainly influence family structure:

* **Health Care.** As people live longer lives, the "sandwich generation" of middle-aged individuals will become increasingly responsible not only for their children but also for their aging parents. One sociologist suggests that this may become a "multi-layered club sandwich" as four- and five-generation families become more common.
* **Technological Advances.** Such innovations as in vitro fertilization, sperm banks, and perhaps even cloning will offer alternative ways to form families and introduce new moral and legal issues.

Despite the potential changes, sociologists believe that families will remain the cornerstone of society.

Chapter 9 Wrap-up
THE FAMILY

Families are the most basic and influential social group. Individuals belong to different families—their family of orientation, their family of procreation—as well as to their larger kinship group. Descent patterns and patterns of authority as well as residence differ among the world's societies along gender lines. Marriage norms differ as well.

Different sociological perspectives have informed our understanding of families. Functionalists have pointed to the important functions families serve: socializing children, regulating sexual activity, replacing generations, providing protection and economic security, providing emotional support, and stabilizing society. Conflict theorists have pointed to ways in which families can exploit weaker members of society. Interactionists have looked at the ways family members negotiate their relationships and their needs for power.

Family life is changing in the United States. Where the nuclear, patriarchal family was once the norm, there are now many different types of families, including blended and single-parent families. Families today are confronted with many problems when both parents work or when there is only one parent in the family. Long-term trends in family composition are expected to continue, resulting in smaller and more socially diverse families and a change in the roles of males and females.

egalitarian family—family where authority is shared equally between spouses. *p. 167*

endogamy—marriage within a particular group in accordance with social custom or law. *p. 168*

exogamy—custom of marrying outside the tribe, family, clan, or other social unit. *p. 168*

extended family—family members of several generations who share a household and are economically and emotionally bound to one another. *p. 164*

family—relatively permanent group of people connected by ancestral lineage, marriage, or adoption. *p. 164*

family of orientation—family into which a child is born and receives an initial orientation into society. *p. 164*

family of procreation—(also called family of marriage) family that people form as adults when they marry. *p. 164*

heterogamy—practice of selecting a mate from among a range of social groups within a society. *p. 175*

homogamy—practice of selecting a mate within one's social group; similar characteristics such as education, race, religion, age, and social class govern the choice. *p. 175*

kinship group—complex network of people whose social relationships are based on common ancestry, marriage, and adoption. *p. 165*

matriarchy—social system in which the mother is head of the family and descent is traced through the mother's side. *p. 166*

modified extended family—different generations do not necessarily live in the same household but do maintain regular contact and support each other with daily life issues. *p. 164*

monogamy—practice of being married to only one person at a time. *p. 168*

nonlineal descent—ancestry traced through both parents. *p. 166*

nuclear family—parents and their children who live together but apart from other family members. *p. 164*

patriarchy—social system in which the father is head of the family and descent is traced through the father's side. *p. 166*

polygamy—practice of having more than one spouse at a time. *p. 168*

unilineal descent—ancestry traced through only one parent. *p. 165*

CHAPTER 10

Education and Religion

In this chapter, you will learn about:

- **the structure and function of education**
- **the structure and function of religion**
- **issues in U.S. education and religion**

In July 1925, religion and education fought it out in a hot courtroom in Tennessee.
Two of the greatest legal minds in the United States, William Jennings Bryan and Clarence
Darrow, faced one another over what Bryan called a "contest between evolution and
Christianity . . . a duel to the death."

The trial was held to determine if a science teacher, John Scopes, had broken the law when
he taught the theory of evolution in his classroom. At issue was the right of a state to pass a
law prohibiting teachers from including certain content because it challenged religious beliefs.

Education and religion are two highly influential social institutions. Both have functions that
serve and control society. In this chapter, you will learn about how these institutions function
and how societal changes affect both institutions.

Bureaucratization of Education

One educational issue of concern is the increasing consolidation of school districts and the bureaucratization that results. The graph shows how the number of school districts in the United States decreased in the last half of the 20th century. As the number of districts got smaller, the size of each district got larger.

School District Consolidation

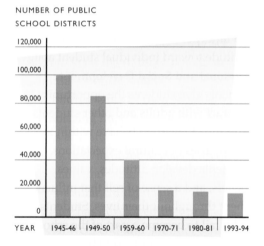

NUMBER OF PUBLIC
SCHOOL DISTRICTS

YEAR   1945-46   1949-50   1959-60   1970-71   1980-81   1993-94

Source: U.S. Department of Education

Advantages of large districts:

* *Course offerings are the same from school to school.* Uniformity of courses allows easy transfer from one school to another.
* *A wide variety of courses and subjects is offered.* Students have more options to explore and more opportunities to expand their horizons.

* *Teachers have a strong background in the subjects they teach.* Larger schools can hire more teachers with specialized training.
* *Policies and rules are standard.* Parents, students, teachers, and administrators know what to expect. Procedures are in place to express diverse viewpoints, resolve conflicts, and protect people from arbitrary decisions that affect their lives.

Disadvantages of large districts:

* *The bureaucracy makes parents, teachers, and students feel they have little power or control.* Teachers in particular become frustrated with red tape and demands on their time for activities that have little to do with teaching. They may become disillusioned and experience "burnout." Some may become authoritarian in dealing with students.
* *Students are dehumanized.* In a large system, students may be treated as products on a factory's conveyor belt rather than as individuals.

One solution to the problem of huge bureaucratic districts is a push toward "schools within schools"—smaller units within a large district in which students and teachers stay together over several years.

Opportunity

You have already seen several ways in which children from lower levels of the economic scale can be shortchanged in the educational process. **Two** programs attempt to equalize opportunities for disadvantaged children.

Did You Know?

The Digital Divide

The digital divide refers to the growing gap between people with access to computers and the Internet and those without.

According to the U.S. Department of Commerce:

* Households with incomes over $75,000 are over 20 times more likely to have home Internet access than those at the lowest income levels.

* Only 6.6 percent of people with an elementary school education or less use the Internet.

* In rural areas, families in which a parent has a college degree are 11 times more likely to have a home computer and 26 times more likely to have home Internet access than those with only an elementary school education.

1. **Head Start.** Many students enter school already "behind" due to poor nutrition or the absence of such school readiness activities as learning the ABCs and numbers at home. Head Start is a *compensatory program* that attempts to make up for those deficits by teaching three- and four-year-olds skills and vocabulary that middle-class children learn at home. Classes for parents are part of it too. Since its inception in 1965, Head Start programs have helped 18 million children. Those years have seen dramatic increases in reading achievement in the first three grades. Over time, studies show that when children who were in preschool programs such as Head Start reach ages 9 to 19, they do better in school than peers who were not. They have higher reading scores, are less likely to be held back a grade, and are more likely to graduate from high school and attend college. They are also less likely to go on welfare or get involved in delinquency and crime.

2. **Magnet Schools.** In 1985, the U.S. government provided seed money to multi-school districts so that they could create *magnet schools* whose programs would attract students from outside the neighborhood enrollment area. Magnet schools offer specialized programs in humanities, the arts, science, and technology as well as foreign language immersion and career/vocational training. They often employ diverse learning approaches. Magnet schools have been somewhat successful in attracting a diverse student population, although low-income and limited-English-proficient students have been less likely than others to take advantage of them.

School Choice

With a national dropout rate in excess of 11 percent—a rate that can exceed 70 percent in urban areas—some policy makers look to economic theory to find solutions. They suggest that if schools have to compete for "customers," they will be forced to improve. This idea has led to **three** proposals for educational reforms.

1. **Vouchers.** Public schools are funded by tax dollars. Some reformers suggest that parents should receive public funds in the form of *vouchers* exchangeable for tuition at the school of their choice. This could include private or church-sponsored schools. Opponents argue that by taking money out of the public school system, vouchers will weaken public education. They fear that racial discrimination may be magnified if parents choose schools based on ethnic or racial composition. They also point out that a voucher system could violate the principle of separation of church and state.

2. **Charter Schools.** Another form of school choice is the establishment of charter schools. These schools are private in that they do not answer to local school boards. However, because they are supported by tax dollars, they must prove that they are providing at least as effective an education as public schools. Estimates suggest that by the end of the year 2000, there were nearly 2,000 charter schools serving almost half a million students.

Does Parent Education Level Predict Student Achievement?

Home School Achievement– Basic Battery Test

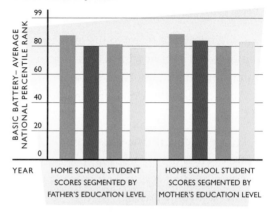

Public School Achievement– Writing and Math Tests

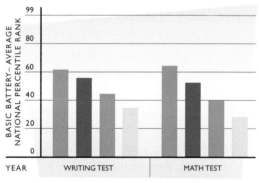

Source: U.S. Department of Education

3. **Home Schooling.** An increasing number of parents opt to keep their children out of the school system entirely and teach them at home. Many curriculum

programs are now available for home-schooled children. Critics say these children do not have access to the resources available in public schools and miss opportunities to develop social skills. Data like those in the charts opposite seem to indicate that home schooling has benefits. Parents, regardless of education, who are willing to teach their own children spend more time with them, thus making such statistics more complex than they appear.

Accountability

In recent years, business and community groups have demanded that schools be more accountable for their results and meet minimum standards of achievement. This has made assessment a driving force in many schools. This demand includes **two** ideas:

1. It assumes that assessments are a true measure of learning.
2. It assumes that every student should be held accountable for the same material at the same age.

Both assumptions have been called into question by research. In addition, teachers point out that other demands, such as courses on alcohol and drug abuse, pregnancy, AIDS, and other social issues, dilute the time schools have to teach "the basics."

School Violence

Violence in schools mirrors the violence in society. In a typical month, more than 150,000 crimes occur in U.S. schools. Estimates are that more than 100,000 guns are brought to schools daily—a frightening fact.

The American Psychological Association blames much of the increase in school violence on the social isolation many students feel, as well as on easy access to weapons. Some people argue that violence in the media and in video games may make students numb to the real effects of violence.

In 2001, the Metropolitan Center for Urban Education at New York University was conducting research that explored the principal issues surrounding school violence. They warned that the problems educators face are "complex, multifaceted, and deeply rooted in the conditions of the dominant culture, which chooses to disregard adolescents, especially the poorest of them." The Center insisted there are no "simplistic, single-shot solutions."

Religion and Society

All societies have religion. Religious beliefs provide answers to the most fundamental questions people have about their existence. Religious practices accompany the most significant events in people's lives: the birth of a child, the transition from childhood to adulthood, marriage, and death.

Religion is not the activity of an individual alone. It is the practice of a community of believers. Even the most solitary hermits have belonged to a community of people with faith. It is precisely because religion is a communal activity that sociologists study it.

Religion as defined by sociologists is a system of shared beliefs and rituals that surround the realm of the sacred and deal with fundamental questions of life. The world's religions share such features as:

* *Rituals*—such as prayer, fasting, sacrifice, initiation, and ceremonies of baptism, naming, marriage, and end-of-life.
* *Symbols*—such as the Star of David, the crucifix, or the crescent moon and star.
* *Places of Worship*—such as churches, synagogues, mosques, temples, and even cities such as Jerusalem and Mecca.
* *Sacred Writings*—such as the Bible, the Torah, and the Koran.
* *Sacred Objects*—prayer wheels, statues, holy water, shamanic medicine bundles, and others.

Sociologist's Perspective

Emile Durkheim on Religion

Emile Durkheim wrote the classic statement of the sociological perspective on religion in his 1912 work *The Elementary Forms of the Religious Life*. Here he defined religion as "a unified system of beliefs and practices relating to sacred things that unite into one single moral community all those who adhere to them." He characterized religion as an institution that deals with the sacred, rather than the profane. The *sacred* involves anything that is beyond the ordinary and for which believers feel awe or reverence. The *profane* represents ordinary objects and events that people encounter in their daily lives.

Context determines whether an object or event is sacred or profane. For example, eating bread is profane in daily life, but sacred during the Christian rite of Holy Communion and the eating of unleavened bread in Jewish Passover.

Durkheim focused on practices relative to the sacred, and his approach continues to be the basis of sociological understanding of religion.

Types of Religion

The beliefs of the world's many religions can be viewed as falling into **four** categories:

1. **Theism** is the belief in one or more supreme beings whose actions influence human affairs and who deserve to be worshipped. **Polytheism** is the worship of several gods who have varying degrees of power.
   EXAMPLE: Hinduism, the world's third largest religion, believes in one divine principal but worships many gods as different aspects of that unity.

   Monotheism is the belief in and worship of a single, supreme God.
   EXAMPLES: Judaism, Christianity, and Islam believe in one God who is the creator and absolute ruler of the universe.

2. **Ethicalism** is a belief that moral principles have a sacred quality. These religions do not involve the worship of gods, spirits, or forces.
   EXAMPLES: Buddhism, Confucianism, and Taoism have widely different practices and beliefs and can include a belief in the saving grace of higher beings. They are similar in their emphasis on living a right and just life.

3. **Animism**, or spiritism, is the belief in the existence of spirits that occupy the same world as humans, but in a different plane of existence. While some cultures practice an animistic religion solely, many believers in animistic religions also practice one or another of the major religions.
   EXAMPLES: In the **totemism** of many indigenous peoples, **shamans** interact with spirits found in natural objects such as trees or mountains, in birds or animals, or in natural phenomena such as the sun, moon, or lightning. Guardian angels, devils, fairies, ancestral spirits, and demons are all animistic spirits. Seventy percent of Americans polled in the 1990s said they believed in angels.

4. **Supernaturalism** is a belief in the existence of supernatural forces that influence human events for good or evil. These forces don't take any specific form. Like animism, supernaturalism can be the basis of a religion or it may be found in the practices of believers in other religions.
   EXAMPLE: Traditional societies in the Pacific Islands believe in a force called *mana* that is neither good nor evil, but is a supernatural energy that some people who have special gifts and knowledge can make work for them.

Sociological Perspectives on Religion

There are primarily two contrasting perspectives on religion in sociological thought, those of the functionalist Emile Durkheim and those of the symbolic interactionist Max Weber. Research since their time tends to follow one or the other of these traditions.

Membership in World Religions*	
Religion	**Followers**
1. Christianity	2 billion
2. Islam	1.3 billlion
3. Hinduism	900 million
4. Secular/Nonreligious/ Agnostic/Atheist	850 million
5. Buddhism	360 million
6. Chinese traditional religion	225 million
7. Primal-indigenous	190 million
8. Sikhism	23 million
9. Yoruba religion	20 million
10. Juche	19 million
11. Spiritism	14 million
12. Judaism	14 million
13. Baha'i	6 million
14. Jainism	4 million
15. Shinto	4 million
16. Cao Dai	3 million
17. Tenrikyo	2.4 million
18. Neo-Paganism	1 million
19. Unitarian-Universalism	800 thousand
20. Scientology	750 thousand

*These numbers are approximate estimates. The list accounts for the religions of about 98 percent of the world's population.

Source: Adherents.com (2001).

Functionalist Perspective

Durkheim was interested in the social functions of religion. These can be grouped around the following **four** needs:

1. **Social Cohesion.** Religion provides a shared set of values, beliefs, and norms. When people share beliefs and rituals, social bonds form that contribute to the solidarity of the community.

2. **Comfort and Support.** Religious beliefs often provide consolation in times of personal suffering or natural disaster. The support of others and the rituals surrounding life transitions such as birth, marriage, and death provide a sense of continuity. Strong religious belief can lead people to endure hardships.

World Religions

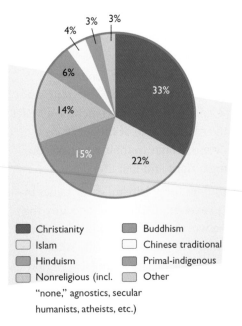

33%
22%
15%
14%
6%
4%
3%
3%

Christianity — Buddhism
Islam — Chinese traditional
Hinduism — Primal-indigenous
Nonreligious (incl. "none," agnostics, secular humanists, atheists, etc.) — Other

Source: www.adherents.com

3. **Meaning.** Religions satisfy the need to understand the world and one's role in it. Religions offer answers to large questions about the meaning of life and death and the ways in which people should lead their lives.

4. **Social Control.** Religion strengthens conformity to society's norms by defining some of them as sacred. Commandments such as "Thou shalt not steal" and "Thou shalt not kill" add religious weight to social laws. The Golden Rule ("Do unto others as you would have others do unto you") encourages helpfulness and cooperation. Laws have even taken on religious names, such as the Good Samaritan Law that protects those who help others during emergencies.

Nonreligious belief systems such as communism, nationalism, fascism, and humanism may meet some of the same needs as religion. These systems draw their power from ideologies that are considered "noble" rather than from the realm of the sacred.

Interactionist Perspective

While Durkheim was interested in the social functions religion perform, Weber was interested in the way religion explained fundamental moral problems of death, suffering, and evil and how religious views operated in a given society's efforts to reach its goals. He described his most important work in this area in *The Protestant Ethic and the Spirit of Capitalism*. In it he tried to show that the roots of Western capitalism lay in the religious beliefs of Protestants.

Sociologists after Weber looked at postindustrial society. Some saw a severe religious decline, or secularization, and tried to show that it was the result of urbanization and cultural pluralism. Others said that religion was transformed in the 20th century, becoming more accepting of other religious views, more inclusive, and thus different but not undermined.

Religion, because it seeks to understand the human situation, makes great use of symbols, and is fundamentally social.

Religion in the United States

Religion in the fabric of U.S. society is related to our history, to the different cultural groups that make up our population, and to the change we are continually experiencing.

Separation of Church and State

For Puritans, "theology was wedded to politics and politics to the progress of the kingdom of God." They had come to this land to escape religious persecution and planned to establish a "holy commonwealth" to be ruled by church officials. They were not tolerant of diverse opinions within their society.

One hundred fifty years later, during the debates on the articles of the Constitution, the founding fathers recalled the history of religious persecution. They wanted to guarantee religious freedom. In the Constitution, they would have no official state religion and forbade government interference in religious activities. Over time, court rulings have interpreted this to mean that activities of the church and state must be kept separate. National, state, and local governments must not, therefore, promote any particular religion.

In practice, this separation is incomplete. U.S. currency states "In God We Trust" and the phrase, "under God" is present in the pledge of allegiance. Governmental events frequently open with a prayer, and churches are tax-exempt. Many citizens have no problem with these things as long as all beliefs are treated equally.

Religious Diversity

The United States is one of the most religious nations in the world. Over 90 percent of Americans believe in a "supreme being." More than 50 percent say that religion is "very important" in their lives.

Religious beliefs are extremely diverse, encompassing more than 1,000 denominations, sects, and new religious movements.

Religions in the United States

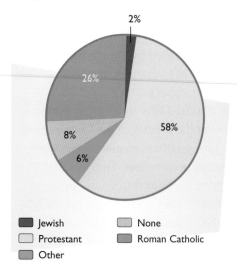

- Jewish
- None
- Protestant
- Roman Catholic
- Other

2%
26%
8%
6%
58%

Source: *Statistical Abstract of the U.S. 1998*

The graph shows the religious membership of people in the United States. Preferences for "other" religions, such as Buddhism and Islam, have been growing.

Sociologists who have analyzed U.S. religious group membership have found certain generalizations can be made:

* **Age.** Adults tend to be more active in churches than younger people. Many baby boomers who dropped out of their religions in their teens or 20s have now returned.

* **Class Differences.** There are noticeable differences among the median incomes of members of different religious denominations. Also, in some communities, the more prestigious members may all belong to the same religion.

* **Ethnicity.** As you have learned, members of ethnic groups tend to share religious beliefs and practices. Many African Americans are Baptist or Methodist, and many Latinos are Catholic. However, most of the major religious groups have members across the cultural spectrum.

* **Gender.** Women seem to be more religious than men. In a 1995 study, 69 percent of women said that religion was important to them, compared to 51 percent of men. Women were 20 percent more likely to have attended a church service in a given week than men. Women's religious decisions differ from those of men in other ways. A woman more often converts to a religion because of a personal contact. Men tend to choose religious affiliation based on their own research.

Hi-Tech Religion

Emerging technologies have added a new dimension to religion. For many years, television ministries and **televangelism**— the zealous preaching of religious doctrine on television—have grown increasingly popular. Services once held in tents are now beamed into living rooms from high-tech "cathedrals." Evangelical Christians buy more than 90 percent of television time allotted to religion.

Searchable scriptures are available on CDs, and gospel music has its own category of music awards.

Over 10 million Internet sites are devoted to religion. With a click of the mouse, people can jump from a mosque to a virtual mass to an Inca sun ceremony. They can choose from a selection of Bible verses or join a heated discussion of religious doctrine in an on-line chat room. In the fall of 2000, there were more than 32,000 web sites where people could learn about different faiths and religions, ranging from "African Religions" to "Zoroastrianism."

Will people use these resources to add to their knowledge of religion or to replace their attendance at live religious services? Some sociologists worry that current trends will lead to isolation and social fragmentation if traditional worship communities are replaced by TV and the Internet.

Changing Beliefs

Several trends are changing the nature of religion in the United States:

* *Members of different religions are exchanging ideas.* Increasingly, members of religious groups are coming to believe that they have made too much of their differences in the past. In some cases, different Protestant denominations are merging. Among the world's religions, groups of people have come together to share their experiences and understandings of the divine. This **ecumenical** movement represents a major shift away from an insistence on having the only truth and a recognition that there may be more than one expression of truth.

* *A fundamentalist revival is taking place.* In reaction to what they see as an increasingly liberal and permissive society, some Christian groups have reasserted **fundamentalist** positions, emphasizing a belief in strict rules and a literal interpretation of scripture. Fundamentalist groups, such as the Christian Coalition, have used the voting power of their members to seek changes in society that conform to their views of what is right.

* *The quality of some religious experience has become more secular and less sacred.* The word *secular* means "worldly," that is, profane. One example is church services offered on television. Sociologists point out that, unlike participating in a solemn religious service in a place of worship, people can now sit on their sofas munching snacks while "attending" church. There are also "drive-through" funeral parlors, and weddings take place in all sorts of "profane" locations. Some feel this compromises the distinction between the sacred and the profane.

* *People are seeking religious answers outside the traditional religions.* This recent trend is sometimes called **New Age.** It is a unique blend of magic and religion, ancient and futuristic beliefs, and both practical and mystical philosophies. People who adopt new-age ideas often refer to themselves as spiritual rather than religious, meaning that they are seeking a direct personal connection with "spirit" rather than relying on the traditions and interpretations of organized religion.

Various factors motivate people to search out different religious practices. These include:

* Major developmental phases, such as adolescence or midlife, in which an individual reexamines his or her identity and basic beliefs.
* Life crises, such as a crippling accident, that can cause an individual to reevaluate the way in which he or she will live going forward.
* New relationships, a close friend, or future spouse who introduce the individual to new ways of worship.
* Disenchantment with organized religions that are run like businesses and seem lacking in spiritual depth.

Education and religion are highly influential institutions. Education performs the functions of socialization, cultural transmission, assimilation/social control, social placement, and change and innovation. Yet conflict theorists say that through some of their practices, U.S. educational institutions maintain social inequalities. Several school programs have addressed these issues.

Religion provides social cohesion, comfort and support, answers to questions about the meaning of life, and social control. Separation of church and state and religious diversity characterize religion in the United States.

Sociology

animism—belief in the existence of spirits that occupy the same world but in a different plane of existence. *p. 195*

apprentice—one who works for an experienced worker, exchanging labor for instruction in a trade. *p. 184*

ecumenical—referring to a movement that promotes unity among religions or churches. *p. 200*

ethicalism—belief that moral principles have a sacred quality. *p. 195*

ethnocentric—centered on a belief in the superiority of one's own ethnic group; from the perspective of that group. *p. 188*

fundamentalist—based on basic or fundamental principles; in religion, emphasizing a belief in strict rules and a literal interpretation of scripture. *p. 200*

monotheism—belief in and worship of a single supreme God. *p. 195*

multiculturalism—point of view that includes the perspectives of many cultures within a society rather than in only a mainstream culture. *p. 188*

New Age—blend of magic and religion, ancient and futuristic beliefs, and practical and mystical philosophies. *p. 200*

polytheism—worship of several gods who have varying degrees of power. *p. 195*

religion—system of shared beliefs and rituals that surround the realm of the sacred and deal with fundamental questions of life. *p. 194*

shaman—holy person who interacts with spirits of nature on behalf of others. *p. 195*

supernaturalism—belief in the existence of supernatural forces that influence human events for good or evil. *p. 195*

televangelism—zealous preaching of religious doctrine on television. *p. 199*

theism—belief in one or more supreme beings whose actions influence human affairs and who deserve worship. *p. 195*

totemism—belief in spirits within natural objects such as trees, mountains, animals, or natural phenomena. *p. 195*

CHAPTER II

Politics and the Economy

In this chapter, you will learn about:

- politics, power, and authority
- politics and government in the United States
- the economy and work in the United States

In 1947, India was granted independence from British rule, due in great measure to the efforts of a charismatic leader named Mohandas Gandhi. Gandhi was a quiet revolutionary, preaching nonviolence and passive resistance against British rule. He led by example, often fasting in protest to government actions and the inequalities of the caste system.

During the same period, Adolph Hitler engaged in powerful public speaking to push the ideas of the Nazi Party. He used his talent for political agitation to promote violent, racial nationalism and anti-Semitism. Hitler convinced the German people that only a dictatorship could rescue them from their social and economic problems. Of course, he was to be the dictator.

These men were both powerful leaders by virtue of their personalities. Yet their legacies could not be more different. In this chapter, you will learn about political power, the role of the economy in society, and work.

Political Institutions

What does it mean when we say the United States has a democratic form of government? How are societies related to governments? The answer lies in a society's **political institutions.** These are the organizations and customs that a society establishes for its government.

Power and Authority

Through the political process, individuals and groups acquire, exercise, maintain, or lose power. In a world of limited resources, there is always conflict between groups. Governments are society's way of controlling that conflict.

Power itself is neither good nor bad. The people wielding the power and the reasons they use it are the important factors. **Legitimate power** is the power in a society that its people believe or trust.

There are **two** kinds of legitimate power held by individuals and groups in a society:

1. **Authority,** the recognized power to enforce laws, require obedience, command, determine, or judge. Authority is formal and is established by tradition or by law.
   EXAMPLES: Parents, employers, and teachers have authority over others by right of their social relationships. Presidents of the United States get their authority from the Constitution.

2. **Influence,** power arising through persuasion. Influence can be formalized in rules— such as the laws differentiating

bribes from respected means of making financial contributions to a party or candidate—or it can be informal and come from the wealth, fame, charm, or knowledge of an individual or group.
EXAMPLES: Friends or experts may possess power through influence. The power of labor unions comes from the voting strength of their citizen members and the lawful power to withhold workers' services from an employer in a strike.

There is **one** kind of illegitimate power:

Coercion, the exercise of power through force or threat.
EXAMPLE: Bullies wield power through coercion. In some societies a special or secret police force uses kidnapping, torture, and murder to silence critics and terrorize communities into submission to a government's rule.

Sociologist Max Weber identified three types of authority arising from different sources. See the chart on the next page.

Weber's Types of Authority		
Type of Authority	**Source of Authority**	**Examples**
Traditional Authority	Custom, habit, heredity, or tradition, often supported by religion. People obey those in authority because they always have.	Kings and queens, tribal leaders, feudal lords, emirs, princes, and chieftains such as those in the United Arab Emirates.
Charismatic Authority	Exceptional personal qualities of an individual. People follow them often because such leaders possess a persuasive vision. Charismatic leaders operate both inside and outside of governments.	Martin Luther King, Jr.; Mohandas Gandhi; Nelson Mandela; Joan of Arc; Cesar Chavez; Adolf Hitler.
Rational-Legal Authority	Constitutions and other laws that define a ruler's rights and duties. People understand their obedience is part of a contract of mutual rights and responsibilities.	Governors, prime ministers, presidents.

Legitimacy

Legitimacy is achieved in several ways. Leaders may gain legitimacy by effectively using symbols, ideologies, and mass communication to create a sense of national unity and to maintain the loyalty and support of the citizens. Elections, when they are seen as honest and fair, serve to legitimize those who are elected to govern. Governments that rule through coercion are subject to rebellion.

Legitimacy in the eyes of the world occurs when a government is recognized as being sovereign, that is, within its territory, supreme, most powerful, and independent of other governments. After a revolution, a new government usually must go through some efforts to get other nations to recognize it.

Nations of the World

When the United Nations was created in 1946, there were 51 recognized nations. In August of 2000, the United Nations recognized 228 countries of the world. The United States recognizes 190 countries as independent states and another 60 or more as dependent states.

* The largest nation is China with 1.27 billion people.
* India is currently the second largest country, with a population of less than 1 billion. By the year 2050, India is expected to take the top position with more than 1.5 billion people, as compared to 1.2 billion in China.
* The smallest independent state is the Vatican—an independent city-state with a population of fewer than 500 people.

The State

You might think of a state as a place, a government, or a group of people. You would not be wrong. But, to a sociologist, the **state** is a distinct set of institutions that has the authority to make the rules that govern society. It is not unified—not *one* thing—but is a *set* of institutions. Together, they define the rules and boundaries within which political conflicts among the competing elements of society are played out. The state includes:

* The legislature.
* The executive.
* The central government or the bureaucracy.
* Local governments.
* The judiciary.
* The police.
* The armed forces.

Some sociologists have gone further, adding other institutions to the list:

* Religious groups.
* Schools.
* Trade unions.

Sociological Perspectives on the State

The functionalist and conflict perspectives inform our study of the state.

Functionalist Perspective

Functionalists claim that as social order is essential to society, the state maintains it by performing **four** functions:

1. **Enforcement of Norms.** In small tribal societies, norms were supported and enforced by the community. As societies grew and became more complex, a system of formal, systematized laws was created. The political authority of the state enforces those laws.

EXAMPLE: The laws defining what constitutes kidnapping and when the FBI should be brought in are our complex society's way of enforcing a norm against taking a person against his or her will.

2. **Regulation of Conflict.** The very real conflicts about the allocation of resources could easily erupt into bloody battles if there were no system to mediate them. The state addresses and resolves conflicts through many of its institutions. It is most successful when the parties to the conflict perceive it as fair and unbiased.

EXAMPLE: In the dispute over the use of public lands, environmentalists, recreationists, and loggers each have a different viewpoint. State and national lawmakers, government bureaucrats, logging industry groups, environmental protection groups, and concerned citizens all play a part in resolving this conflict.

3. **Planning and Coordination.** The infrastructure needed to keep a large society running smoothly is very complex. The state provides mechanisms for planning and coordinating the many, many activities needed to keep a complex society going.

EXAMPLES: The construction and maintenance of highways and dams, air traffic control, emergency readiness and relief, military preparedness—governments plan and coordinate these important activities of a society.

4. **Conducting Relations with Other Societies.** The state determines foreign policy and defense strategy and makes complex decisions dealing with international economics. It would be impossible for nations to form alliances if different interests within a state were not resolved and the nation could not talk to other nations with "one voice."

EXAMPLE: In forging the North America Free Trade Agreement (NAFTA), the administrations of two Presidents (Bush and Clinton) had to negotiate with Congress, representatives of various state legislatures, lobbyists from unions and other interest groups, and with the governments of Canada and Mexico. The state continues to deal with public concerns about the effects of the agreement.

Conflict Perspective

Sociologists and political scientists disagree about the fairness of the activities of a complex, postindustrial state. Some sociologists say that the different groups within a society have representation through the various institutions within it. They believe there is a balance among conflicting groups and that systems for expressing needs and negotiating among conflicting demands are in place to achieve smooth operation. They see the state as acting in the interest of the groups within it.

Other sociologists see the state as captive to the special interests within it.

Marxist conflict theorists argue that the state serves the interest of the "ruling class." Because those in power can pass laws that maintain their own economic and social privileges, class differences become even more pronounced. Marxists suggest that, rather than exerting legitimate power, the state engages in coercion to maintain the ruling class.

EXAMPLE: The use of troops or executive orders to send striking workers back to work can be seen as benefiting big business at the expense of the working class.

Forms of Government

The modern industrialized state traces its development through **four** stages in Western civilization.

1. **The city-state of ancient Athens in Greece,** around 500 B.C., is credited with being the origin of democracy, in which sovereignty rested with the free citizens of an independent city.

2. **The feudal systems of early medieval Europe,** from about 800 to 1500 A.D., were small, self-sufficient economic units governed by feudal lords, who in turn swore allegiance to kings. The society understood a contractual agreement among the groups: Nobles agreed to provide protection (especially military) and various judicial functions, and to care for those who could not care for themselves; peasants agreed to provide labor in exchange. All agreed to love and serve the king, who agreed to provide justice and rule. But feudal lords often were rivals to the king, and kings were often nothing more than super feudal lords.

3. **The national monarchies of the late middle ages** were characterized by a centralized authority, urbanization, and a growing middle class. Economic changes, such as the expansion of trade, necessitated and supported the creation of these larger political units. Monarchs became increasingly powerful as they could exercise authority with large armies and large treasuries.

4. **17th- and 18th-century nation-states.** **Nation-states** are political entities whose governments hold jurisdiction over a large territory. Their people share a common history, language, and independent government. The development of **nationalism,** or a people's sense of its right to have its own nation, spurred revolutions in Europe and on the American continent. Written constitutions, a bill of rights, and representative democracy resulted from the American and French revolutions.

Continuum of Types of Government

Governments can be thought of as lying on a continuum. The most liberal governments (on the left) are democratic, with authority coming from their citizen members. The most repressive governments (on the right) are totalitarian, with authority consolidated in one person, or in a small, elite group, that has complete power over the people.

You can get a chilling picture of what life can be like in a totalitarian government by reading *1984* by George Orwell. He

Power in Government		
	Democratic	**Monarchic**
Description	Authority resides in the citizens of the state. People participate directly or indirectly in their own governance. In direct, or pure, democracy, all citizens are directly involved in the decision-making process. In representative democracy, citizens choose others to represent them in political decision making through regular elections.	Power to govern is passed from one generation to another within a single family. In an absolute monarchy, the ruler governs with no legal restrictions. In a constitutional monarchy, the monarch is the symbolic head of state, but political power rests in a government with a constitution.
Examples	**Representative Democracy:** The United States and France **Direct Democracy:** Town government in New England.	**Absolute Monarchy:** Saudi Arabia, Kuwait, and Jordan **Constitutional Monarchy:** Great Britain, the Scandinavian countries, and Japan.
Issues	How widely can political power be distributed and still produce effective government? In the United States, power is distributed among the three branches of government in a system of checks and balances. States also share in the power.	Royals in Britain have been criticized for excessive spending and an antiquated monarchy. The royal family has had to become more sensitive to the concerns of the people.

wrote in the years following the end of World War II, and was inspired by the horror of the excesses of communism under Stalin and from concern about the ability of such a government to use the emerging communications technology against its people. But England in the future, not Russia of the late 1940s, is the setting of his book. There the government uses the language of socialism to mask the reality of totalitarianism.

The chart below describes the most common forms of modern governments.

Authoritarian	Totalitarian
Authority is concentrated in rulers who limit citizen participation in government. Leaders come to power through inheritance, by preselection (by a former leader), by membership in a small, elite group that assumes power (an oligarchy), or as military officers who seize power (a junta).	The government recognizes no limit to its power and can control all aspects of people's lives. There is no organized opposition, and information is controlled by the government. Dissidents are dealt with harshly. Travel both within and outside the country is tightly controlled.
Dictatorships: Juan Peron in Argentina, Ferdinand Marcos in the Philippines **Juntas:** (in the past 50 years) Myanmar (Burma), Nigeria, and Chile.	Nazi Germany under Hitler, the Soviet Union under Stalin, China under Mao Zedong, and Iraq under Saddam Hussein.
Dictatorships are often succeeded by oligarchies or military juntas. People have no legal recourse to remove leadership. Revolutions are common.	Totalitarianism is fairly recent. Advances in technology have made surveillance of large populations possible and permit control of mass media and, therefore, information.

Politics and Government in the United States

The representative democracy in the United States depends on participation by the country's citizens. For two centuries, much of this participation has taken place in the context of two major political parties and a number of smaller parties. In recent times, a variety of interest groups has also encouraged political participation.

Political Participation

In a country founded on principles of democratic rule, it is surprising that the percentage of the voter age population (VAP) who actually vote has been steadily

Sociologist's Perspective

Theories of U.S. Political Power

In the United States, political power is theoretically in the hands of the people. However, several theories have arisen about where the power really lies.

* Conflict theorist C. Wright Mills suggested that a power elite controls the government. This is a group of wealthy and influential individuals who hold important positions in government, business, and the military. They share common ideologies and often move from one area of influence to another. You can observe this movement when business leaders and military officers become government advisors.
* President Dwight Eisenhower, who led the Allied forces of World War II before he was elected to the presidency, suggested that there was a "military-industrial complex" that had enormous

power in the United States. By this he meant that the top levels of the military and the leaders of businesses that supplied weapons and goods to the military had economic interests in common that were not always the true interests of the country. Yet, as a group, they were tremendously influential among legislators and other government policy makers.

* Social scientist Robert Dahl and others wrote that U.S. political power is actually distributed among many interest groups, each of which seeks to influence, rather than control, government policy. This is called the *pluralist model*. The passage and enforcement of antitrust legislation, which prevents big business from monopolizing an industry, supports the view that an elite does not control political processes.

Compulsory Voting

In many countries, such as Ecuador, citizens over the age of 18 are required to vote in city, regional, and national elections. Elections are often held on Sunday to enable people to get to the polls. Even if people are working the day of the elections, they must still "present themselves" and obtain a slip of paper enabling them to vote later. Failure to vote results in fines or refusal of government services, such as driver's licenses and passports.

Arguments have been made both for and against compulsory voting.

For:

* Voting is a civic duty. Like other duties, such as paying taxes, sending one's children to school, and serving on a jury, it should also be required.
* When everyone votes, the government more accurately reflects the will of the people and will better serve everyone's needs.
* It would force candidates to consider the total electorate, instead of only groups of "likely voters," so policy formulation and management would be better.

Against:

* It is undemocratic and an infringement of liberty to force people to vote.
* Votes cast by uninformed or uninterested people could have strange results; the elected people might not really represent any broad-based interests.
* Larger numbers of wasted or invalid votes would result.
* Needed reforms might not happen because elected officials and candidates would not want to offend some segment of the population.

WHY WE VOTE

His daddy was president...

He used to play basketball...

He has a war injury...

His father was a senator...

His opponent is so ugly!...

He reminds me of my first husband...

declining. In 1998, the United States ranked 138th in voter turnout among countries holding elections. Less than half the VAP voted.

Reasons for nonparticipation include:

* Complicated residency and registration requirements.
* Too many elections.
* General satisfaction with things as they are. People feel no "need" to vote.
* People are "too busy."
* Lack of interest in the issues.
* Perception of campaigns as mean-spirited or lacking in substance; voters may say none of the candidates is worth voting for.
* Belief that a single vote won't make a difference.

Political scientists warn that voter apathy poses a threat to democracy because when a government doesn't have the support of the people, it lacks legitimacy. Others say that low turnout means that people are satisfied with the status quo.

Political Parties

Political parties are organized groups of people who work together to win elections and shape public policy. The services provided by a political party include:

* Recruiting people to back a platform—the set of policies on which the party "stands."
* Nominating candidates.
* Raising funds to present candidates and their views to the public.
* Providing continuity of government from one administration to another.
* Recruiting and recommending responsible individuals for government service.

Two Parties

Unlike European democracies, which may have ten or more parties, the United States has traditionally had two major parties—the Democrats and the Republicans. Occasionally, third-party candidates run for office. In national elections, they rarely win. They can, however, draw enough votes away from one of the major-party candidates to affect election results. They also serve to let the major parties know that some issue they have neglected is of great importance to a large number of voters.

Differences Between the Parties

While there is heated rhetoric between the two parties, their real differences are not very great. They each, after all, are trying to capture the largest number of voters, so they address issues that most Americans are concerned about. Their solutions to the problems of society do have some distinctions.

* **Republicans** are generally more *conservative,* or to the "right." This means they value local solutions over national ones, argue for tax policy that encourages investment in the economy, seem to favor business interests over labor interests, and generally seek to reduce government spending in social areas and increase it in military ones.
* **Democrats** are more *liberal,* or to the "left." They tend to emphasize the national government's role in social welfare and look there for solutions to unemployment and poverty. They tend to favor tax programs that "take from the rich and give to the poor." Traditionally, they have represented organized labor and have been the party that claims to represent minorities.

Individual citizens in our society are not required to belong to a party. Many voters describe themselves as *independent* and vote for candidates of either party.

Many voters have mixed feelings about the role of government. While they don't want "big government" interfering in their affairs, they are in favor of more government services.

Interest Groups

An **interest group** is an organized collection of people who attempt to influence the political process and decisions. Such groups represent a wide variety of people, from tobacco growers to members of the National Rifle Association; from

foreign businesses to American workers' organizations such as the AFL-CIO; and from women's rights advocates to senior citizen groups.

Interest groups serve **three** general functions:

1. They give voice to the needs of their members in the halls of government.
2. They pressure legislators to consider issues that might otherwise be ignored.
3. They educate legislators about specific issues, providing them with information to make informed decisions.

Interest groups influence policy in **five** key ways:

1. They influence public opinion through media and advertising.
2. They encourage people to write or call government officials.
3. They work for the election of candidates sympathetic to their cause, often by donating money to campaigns.
4. They file lawsuits to try to stop legislation that is not in their interest.
5. They hire *lobbyists* to directly influence public officials.

Interest groups are extensions of our constitutional rights to free association and free speech. They are people's ways of joining together to influence the distribution of power and resources. Nonetheless, they tend to get a bad name when people see them as having more influence than they deserve. **EXAMPLE:** Most Americans think there is too much gun violence in U.S. society. The National Rifle Association, which lobbies

Data from Polls

Politicians use public opinion polls to learn everything from which candidate the public favors to what "buzzwords" people want to hear in speeches. Even George Washington had a friend mingle with "ordinary folks" to find out what they thought of his presidency.

Pollsters must be careful in their research design if they hope to get accurate data.

* The population sample chosen for the survey must represent the people who will actually vote, not simply those of voting age.
* Questions must be carefully worded to avoid leading the responder. For example, questions about *Governor* Smith rather than John Smith will increase his approval rating.
* The appearance or tone of voice of the surveyor may cause people to try to impress the questioner with the answer they think he or she wants to hear, or, on the other hand, may put people off so that they don't bother to respond.

Interpreting the data from polls is also challenging. A famous error in data interpretation came in the 1948 presidential race between Harry Truman and John Dewey.

Polls predicted a big win for Dewey. The *Chicago Tribune* even printed the headline "Dewey defeats Truman" before election results were released. But Truman had won!

How did it happen? The survey had included all eligible voters, and a majority said they would vote for Dewey. However, his supporters were so sure their candidate would win that many didn't bother voting. Truman supporters came out in large numbers.

against controlling weapons, including those only soldiers are meant to carry, may thus appear to be acting against the will of the majority of citizens.

Political Action Committees

Interest groups set up political action committees (PACs) to collect contributions and make donations to political campaigns. From the 1970s to the present, PACs grew in number from about 600 to 4,000. While most campaign funds come from individual donors, often from people who are not rich, PACs have come in for criticism on many fronts.

We call it "influence peddling" when an interest group buys the support of lawmakers through campaign contributions and other favors. Legislators struggle with issues of campaign finance, and campaign finance reform was a major plank in the platforms of many candidates running for office in the 2000 elections.

Sociologists have pointed out several possible effects of PACs.

* "Power elite" theorists say that PACs stack the deck against challengers whose loyalties are unknown.
* "Pluralist" theory supporters argue that PACs give many different groups input into the political process.
* Conflict theorists insist that PACs favor upper-middle-class people because poor people have neither the resources nor the organization to compete on an equal footing.

Economic Institutions

An **economic institution** is a system for producing and distributing goods and services. It includes the beliefs, values, norms, and activities—including work— that regulate an economy. Economists focus on scarcity and resource allocation and examine such things as productivity, wages, prices, and profits. Sociologists are interested in how work affects the lives of people and the relationships among the economy, the political system, social structures, ideological systems, and culture.

The Economy

The **economy** consists of the systematic production, distribution, and consumption of goods and services in society. The Industrial Revolution transformed both the economies and societies of the world. It had **five** principal effects. It:

1. **Changed the nature of work** from agricultural work and hand work to factory jobs and others that required formal education.
2. **Changed demographics** as people moved from farm to city. Population growth slowed over time, and the number of elderly rose.
3. **Changed human relations** as more people joined large communities.
4. **Raised the standard of living** for everyone as many more goods became available at lower prices.
5. **Changed the values of society,** downplaying traditional ways of living and increasing the pursuit of material things.

Recent Changes

Recent events are changing the face of economics, creating a postindustrial society. These events include:

* The switch from a manufacturing focus to an information focus.
* The globalization of the economy made possible through modern technology—air travel, satellite communications, computers, and the Internet.

Advertising has changed over the years, and so has its effect on the economy. In 1967, businesses spent about $50 million to advertise their products. By 1998, that figure had risen to more than $330 billion. On-line advertising is reshaping the economic community and is now a multibillion-dollar industry.

Electronic commerce is still in its infancy, but it is having a profound influence on economics. Many people became wealthy almost overnight when "dot.com" companies started up in the late 1990s. They just as quickly lost money when many companies failed to produce the expected earnings.

Production

The work that creates products or provides services is done in the production systems of an economy. Production is generally described as having **three** sectors:

1. **Primary production** obtains or generates resources from the environment.
   EXAMPLES: Mining, fishing, logging, agriculture.

2. **Secondary production** manufactures goods from raw materials.
   EXAMPLES: Factories, automakers, food processors.

3. **Tertiary production** provides services rather than goods.
   EXAMPLES: Teachers, doctors, information providers, store clerks, personal trainers. This sector has been increasing while the others have been shrinking.

Distribution

A society's systems for getting goods and services from the people who make or offer them to the people who need or want them are its distribution systems. These can vary widely in different societies. In the planned economies of communist societies, a central government employs bureaucrats to figure out how and in what quantity to move agricultural products from the countryside to cities. In the United States, we rely on the "marketplace" to achieve that.

Consumption

Consumption is the process of accumulating and using goods and services. Initially, consumption is based on *need* for the basic goods and services. In more developed countries, consumption is increasingly based on *want*. *Conspicuous consumption* is the desire to express social standing by having, displaying, or consuming goods and services beyond one's needs, such as expensive cars, fancy jewelry and watches, and expensive homes that are lavishly furnished.

How Technology Is Changing the Economy

Early sociologists believed that when money replaced bartering as a means of securing goods and services, social problems such as wastefulness, bribery, and fraud became more common.

Today, money has been replaced by credit cards—not only in the United States but throughout many areas of the world. Travelers no longer find it necessary to exchange money when they travel abroad. Many businesses, especially those that cater to tourists, accept credit cards. Foreign ATM machines return local currency in exchange for credit card information.

Credit cards can also be used on the Internet to make purchases of goods and services from all over the world.

What do today's sociologists make of these changes? Sociologist George Ritzer warns that the global use of credit cards helps "Americanize the globe and erode national differences. . . . A world of sameness is a world of decreasing interest."

Look at these examples of our global economy:

* U.S. manufacturers use parts made all over the world.
* Fruit grown in Montana appears on a table in Japan within 48 hours.
* U.S. investors buy and sell stocks on the Asian stock exchanges over the Internet.
* Two-thirds of the sales of Coca-Cola are outside the United States.

Three Types of Economic Systems

Economic systems are often closely tied to types of government. Three common economic systems in the world today are capitalism, socialism, and democratic socialism.

Capitalism: The Market Economy

Capitalism features the private ownership of property, competition in the production and distribution of goods and services, and maximization of profit. In a capitalist economic system, supply and demand in the marketplace determine prices.

Societies have considered **three** forms of capitalism:

1. **Unregulated Capitalism.** Trade is unrestrained and production is not regulated. Supply and demand determine both the availability and price of goods and services. Monopolies can occur. In a **monopoly,** a business becomes so powerful that it has forced all its competitors out of the marketplace. When that happens, supply and demand no longer operate on price and availability. The monopoly can charge as much as it wants for its product and can offer it or limit it any way that it wants. No regulation safeguards consumers against dangerous or shoddy goods.
   EXAMPLES: There are no examples of major societies with unregulated capitalism. This is a theoretical ideal that does not operate in the public good, as the above description makes clear.

2. **Welfare Capitalism.** Government plays a significant role in assuring fair competition, worker compensation, and the welfare of the consumer. Environmental issues and working conditions are also regulated through legislation. Societies that practice welfare capitalism struggle to find the balance between letting market forces operate and providing safeguards against excesses. They tend to lean more heavily on regulation at one time and on "hands off" approaches at others.
   EXAMPLES: United States, Canada, Great Britain.

3. **State Capitalism.** Companies are privately owned but often receive financial assistance from the government and are aided by governmental control of competing imports. This causes other countries to charge them with unfair practices.
   EXAMPLES: Japan, Korea.

Sociological perspectives on capitalism differ:

* *Functionalists* see that private ownership motivates people to be efficient and productive. Free competition compels businesses to make the most efficient use of resources, produce the best possible goods and services, and sell them at the lowest possible prices.

* *Conflict theorists* say that private ownership enriches owners and encourages them to keep workers' wages low to increase their own profits. Workers experience alienation because they lack

control or ownership over the goods they produce.

* *Interactionist* Max Weber saw a relationship between the value early U.S. Protestants put on the ethic of hard work and investment of profits in their workplaces. He theorized their business interactions led to capitalism.

Socialism: Centrally Regulated Economy

In **socialism,** the means of production are owned and controlled by the state. Goods and services are distributed as a cooperative enterprise without regard for personal profit. Ideally, all citizens share in both work and profits.

Proponents of socialism argue that centralized planning can control inflation and recession. Manipulation of production and consumption can ensure full employment. Growth is steady and does not undergo the rapid fluctuations that can occur in a capitalist society. In practice, however, none of these benefits has been fully realized.
EXAMPLES: The former Soviet Union, Cuba, North Korea, China (though it is moving toward a market economy).

Mixed Economy: Democratic Socialism

Democratic socialism combines private ownership of property and competitive markets with state ownership of large corporations that are run for the benefit of all citizens. The state owns the largest industries and services, such as transportation, health care, utilities, and the media. Although taxes are high, many public programs are provided, such as low-cost housing and pensions for retired people.
EXAMPLES: Sweden; to a lesser extent, Holland, Germany, France, and Italy.

The U.S. Economy and Work

Sociologists look at how the economy influences people's attitudes, changes their goals, and affects values. They also look at how people experience work and whether they find it satisfying.

A Strong Economy

The United States is primarily a capitalist economy. The success of the economy is measured in **two** ways.

1. **Gross Domestic Product (GDP),** the total dollar value of all goods and services produced in one year by a nation's people.
2. **Productivity,** the nation's efficiency in producing goods and services. It is defined as the ratio of output to input. Output is represented by the GDP, and input is represented by the dollars spent on labor and materials.

When GDP is divided by population, the United States ranks as the "richest" country in the world. The inequity that this represents worries many people. When one nation controls so much of the world's resources and can control even more through the use of its economic power, there are moral and practical problems. The moral ones create a need for

Americans to be just and wise in their exercise of power. The practical ones create a need for vigilance against terrorism and other expressions of frustration and anger.

Taxes

Governments have collected taxes for thousands of years. The ancient pharaohs made people pay taxes in the form of grain, which was then stored as a surplus to protect against times of famine. Conquered peoples were required to pay taxes to their conquerors, and the powerful also became rich.

With the growth of democracy came the idea that those who paid the taxes should have a voice in how they were raised and spent. The American Revolution, you'll recall, was fought in part over "taxation without representation."

Taxes are collected in the United States by every level of government:

* *The federal government* collects income taxes and social security taxes from individuals and businesses.
* *State governments* also collect income tax in most states. Fees paid for drivers' licenses and automobile licenses, highway tolls, and sales taxes are some of the other ways the states raise money.
* *Local governments* most commonly raise money through taxes on property. Homeowners pay these on the value of their homes. Renters pay them, though they don't see them as clearly, in the rent they pay to landlords. Cities can also levy sales taxes and other taxes.

In all, the average U.S. family spends nearly 30 percent of its income on taxes. In addition, business and other corporations pay close to 50 percent of their profits. Almost everyone agrees that they must pay taxes because the money is needed for the smooth running of a myriad of things—highways, school systems, waste removal from our cities, police protection, and so on.

Tax policy is a major issue, because not only does the money raised help our society run smoothly, but how it is collected can have a major effect on our economy. When taxes are raised, individuals and businesses have less to spend. Shoppers buy less; manufacturers cut back on production and may lay off workers. When taxes are lowered, the opposite happens. When legislators design new programs for such things as improved health care or new weapons and military innovations, part of the public debate always revolves around how the programs will be paid for.

A Regulated Economy

The economy in the United States is regulated in a number of ways to achieve **three** important goals:

1. To protect the value of the money people earn so they can plan to meet their current and future needs.
2. To protect the economic climate in which businesses operate so they can plan for their growth and make profits for their investors.

3. To provide security to the nation's business partners around the world and protect the world from major economic downturns that could cause massive unemployment, cause starvation, topple governments, and cause civil rebellions and revolts.

The Federal Reserve System ("the Fed") is the central banking system of the United States. By "tightening" or "loosening" the amount of money available at any time, the Fed attempts to control the rate of economic growth. When the economy grows too quickly, inflation can result, bringing a reduction in the buying power of money (prices go up).

When the members of the Federal Reserve Board believe that the economy is growing too quickly, they can raise interest rates. This makes it more expensive to borrow money. Individuals feel that money is "tighter," and they tend to reduce their spending, slowing the economy. Businesses find it harder to borrow the money to invest in raw materials or in improvements, and this too slows the economy. Lowering interest rates has the opposite effect.

Not only do the actions of the Fed affect producers and consumers, they also affect investors in the stock market. Announcements of interest-rate changes by the Fed can create rapid and major changes in stock prices.

An increasing number of Americans are investing in the stock market through programs in which their employers add to the savings they set aside for retirement in Individual Retirement Accounts (IRAs). Thus the effect of decisions by the Fed on the stock market has become a matter of serious interest to many.

Corporate Capitalism

Even though small business owners and service providers represent the largest segment of a capitalist society, large businesses dominate the wealth. This is as true in the United States as it is elsewhere. There are **two** main types of large businesses:

1. **Corporations,** formal organizations that have legal status, power, and liabilities that are separate from the people who own or manage them.
   EXAMPLES: ExxonMobil, McDonald's, Microsoft.

2. **Conglomerates**, huge corporations consisting of smaller corporations or subsidiaries engaged in different kinds of business. Their size and presence in different areas of business give them tremendous influence.

   EXAMPLE: General Electric owns subsidiaries providing aircraft engines, broadcasting, appliances, financial services, medical systems, power, real estate, and transportation.

Many large businesses are also *multinational corporations*, with manufacturing, sales, or service subsidiaries in one or more foreign countries. Typically, a multinational corporation develops new products in its native country and manufactures them abroad, thus gaining trade advantages and lower costs of labor and materials. These corporations also provide significant economic influence for the United States in the economies of other countries.

EXAMPLE: General Motors is a conglomerate with manufacturing operations in 50 countries. Its income in 1999 was over $176 billion, more than the GDP of many countries.

Capitalistic Values

Capitalistic societies tend to have particular values in common. See if you can recognize any of the following as values in the United States:

* Material rewards for an individual's efforts.
* The ability to "get ahead."
* Change—sometimes for its own sake, as in "new, improved" products.
* Openness to diversity.
* Creativity and individualistic pursuits.

Some people in capitalist societies, uncomfortable with the rapid changes society is undergoing, seek more security and stability. Others are less concerned with control and order than with personal improvement.

Work and Society

"What do you do?" This common question asked when people first meet demonstrates the importance we place on our work as a part of our identities. Work not only provides people with necessary income but also contributes to their sense of self. The onset of a knowledge-based rather than labor-based economy has changed the concept of work for many people.

Job Satisfaction

In the United States today, economists divide the workforce (or labor market) into **two** broad categories. The category in which one works can influence one's satisfaction with the job.

1. **The primary labor market** includes occupations that provide high income, prestige, and extensive benefits.
2. **The secondary labor market** includes jobs that provide low wages and few benefits.

Sociologists are interested in how much job satisfaction different kinds of work offer. Job satisfaction is a good indicator of such things as a society's perception of the quality of life and the role people feel they play in the work of their society. Repetitive jobs done under heavy supervision get low ratings on a job-satisfaction scale. Skilled jobs with a certain amount of self-direction and fair compensation rate higher. Many managers involve workers in decision-making processes to enhance job satisfaction.

Another factor that affects job satisfaction occurs when people are forced to accept jobs for which they are overeducated. This *underemployment* leads to frustration and emotional distress.

Changing Jobs

In the postindustrial age, manufacturing jobs are decreasing in number. New jobs come from the high-technology and service sectors. Service occupations include those in education, health care, tourism, banking, real estate, and insurance. Jobs in this sector range from the higher-paid kind held by computer programmers to the lower-paid jobs of childcare or fast-food workers.

Automation and environmental pressures decrease the number of jobs requiring physical labor. People who once worked in industry or in resource jobs, such as mining and logging, must either retrain for "information" jobs or take lower-paying jobs. Other U.S. workers have even seen their jobs disappear as businesses hire lower-paid workers in other countries to do their jobs.

Chapter 11 Wrap-up
POLITICS AND THE ECONOMY

Politics is the social process through which people and groups acquire, exercise, and maintain power. Authority is legal, legitimate power that can be obtained through tradition, charisma, or rational-legal procedures.

The state is the main political authority in most societies. Functions of the state include enforcing norms, regulating conflict, planning and coordination, and conducting relations with other societies. In the United States, political parties and interest groups have a major effect on politics and political participation.

An economy is the systematic production, distribution, and consumption of goods and services in a society. Economic systems include capitalism, socialism, and democratic socialism. In the United States, corporations control most business income. Work provides individuals with both an income and a sense of identity.

authority—legitimate, recognized power to enforce laws, demand obedience, command, determine, or judge. *p. 203*

capitalism—economic system in which the means of production and distribution are privately owned and operated for profit by competing entities. *p. 218*

coercion—illegitimate exercise of power through force or threat. *p 203*

conglomerate—huge corporation consisting of smaller corporations or subsidiaries engaged in different kinds of business. *p. 222*

corporation—formal organization with legal status, power, and liabilities separate from the people who own or manage it. *p. 221*

democratic socialism—economic system that combines private ownership of property and competitive markets with state ownership of large corporations that are run for the benefit of all citizens. *p. 219*

economic institution—system for producing and distributing goods and services. *p. 215*

economy—systematic production, distribution, and consumption of goods and services in a society. *p. 215*

Gross Domestic Product (GDP)—total dollar value of all goods and services produced in one year by a nation's people. *p. 219*

influence—legitimate power arising through persuasion. *p. 203*

interest group—organized collection of people who attempt to influence political processes and decisions. *p. 213*

legitimate power—power in a society that its people believe or trust. *p. 203*

monopoly—business that has exclusive control of a market because it is without competitors. *p. 218*

nationalism—people's sense of its right to have its own nation. *p. 207*

nation-state—political entity whose government holds jurisdiction over a large territory. *p. 207*

political institutions—organizations and customs that a society establishes for its government. *p. 203*

political party—organized group of people who work together to win elections and shape public policy. *p. 212*

productivity—efficient use of productive resources in making goods and services; it can be measured by the ratio of output (GDP) to investment in labor and materials. *p. 219*

socialism—economic system in which society owns the means of production and distribution and all citizens share in work and profits. *p. 219*

state—distinct set of institutions that has the authority to make the rules that govern society. *p. 205*

CHAPTER 12

Sports and Entertainment

In this chapter, you will learn about:

- sport as a social phenomenon
- how sports and social institutions interact
- how entertainment influences the culture
- effects of the media on U.S. society

In the summer of 2000, Texas suffered an ongoing drought and severe water shortage resulting in a $600 million loss to farmers and ranchers. On the evening news, trucks were shown carrying water to the blighted region. One might assume that the water was meant for failing crops. Instead, it was being trucked in to water the local high school football field!

Such an example, as well as the extent of sports coverage in newspapers and television, demonstrates the role sports play in Western culture. Are other cultures equally focused on sports? How does the culture influence sports, and how do sports influence the culture?

People once entertained themselves by playing board games or reading books. Today the choice of entertainment is staggering. How has this change affected society? This chapter will examine the roles of sports and entertainment in our lives.

Sports and Society

People often think of sport as simply a diversion—a form of recreation apart from their "real" lives. Sociologists see sport as a sociocultural phenomenon with both positive and negative implications.

What Is Sport?

Sport is a game, contest, or other pastime requiring skill and physical exercise. Sociologists defining sport begin with the concept of play. Animals, children, and adults all naturally engage in play. People play football or soccer. They play against an opponent in tennis and against the course in golf.

Play has been said to serve a number of functions:

* Discharge of excess energy.
* Safe outlet for harmful impulses.
* Wish-fulfillment.
* Training for other functions in life.
* Satisfaction of an innate urge to dominate.

These ideas assume that play is a means to an end rather than an end in itself. In 1938, sociologist Johan Huizinga defined play differently. He suggested that play is "a voluntary activity or occupation executed within fixed limits of time and place according to rules freely accepted but absolutely binding, having its aim in itself and accompanied by a feeling of tension, joy and the consciousness that it is 'different' from 'ordinary life.'"

Notice that Huizinga claims **three** conditions are necessary for play:

1. It is voluntary.
2. It occurs at certain times and in certain places.
3. Participants freely accept the rules and expect to enjoy it for itself and for the feelings they get from it.

Huizinga believed that play was a necessary element in sport. When games are compulsory, such as those in which students are expected to engage in school, at least one of these three conditions is missing—the freedom to participate or not. The contempt some students feel for sport may be due to the loss of the play element during school.

Thinking About Sport

There are many approaches to describing what makes an activity a sport. Games of chance and games such as chess, though they can be competitions, do not require physical activity. They are usually not included.

As the chart below shows, sports have been defined by type, as contests, and according to motives.

What is Sport?	
Ways of Defining Sport	**Types and Examples**
Types of Sport	**Competitive:** track, football. **Noncompetitive:** recreational swimming, running. **Predatory:** hunting, fishing.
Sport as Contest	**Direct Competition:** two individuals or teams engage each other physically (baseball, soccer, basketball). **Indirect Competition:** participants take turns at the same skill (diving, bowling). **Competition against a Standard:** figure skating, gymnastics.
Motives in Sport (may be competitive or noncompetitive—individual sports may fall in different categories)	**Evidence of Personal or Team Skill and Superiority:** basketball, diving, auto racing. **Combat/Personal Contact:** boxing, wrestling, fencing. **Conquest of Nature:** mountaineering, cycling, golf. **Physical High/Mastery of Self:** skiing, mountain climbing. **Expression of Ideas/Feelings:** gymnastics, eurythmics, dance (dance was a recognized sport in early cultures).

FoxTrot by Bill Amend

▲
Conquest of Nature?

History of Sport

The first sports may have been playful exhibits of physical skills related to survival activities such as fishing or hunting.

2697 B.C.: Chinese emperor Huang-ti is said to have invented a form of soccer played with a leather ball stuffed with cork and hair.

c. 1500 B.C.: The ancient Minoans engaged in a gymnastic type of "bull dancing" in which athletes leapt over bulls. It probably was part of a religious ceremony.

750 B.C.: The ancient Greek poet Homer wrote that Odysseus, hero of the *Odyssey*, participated in foot racing, archery, discus throwing, chariot racing, and wrestling.

776 B.C.: The first Olympian Games may have had a religious origin. Competitors ran around a track decorated with the signs of the zodiac. This mimicked the movement of the sun and moon across the heavens.

1st Century A.D.: Roman athletes joined together in guilds that were supported by the state. They had training facilities, trainers, and veterinarians for their horses.

Physical fitness was important to Roman citizens. Both men and women worked with weights and did gymnastics; the women displayed their skills in intricate dancing and movement with small balls.

Middle Ages: Some sports, such as early rugby, were "played" by thousands of people at a time and with few rules. People often took the opportunity during these games to take revenge on others. Such group "games" are played in some developing countries today.

Sport Around the World

Relationships can be seen between the type of culture in a country and the popularity and development of specific sports. For example:

* In baseball, although it is the team that wins or loses, each player remains in a particular position and has a specific role to play. In Japan, baseball mirrors state values of order and harmony. Emphasis is placed on team loyalty and cooperation.

* Soccer is the most popular sport in the world. The "pregame" show at a soccer match among the Zulus in South Africa includes incantations and ritual incisions done on the players by traditional religious healers.

In the 1200s, the French had a game similar to hockey. In the 1400s, tennis became popular in England. Track and field competitions were held in 1510. Mary, Queen of Scots, popularized the game of golf during her reign.

19th Century: The organization and institutionalization of many sports increased.

* The first modern track and field meet was held in England in 1825.

* One of the earliest intercollegiate competitions was a boat race in England in 1829.

* Baseball was first commonly played in the United States in 1845 and professionally in 1869.

* Football, a cross between rugby and soccer, was first played between Princeton and Rutgers universities in 1869. College football dominated the sport for many years before professional football became popular.

* Basketball was invented in Springfield, Massachusetts, in 1891.

* In 1896, the ancient Olympian Games were revived as the Olympic Games. Achievements were recorded with tape measures, stop watches, and photographs.

20th Century: In industrial countries, sport became a multimillion-dollar industry and an established social institution.

International competition resulted in recognized rules, formal sports organizations, and specialization of players.

Technological improvements in equipment and training resulted in many physical records being broken and in games becoming increasingly complex.

* Emphasis on competition is much greater in Western cultures than in Eastern and indigenous cultures, where personal *development* has a higher cultural value than personal *achievement*.

* In some cultures, such as the Q'ero in Peru, competition has a spiritual component. It becomes the winner's responsibility to teach the opponent how he or she did it.

In developing countries today, there is low participation in highly competitive sports because of differences in values and resources as well as cultural patterns. As industrialization occurs, a society tends to move away from traditional sports and folk-games and adopt modern sports.

Sport in the United States

Sport is a social institution in that it has values and generates distinctive modes of social interaction. Sports both reflect the values and social stratification of the larger society and influence other social institutions, such as the economy and politics.

Sports and Cultural Values

Among sociological views of how sport relates to society and culture are these **three**.

1. **Reflection Thesis:** Sport *reflects* the values and social stratification of the larger society. Sports are said to "prepare one for life." In the United States,

that is a life of competition, thought of as essential for personal achievement. The emphasis on competition and "winning" in U.S. sports *reflects* the role of competition in the economic rise of the country and the desire for power and control over nature.

EXAMPLE: Many high school athletic coaches embody a "work ethic" and promote the values of hard work, sacrifice, and discipline necessary to achieve mastery, domination, control, and eventual victory. The coach values power and control over both the team and opponents. Players become socialized into this way of thinking, reinforcing lessons about what adult behavior

University Sports

In the United States, collegiate sport is a big business. The National Collegiate Athletic Association (NCAA) projected revenues of over $350 million for 2000–2001, with 78 percent of that coming from television. Coaches at large universities often earn more than the university president.

By contrast, sports at universities in Great Britain, Australia, Germany, Japan, and many other countries are organized by clubs. Each university club sends a representative to a governing council where

competitions with other universities or community teams are arranged. Universities have no athletic departments and no full-time athletic directors. Some other differences include:

* Games are not televised.
* Spectators pay no admission fees.
* Athletes do not see participation as a step toward playing professional sports.
* Competition is available at several different levels of ability.
* Players do not receive athletic scholarships to school.
* Coaches are often volunteers.

entails. As in the world after school, there can be tension between these values and the values of cooperation and fair play.

2. **Reinforcement Thesis:** Sport *reinforces* the values and social stratification of society. The sports analogies we use in common speech are indicators of the degree to which we use sport to support our values.

   EXAMPLES: Employers emphasize teamwork. Consultants coach employees. People write winning proposals, reach a goal, or come up with a successful game plan. Someone scores when he or she reaches a personal goal. (Interestingly, we rarely use that word to describe the accomplishment of a group's goal.)

   School sports *reinforce* the value of competition for young people. Sociologists have studied the way in which too much emphasis on competition can cause students to lose sight of such values as personal growth, freedom, creativity, love, reason, and justice. Can you think of times when the values of fair play and sportsmanship were sacrificed for the sake of "winning"?

3. **Resistance Thesis:** Sport *resists* the values and social stratification of society. This conflict view emphasizes the ways in which sports participants are at odds with the norms of society.

   EXAMPLES: The ongoing arguments between athletes and their employers are not just about how rich an athlete can get. They also express discontent with a power structure that does not put the athlete at the very top. Sport has also provided an arena for the protest of gender and race inequality. As athletes were able to break these barriers, they assisted a growing movement in society to reject discriminatory norms.

Sociologist William A. Sadler warns that "we should not make the mistake of equating meeting a challenge with competition." Sadler points out that many sports can challenge participants to improve their abilities and skills and provide healthful exercise and change from the workaday world without an excessive emphasis on competition and winning.

Athletes as Role Models

According to Gallup polls taken in the late 1990s, only one athlete, Michael Jordan, was among the top ten most admired people. These polls reflected the views of adults. If you were to poll your classmates, would athletes appear near the top of their list?

Should athletes be held accountable as role models? Society honors athletes for their athletic skill, not for their honorable behavior. But it's not "just sports." When athletes are involved in drugs, gambling, or violence, or when they exhibit racist behavior, parents are advised to discuss such behavior openly with their children and to reinforce social norms that condemn it. Such advice comes from educators and other leaders who recognize the influence of heroes on the moral development of children.

Sports and Social Class

In the original Olympian Games, participation in some sports was related to wealth and status. Equestrian sports required that participants be wealthy enough to keep horses. Athletes from families with wealth had the time to train and access to training facilities. Poorer people were limited by their ability to find sponsors and access to training facilities. The same is true today.

EXAMPLES:

* Sports such as polo and yachting are considered "elite," engaged in and watched by people with wealth and high status.
* Class distinctions are maintained among spectators, with the wealthy or powerful watching from skyboxes or courtside seats.
* The cost of attending both collegiate and professional games has risen sharply. Taxpayers who subsidize the building of sports arenas often cannot afford to attend events at those facilities.
* Major colleges and universities generate huge amounts of revenue from sports,

but athletes are prevented by NCAA rules from benefiting monetarily from playing. Conflict theorists suggest that this is slave labor.

* The perception that sports provide opportunities to the disadvantaged with sufficient skill is misleading. For example, according to NCAA data, only .03 percent of male and .02 percent of female high school basketball players become professionals. Less that 1 percent of high school football players eventually play pro ball.
* Although more than half of the players in Division I collegiate basketball are African American, only one percent of the schools has a black athletic director and only 17.6 percent have black coaches. Professional team ownership exhibits the same imbalance.

Sport and the Economy

In the United States alone, sports were a $50 billion annual industry by the late 1980s. Professional athletes have become business men and women. They have ownership in clothing lines and sporting equipment. Product endorsements of everything from cereals to automobiles earn them millions. Michael Jordan earned $45 million in endorsements in 1998 (his salary was $34 million). Professional golfer Tiger Woods earned $28 million in endorsements that same year.

In 1989, the U.S. sporting goods industry did over $40 billion in business. Corporations and small businesses sponsor teams, stadiums, and the Olympics.

Clothing and equipment tied to professional teams and athletes are big sellers. In addition, there is a huge underground economy in gambling on sporting events.

Business people commission surveys to pinpoint the type and brands of food and beverages consumed while watching sporting events on television. Correlations of product to type of sporting event produce data that help marketers decide how to promote products and which sporting events to sponsor.

Industries and businesses that benefit from sports include:

* Tourism: airlines, hotels, restaurants.
* Construction: sports facilities.
* Sporting-goods.
* Health clubs.
* Souvenirs and collectibles.
* Food concessions.
* Advertising.
* Entertainment.
* Promotion.
* Publishing.

Professionals specializing in sports include:

* Lawyers.
* Business managers.
* Agents.
* Sports physicians.
* Sports psychologists.
* Media personalities.

Often, when very large amounts of money are involved, some are tempted to violate norms. At the Olympics, fair play and sportsmanship are held up as ideals. However, the economic and social benefits to a city hosting an Olympics led to corruption in the late 20th century. It became almost common practice for officials of contending locales to bribe members of the Olympic Organizing Committee in an attempt to have the games awarded to their city or country.

Sports and Politics

Local and state governments have become involved in the business of sport because of the economic advantages big sports can bring to their area. Sometimes cities subsidize sports facilities in an attempt to attract teams. They may also offer such enticements as lowered taxes. As with other government activity, heated debate often accompanies such efforts. The people of the Phoenix metropolitan area paid $355 million for a baseball stadium and $130 million for the team's admission into major league baseball. Many people felt this money could have been used in better ways to benefit the area. In addition, the city condemned property to build a parking lot for the stadium, and this seemed unfair to those whose property was taken as well as to others who did not support the city's actions.

Politicians like to be associated with events that draw large crowds. You have probably noticed that presidents, governors, and mayors are often photographed at sporting events and may phone winners during prime-time post-game television shows. Appearing to be a "good sport" may help enhance a political candidate's image.

Sociologist's Perspective

High School Sports

In his book *Sport in Society: Issues and Controversies*, sociologist Jay J. Coakley lists a number of arguments in favor of and against the participation of high school students in sports.

Arguments **for** participation are based on the belief that sports:

* Involve students in school activities and increase interest in academic activities.
* Build responsibility, orient students toward achievement, and promote teamwork skills needed for participation in adult society.
* Encourage physical fitness and interest in physical activity in all students in the school.
* Generate spirit and unity that give substance to the school.
* Promote parental, alumni, and community support for all school programs.
* Give students opportunities to develop and display skills in activities valued by society.

Arguments **against** participation claim that sports:

* Distract students from academic activities.
* Encourage a focus on physical prowess rather than on other mental and human qualities.
* Focus on "macho" values no longer appropriate in society.
* Force most students into the role of spectator.
* Cause too many serious injuries and developmental problems for participants.
* Create a superficial spirit based on competition rather than educational goals.
* Deprive educational programs of resources, facilities, staff, and community support.
* Apply inappropriate pressure to student athletes.

Women and the Olympics

When the Olympic Games were reestablished in 1896, women did not participate. Twelve women were permitted to compete in 1904—in golf and tennis. Female participation has increased ever since, but for over 30 years, Pierre de Coubertin, the first president of the modern Olympics, expressed the following views:

1901—"The role of women [is] to applaud the male victor as a means of reward."

1902—Women's sport "could well be contrary to the Laws of Nature."

1908—Women's tobogganing is "the most unaesthetic sight human eyes could contemplate."

1912—"The Olympic Games should be reserved for men."

1924—"Women should be expelled from the games."

1934—"Contact with female athletes would be bad for [male athletes]."

1935—"At the Olympic Games [women's] primary role should be, as in ancient tournaments, to crown the [male] victors with laurels."

Women and Sports

Although women in many cultures are known to have participated in sports throughout history, social customs during the 19th and the early 20th centuries excluded women from mainstream sports. Reasons given stemmed from cultural concerns that athletics were "unseemly for the fairer sex" or would damage women's ability to bear children.

Among the reasons given for continued underrepresentation of women in sports are these **three:**

1. Lingering prejudices and stereotypes.
2. Lack of qualified women to coach and administer athletic programs.
3. Failure of women to apply for leadership positions.

Some also cite a lack of female role models and the responsibilities of childbearing as elements in society that discourage women from participating in sports.

But several factors have increased the participation of women in sports in recent years:

* The women's movement of the 1970s and 1980s.
* Increased societal emphasis on health and physical fitness.
* Legislation that mandates equal funding for women's and men's programs at publicly funded schools.
* Increasing numbers of female role models in sport. The success of women's soccer and softball at the international level has done much to promote participation in local teams in the United States.

Despite the popularity of some women's sports, inequalities still exist:

* Boys and girls are offered different play experiences at an early age.
* Girls receive less encouragement from parents to participate in sports.
* A 1998 report found that athletic departments spend only one-third or less of their budgets on women's teams.

* Fewer sports and athletic scholarships are available to women.
* Females are allotted fewer hours to practice in sports facilities and are given shorter playing seasons than males.
* Professional female athletes receive lower pay and less prize money than males in the same sports.
* There is much less media coverage of women's sports than men's sports.

Violence in Sports

Sociologists point out that while sport can provide an outlet for aggressive tendencies, it can also serve to undermine social norms that seek to control aggression. Actions that are deviant in normal society are accepted and even encouraged in many sports. **EXAMPLES:** Ramming your 300-pound body into another person and knocking him to the ground, rendering someone unconscious, or driving your car at 195 miles per hour are all illegal. In sports, they are not only legal, but admirable. They are within the rules of the sport.

Society is concerned, however, when violence in sport is excessive. In a 19th-century case, a player was accused of manslaughter in the death of another player. The British judge instructed the jury that no rules or practices of a game can make legal something that is otherwise illegal.

Are we losing sight of this principle? Recently, some cases of blatant violence have not been prosecuted or have been dismissed. And observers note that violent behavior is on the rise among spectators, even among parents at their children's sporting events. What do you think?

Sports and the Media

Television has brought about changes that make sports more "salable":

* Baseball, once played mainly in the afternoon, is now played largely at night to attract a larger television audience.
* In basketball, the 3-point basket and the 20-second rule have been added to speed up the game.
* In football, the number of time-outs has been increased to allow for commercials.
* End-of-season tournaments run for several weeks to attract weekend viewers.
* In 1994, the Olympic Games were rescheduled so that they fell during "sweeps" month (when viewer surveys are taken to determine advertising rates).

On a positive note, the availability of sports on television and cable has increased public awareness of teams from different countries and of unfamiliar sports.

Sociological Perspectives on Sport	
Functionalist Perspective	* Sports reinforce the social norms and values of the culture. * Young people learn the consequences of obeying or breaking rules. * Participation encourages moral judgments. * Hierarchies within sports reinforce hierarchies within the larger society. * Participation promotes healthy development of the body and mind. * Sports provide an outlet for relieving tension in a socially acceptable way for both participants and spectators. * Sports unite communities and provide opportunities to interact with other nations.
Conflict Perspective	* An individual's contribution to "winning" determines his or her status. * Groups with control over sporting activities benefit at the expense of players and spectators. * Sports discriminate against minorities and women. * The health of athletes is secondary to profit. * Sports reflect patterns of inequality in society. Some are so expensive to participate in or to watch that they exclude all but the wealthy. * Because those in control determine the reigning values and rules, sports reinforce the dominance of one class over another. * Sports legitimize violence. * Sports divert attention from issues in the "real" world.
Interactionist Perspective	* Sports contribute to teamwork and friendships. * Sports encourage parent-child interaction and involvement. * Sports help define relationships and role performance. * Sport is a social world with meaningful symbols. * Sports encourage unity among people in a particular geographical or social environment.

Entertainment and Society

Entertainment is defined as something that amuses, pleases, or diverts. It encompasses a wide variety of activities and experiences, from playing a game to reading a book, from attending a play to listening to music.

Some popular forms of entertainment—such as movies, television, music, and printed materials—are also forms of mass communication, commonly known as **mass media**. Each form of entertainment interacts significantly with society.

During early human history, people probably entertained one another by telling stories around the campfire. Today, entertainment includes, but isn't limited to:

* Games—bingo, card games, board games, arcade games, electronic games.
* Music—from opera to rap.
* Live performances—theater, dance, pantomime.
* Outdoor recreation—hiking, fishing, sailing, hunting, bird watching.
* Participation in and watching sports.
* Celebrations, festivals, circuses.
* Reading.
* Radio.
* Motion pictures.
* Television.
* Recreational use of the computer.
* Amusement parks.

Historical Background

Other than sports, the entertainment forms that most influence society are those grouped as media—forms of mass communication. Communication began with the development of speech and language. Writing developed around 2400 B.C., but the printing press was not invented until A.D. 1450.

In the 1830s, newspapers were first published. These contained local, national, and foreign news as well as human-interest stories. In the early 1900s, radios and motion pictures were introduced, and by the 1920s the number of radios owned by private citizens had jumped from 60,000 to 10 million. The first movie with sound was released in 1927. The 1940s saw the invention of the television, and in the 1950s the computer revolution began.

Who Controls the Airwaves?

Radio and television are not the same the world over. In some countries, they are completely controlled by the government. In others, some stations are government stations and others are financed by private investments or the public. In Great Britain and Canada, for example, government stations were begun in an effort to prevent commercialization from influencing programming.

In contrast, in the United States almost all radio and television stations are commercial enterprises. Advertising supports most of the programs that appear on TV. Public television and National Public Radio, however, are supported by donations from private individuals, corporations, and foundations.

Trends

The concept of "daily news" did not exist before the era of rapid mass communication. Today, newspapers and the news of the day on radio and TV are sometimes called **edutainment**. This term reflects their dual functions of educating and entertaining.

The distinction has further blurred with the introduction of talk shows on radio and television, newsmagazines, tabloid newspapers and TV, "reality" programming, and docudramas. U.S. tastes in entertainment change over time.

With each new invention—motion pictures, television, computers—doomsayers insist that books and other print materials will become extinct. Their worries have not been borne out.

* In 1995, more than 2 billion books were sold in the United States. Consumers spent over $25 billion on them. The chart at upper right shows approximately how those books break down.
* The number of U.S. magazines rose from about 1,000 during the Civil War to 10,000 in the 1990s. More than 500 new magazines were started in 1996 alone. Twenty percent of those dealt with sports.

Book Sales

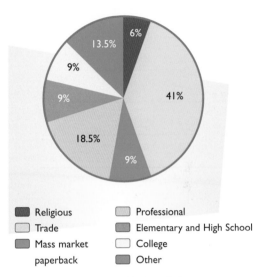

Religious — 6%
Professional — 13.5%
Trade — 9%
Elementary and High School — 9%
Mass market paperback — 18.5%
College — 41%
Other — 9%

Source: Veronis Suhler Media Merchant Bank

Daily Newspaper Subscriptions

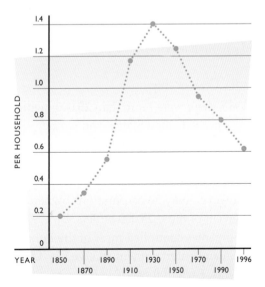

Source: DeFleur/Dennis, *Understanding Mass Communication.*

TV Viewing Habits

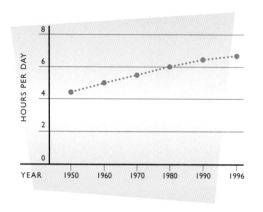

Source: DeFleur/Dennis, *Understanding Mass Communication.*

Weekly Attendance at the Movies

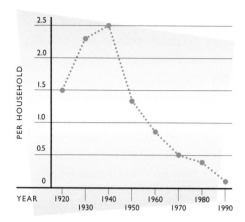

Source: DeFleur/Dennis, *Understanding Mass Communication.*

The Media in the United States

Everybody's talking about the effects of the media on U.S. society. Questions are being asked about media ownership, media and the economy, and media and politics. Researchers are also involved in investigating how the media influence socialization and problem solving in communities.

Media Ownership

In 1983, there were more than 25,000 media outlets in the United States. You would think that would be more than enough to provide diverse viewpoints and a balanced picture of society.

However, only 50 corporations owned 80 percent of those 25,000 outlets. By 1997, 10 companies controlled most of the information and entertainment received by U.S. residents. Each of those 10 companies owns stock in one or more of the others.

Antitrust and monopoly laws have been successful in preventing monopolies on news and broadcast journalism in local markets. But nationwide, they have failed to prevent monopolistic control of the media. Huge international conglomerates own the major TV stations, satellites, newspaper and book publishing companies, movie studios, and Internet access providers. Should you be worried about the free flow of ideas in society?

Ben Bagdikian, media critic and former Dean of the Graduate School of Journalism at the University of California, Berkeley, thinks you should. In 1983, he wrote *The Media Monopoly* to call attention to the consolidation of media ownership and the effects of advertising on programming. This classic book is now in its fifth edition.

In a 1999 interview, Bagdikian said there was no diversity of viewpoints in programming. "We have commercial broadcasting which is so uniform in content, that if you brought in someone from Outer Mongolia and said we're gonna show you all four networks, or we're gonna show you cable, tell us the difference between them, I think they would be hard put to do it." He said that in an effort to make money on news programs, the media offer "that horrid word and horrid idea, *infotainment*, which is supposed to be information that's entertaining, but it's neither good information nor good entertainment." Would you agree with Bagdikian?

Media, Advertising, and the Economy

Movies, radio, television, newspapers, and magazines have one thing in common that makes them desirable to investors: the income from advertising. According to *Advertising Age*, in 1997 advertisers spent over $175 billion on media ads. Product familiarity and subsequent sales of goods and services make that expenditure worthwhile to the advertisers. Whole businesses have grown from their needs.

Sociological Perspectives on Mass Media	
Functionalist Perspective	* The media coordinate, correlate, and disseminate information and ideas valuable to the culture. * The media serve as powerful agents of socialization, communicating cultural norms and values. * The media rapidly communicate information internationally. * The media provide opportunities for relaxation and entertainment. * The media help reduce stress and thus reduce social conflict.
Conflict Perspective	* The media maintain the status quo and express the values of the ruling class. * The media view of violence legitimizes law and order and makes dissenters appear as criminals. * The media develop consumers for capitalist goods. * The media disseminate information that benefits corporations and those who own and control the media. * Some forms of the media are available only to an elite class. * The media encourage passivity and reinforce stereotypes.
Interactionist Perspective	* The media familiarize people with societal symbols, create symbols, and communicate values worldwide. * The media provide access to the ideas and agendas of politicians and others in power. * The media promote commercial products through advertising.

Violence in the Media

For many years, researchers have conducted studies on the effects of media violence on children. Media representatives insist that children view media violence in the same way they view fairy tales. They say the children know it isn't real. Others argue, if the media don't influence people, why do so many businesses advertise in those media?

Some causes of concern include:

* Music lyrics that advocate violence against police and portray women as objects of violence.
* Movies that show violent, bloody scenes, sometimes graphically reenacting actual crimes.
* Violent video games that employ the same strategies the army uses to break down a soldier's aversion to shoot. One officer said, "Pilots train on flight simulators, drivers on driving simulators, and now we have our children on murder simulators."
* Perpetrators of violence on TV shows who go unpunished. This happens in 73 percent of all violent scenes. Only 5 percent of children's programs show long-term consequences of violence.
* Children's cartoons, which contain an average of 32 violent acts per hour.

If the media are agents of socialization, what are they teaching children? Some of the research findings indicate that:

* By the time children leave elementary school, they have seen 8,000 killings and 100,000 other violent acts portrayed on television. By the age of 18, the typical U.S. child will have witnessed 40,000 killings and 200,000 acts of violence on television.
* Children not only become **desensitized** to violence (meaning they learn to react to it unemotionally), but also are more likely to act aggressively after viewing violent acts.
* Adults are not immune to desensitization. Researchers in one study had to train their research assistants to identify acts of aggression, such as hitting and kicking another person. The assistants didn't recognize that such acts were aggressive!

Many companies do nothing but compile demographic data for others to use in making their advertising decisions. Advertising influences the media in many ways.

* In new magazines appearing during 1996, advertising took up more than one-fourth of the pages.
* Commercials make up a third of many hour-long television shows.
* Many web sites make money only through advertisers.
* Televised sporting events are planned to allow commercials.
* Politicians wait to give speeches until the times most citizens are viewing TV.
* The content of radio and television programming is influenced by what advertisers will or will not accept.

The Media and Politics

Imagine toothless George Washington or skinny Abraham Lincoln in one of today's televised campaign debates. Would either man win election? To what extent does a candidate's media presence—his or her appearance or the ability to project personality and charisma to a camera—influence voters?

The immediacy of media coverage gives us instant access to political candidates. This should make voter choices more informed than they were in the past. And yet, today's political activities are carefully staged theatrical events. Most of what people see or hear consists of "sound bites" designed to fit media formats. Political ads are designed to respond to what polls suggest voters want to hear.

Before candidates begin debating, commentators tell the audience what to expect from each candidate. Then, rather than allowing the candidates to speak for themselves, media commentators are quick to "interpret" what each candidate said or did not say. Often, we see more of the interpreters than we do of the candidates. The distinction between politics and the media has blurred.

Social Concerns

Theoreticians have other concerns about the influence of the media on society, including these **five** points:

1. **The change in focus from the written word to images reduces the depth of thought needed to process information.** Even early radio dramas, they say, required people to listen actively, making sense of the words they heard and creating mental pictures to accompany them. Television and movies that contain preconstructed images require much less processing. Will we become a nation of less mentally agile people as a result? What do you think?

2. **Americans are bombarded with trivia and "sound bites."** People are neither invited nor given the time to think deeply about issues. Said one media critic, "The content of much of our public discourse has become dangerous nonsense." Does it seem to you that people believe they are informed when they actually have very little information?

"Welcome to 'All About the Media,' where members of the media discuss the role of media in media coverage of the media."

3. **We are forming an image of our society—both its problems and its strengths—based on what those who select media content choose to show us.** If the media focus is one-sided, will we understand our reality?

4. **TV news is not really designed to inform us.** TV news begins with "bad news" in its lead stories, hooking viewers to receive the "good news"—the wonderful life the sponsor's products can provide.

5. **Media-produced excitement is excessive.** Fast-paced television, electronic games, and movies filled with special effects have increased people's need for stimulation and may make "real life" seem tame by comparison.

The rise in TV "reality" programming that shows disasters or dangerous situations, the increasing popularity of extreme sports, and movies that focus so much on special effects that characters become secondary—all have provoked similar concerns.

In 1932, Aldous Huxley wrote a novel entitled *Brave New World* in which a government enslaved people by "inflicting" pleasure on them. Have Huxley's satirical warnings come close to describing our sport- and entertainment-influenced society? Some questions are:

* How much do media and entertainment contribute to our pleasure, and what are the side effects of them?
* In what ways does our society's focus on competition diminish needed cooperation?

* Does violence in sports and the media cause or reinforce violence in society; does it reflect the violence that already exists; or does it provide a safe outlet for violent tendencies?
* Does the demand for more and better special effects in movies diminish the importance of human characters?
* Are Americans really more interested in violence and mayhem than in the positive aspects of life, as the media's focus suggests?

* Are people's interests and ideas shaped by the media?
* To what extent does the availability of media in the home reduce people's participation in civic, volunteer, and other social activities?

These are just a few questions people must answer to analyze the effect of sports and entertainment on their lives and on society in general.

Chapter 12 Wrap-up
SPORTS AND ENTERTAINMENT

Sports and entertainment are social institutions with far-ranging influence on and interactions with society and culture. They reflect the values and norms of society, but they may exaggerate the importance of some values over others in ways that are harmful.

Sport begins with the concept of play, but in modern society it has developed into big business, both in schools and in the professional arena. Sport reflects the values and structure of society, it reinforces them, and it can resist some of them. Because we make heroes of athletes, their conduct outside the playing field becomes an issue for society. Social issues that surround sport include its undue influence on young people; unequal access to its opportunities and its recreational benefits; concerns about the amount of money society spends on it and the corruption of individuals that can accompany such spending; its relation to violence in society; and how the media have changed it.

Among forms of entertainment are reading, music, motion pictures, radio, and television. At one time, these activities had unique content and were recognizably different. Today, the mass media provide a very substantial amount of the entertainment our society enjoys. The media influence both the economy and politics in the United States and the world at large. Issues include who controls media content; whether the media seriously distort society's image of reality; and whether the media promote violence.

desensitized—made emotionally unresponsive. *p. 242*

edutainment—something that educates as it entertains. *p. 239*

entertainment—something that amuses, pleases, or diverts. *p. 238*

mass media—forms of mass communication, such as newspapers, television, and radio. *p. 238*

sport—game, contest, or other pastime requiring skill and physical exercise. *p. 226*

Population and the Environment

In this chapter, you will learn about:

- **how population changes and is measured**
- **theories of population growth**
- **how population and the environment influence each other**

In 1986, one of the worst catastrophes ever triggered by human technology took place at Chernobyl in northern Ukraine. A nuclear reactor exploded, eventually showering radioactive debris over much of eastern Europe. Normal air circulation carried measurable amounts of radiation as far as Japan and the United States. In many countries, farm animals—even reindeer—that had grazed on contaminated vegetation had to be destroyed, as did milk and crops that had been exposed. An estimated 32,000 people died as a direct result of Chernobyl. Many others suffered serious illness and were unable to work.

The role of humans on Earth has always been a subject of debate. As the growing population continues to alter the environment to suit its needs, previously unheard-of problems multiply. Sociologists use both demographics (the study of populations) and ecology (the study of the interactions among living things and their environments) to better understand how this complex process operates and what might be done to address emerging problems.

The Changing Population

Studying Population

Sociology is the study of human interaction—a complex subject that isn't easily measured quantitatively. One of the areas where sociologists can get meaningful data is in the study of populations.

Demographics

Demographics is the field of sociology that scientifically studies the size, composition, and distribution of populations. It is also concerned with the social factors that influence these variables. The size and composition of a population affect nearly every aspect of people's lives. A sudden change in the population can mean that adequate resources are not available.

EXAMPLE: After World War II, men from what would have been five years' worth of freshman classes returned from war to seek education. All at once there were more students on campuses than there was housing available for them.

Other factors that are affected by the size of a population include:

* Diet.
* Work.
* Marital status.
* Family size.
* Access to medical and social services.

By *composition,* we mean the makeup of different groups within the population being measured. The sizes of different population groups put different kinds of pressure on a society.

EXAMPLE: When many dependent people (children, the elderly) are being supported by a smaller number of employed people, people's priorities change.

Distribution simply refers to the placement of different populations.

EXAMPLE: The elderly in the United States are concentrated in some states—such as Arizona and Florida—and not in others.

Taking a Census

The practice of counting the population of an entire country is called taking a **census.** Census taking has gone on for thousands of years.

EXAMPLE: In ancient China, government officials counted people for the purposes of taxation, military service, and to determine how many people were available to build the Great Wall.

Census Data and Vital Statistics

The census in the United States has been taken every ten years since 1790. Because it is used for everything from assigning congressional seats to locating businesses, accuracy is important. States get certain funds from the federal government based on their demographics, so recent censuses have made a particular effort to count people who would normally be missed, such as the homeless.

Compiling census data involves more than "counting noses." Different segments of our society have urged the government to collect demographic data that can help:

* Legislators enact social policy.
* State and local governments plan for new school construction.
* Educators anticipate changes in the school population that require more or fewer teachers, or teachers with special skills.
* Business people locate shopping malls, factories, and distribution centers.
* Health care providers locate clinics and hospitals and plan for the needs of future populations.

The data gathered in our modern census include a wealth of information on age, sex, education, occupations, ethnicity, and types of residence. During non-census years, more information is gathered on many other facets of society. The graph on the right shows the distribution of workers in various sectors of the economy. It is based on data collected between the 1990 and 2000 censuses.

In addition to the information gathered in a census, other information comes from **vital statistics**. These are records of births, deaths, marriages, divorces, and migration from one region to another.

The United Nations collects global demographic statistics. In 2000, the world's population stood at just over 6 billion people. Through the UN's efforts, we can compare demographic data from different countries and understand worldwide trends.

U.S. Business Distribution

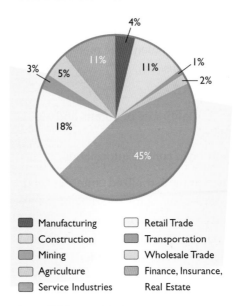

Legend:
- Manufacturing
- Construction
- Mining
- Agriculture
- Service Industries
- Retail Trade
- Transportation
- Wholesale Trade
- Finance, Insurance, Real Estate

Source: U.S. Bureau of the Census

Population Change

Factors that change the population include births, deaths, and migration.

Births

When demographers study birth rates, they look at **two** factors:

1. **Fertility**—the actual number of children born per woman between the ages of 15 and 44, which are considered the child-bearing years.

2. **Fecundity**—the potential number of children that could be born to the average woman of childbearing age.

The economy, health, and customs of a population generally determine the difference between the fertility and fecundity rates.

The birth rate of most industrialized nations is less than 20 per 1,000. Agricultural nations typically exceed 30 per 1,000. In poor countries, women have more children for **three** reasons.

1. Custom.
2. High mortality rate of infants and children.
3. Lack of birth control information.

Women in industrialized countries tend to have fewer babies for a variety of economic and cultural reasons.

The map below, published by the United Nations in 1997, shows world fertility patterns (the average number of children per woman).

Deaths

Mortality (or *death*) **rate** is the number of deaths per year for every 1,000 members of a population. The relative number of young and older people in a population influences its death rate, so the death rate by itself isn't a good measure of health and living conditions. Important are **two** other measures:

1. **The infant mortality rate,** which describes the number of deaths among infants less than a year old for every 1,000 live births. This ranges from about 13 in developed countries to 70 for developing nations.
2. **Life expectancy,** which is the average number of years the average infant born into a population can expect to live.

Factors influencing these rates include:

* Medical practices, such as the availability of immunizations and vaccines.
* Economic conditions and the standard of living.

World Fertility Rates

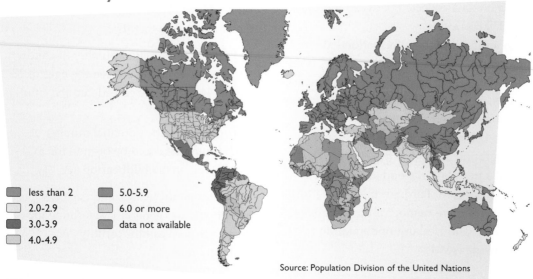

less than 2	5.0-5.9
2.0-2.9	6.0 or more
3.0-3.9	data not available
4.0-4.9	

Source: Population Division of the United Nations

Migration

Migration refers to the movement of people from one geographical location to another with the intent of establishing a new residence. People migrate for many reasons. Factors that *push* people away from a country or a region include:

* Social upheaval.
* Lack of jobs.
* Lack of religious or political freedom.
* Natural disasters such as floods or drought.

Factors that *pull* people to an area include:

* Enhanced economic or social opportunities.

* The locale itself, including climate or geographical features.

Migration can be internal or international. Knowledge of the following **three** terms will help you understand data about migration:

1. **Immigrants** are people who migrate into a country.
2. **Emigrants** are people who migrate out of a country.
3. The **migration rate** is the difference between the number of immigrants and emigrants in a society.

Did You Know?

Migration Trends

Around the world, migration trends have played a major part in changing the populations of many countries—increasing or decreasing populations and changing the cultural makeup.

* During the late 1800s and early 1900s, more than 28 million Europeans emigrated to the United States. In those years, more than 14 percent of U.S. residents were foreign-born.
* Since its establishment as a nation in 1948, the population of Israel has grown 24 percent a year. By 1980, more than 42 percent of Israel's residents were foreign-born.
* Today, there is a worldwide mass movement away from underdeveloped countries and toward countries with greater economic opportunity. This is owing to **two** technological changes:

    1. The information revolution allows people to see what life is like elsewhere.
    2. The transportation revolution makes it easy for people to travel long distances.

Forms of Migration

A country permits immigration only when a person meets certain conditions. Countries restrict immigration in order to preserve resources and limit demographic changes that might alter their own standard of living. Immigration laws in the United States set restrictions on the number of people who can enter legally. Quotas are set for the numbers admitted from each country or region. Preferences are given to people who have family members here.

Sometimes people must be able to show they can find employment. Criminals are not admitted, with the exception of those whose "criminal record" is based on imprisonment for political beliefs.

Refugees are people who flee a region because of its dangers.

EXAMPLES: People who leave an area destroyed by a volcano's eruption, those escaping floods, earthquakes, or a region torn by warfare.

Across Cultures

Refugees and Asylum Seekers

At the end of 1998, the world's population of refugees, asylum seekers, and internally displaced persons totaled more than 30.4 million people. Nearly half of those people were:

* People fleeing the bloody civil wars in Sudan (4.3 million).
* Palestinians (3.8 million).
* Afghans (2.6 million).
* Iraqis (1.5 million).
* Colombians (1.4 million).

Nearly two-thirds of all refugees worldwide go to Middle Eastern or African countries. Eighty percent of all the uprooted people in Africa seek protection in countries that are themselves experiencing internal conflict.

In Europe, countries have been criticized for turning away those seeking asylum. Since the late 1980s, European countries have had a policy that prevents refugees and asylum seekers from choosing the country to which they migrate. According to this policy, refugees must seek protection in the first "safe" country they enter. Thus, a Kosovo Albanian woman who crosses Hungary and Austria (both considered "safe") before asking for asylum at the German border can be refused, even though she is seven months pregnant, traveling with two small children, and her husband is already in Germany. Critics say that such cases should be decided on an individual basis.

Some refugees seek **political asylum**. They can't or won't return to their country of nationality because of persecution. In many countries, a person's race, religion, nationality, or membership in a particular social group makes him or her the target of government oppression. Persons requesting asylum fear physical brutality, jail terms, and often death.

Illegal aliens are people who enter or remain in a country without permission. In 1996, it was estimated that there were about 5 million illegal aliens in the United States, more than half of whom came from Mexico. About 40 percent of the illegal aliens had entered the country legally on a temporary visa, but did not leave when the visa expired.

Population Growth and Society

As populations increase, societies face challenges in providing for the needs of the greater numbers of people. Throughout history, major changes in population have been among the greatest challenges facing civilizations.

World Population

In 1750, there were about 800 *million* people in the world. By the year 2000, there were more than 6 *billion* people on Earth. Nearly 15,000 children are born each hour and about 6,200 people die. Several factors that have contributed to this rise in population include:

* Technological changes in agriculture that have made food more plentiful.
* Improved medical care that has reduced infant mortality rates and cured many adult diseases.
* Improved economic conditions that make food and sanitation available to greater numbers of people.

Growth Rate and Doubling Time

A population's **growth rate** is the difference between the birth rate and the death rate, expressed in annual percentages. If the growth rate is zero, the same number of people die as are born in a year. Growth rate is closely related to fertility rate.

The rate at which a population is growing is often expressed in how long it will take for the population to double. A country with a growth rate of 1 percent doubles in size in only 70 years.

EXAMPLES:

* Kenya's population, with a growth rate of 4.2 percent, will double in just 24 years if it continues growing at that rate.
* If the current growth trend continues, more than 80 countries will double their populations in 30 years or fewer.
* At current rates, the world's population will double in the next 50 years.

Those predictions are all based on growth continuing at its present rate. You must always question statistics. There are reasons why growth may not continue.

A number of different methods are used to predict the growth rate in the future. Both the United Nations and the U.S. Census Bureau currently project that the growth rate of the world population, now 1.3 percent, will decline over the next 50 years, as the chart below shows.

Challenges of Population Growth

Some observers of world population growth worry that the number of people in the world may someday outstrip the world's resources. Certainly, in some regions, local resources cannot sustain populations. Years of drought may create famine and bring death to populations, particularly those in desert regions. Overcrowding causes rats to go berserk, and it has had a similar effect on some urban populations from time to time.

Projected World Population Growth Rate

GROWTH RATE
(PERCENT)

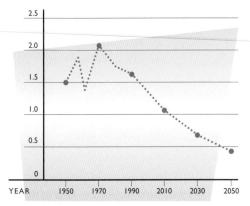

Source: U.S. Bureau of the Census, International Data Base

In 1968, biologist Paul Erlich wrote a bestseller, *The Population Bomb.* In it he warned that not only would population growth lead to widespread food shortages, but also that air and water would become so polluted that life could not be sustained. These are certainly problems to consider seriously. But Erlich also warned that by 1985, there would be worldwide famine, life expectancy would decrease to only 42 years, and the U.S. Midwest would become a vast desert!

Several factors encourage a belief that the challenges of growth can be met:

* Food output is rising significantly, particularly in Asia and Africa.
* Food prices worldwide are coming down.
* Technology to make ocean water drinkable and usable for irrigating crops is available now, and wide-scale use is foreseeable.
* Abundant energy resources—such as solar energy and radioactive minerals—have not yet been tapped to any real extent, and new technologies may one day do so.

There are, to be sure, serious social problems of poverty, starvation, environmental degradation, and pollution in the world. Many argue, however, that these are not the result of too many people but of warfare and of oppressive governmental practice or neglect.

Population Growth and Economic Development

Historically, it has been the case that with industrialization have come reductions in birth rate and the emergence of small families. This has not only been true in Europe and North America, but in other parts of the world as well. Several reasons for smaller family size have been proposed:

* People feel secure and do not feel the need to have children to take care of them in old age.
* People do not need as many hands to do the work as they did in a preindustrial age.
* People do not need to offset high infant mortality rates.

Societies that have high levels of education and high standards of living, and that protect women's rights as well as men's, have lower birth rates.

In most countries, parents decide how many children to have. In some societies, governments try to influence birth rates by providing economic advantages to families who have fewer children. Governments may also use coercion, requiring a license for each new child and punishing couples who disobey.

For the last 20 years of the last century, China enforced a one-couple, one-child policy. As China's population neared the one billion mark, abortions, forced sterilization, and very significant fines were imposed on families who did not respect the policy.

Population Growth in the United States

Population in the United States has been growing since the first census. Although the birth rate is decreasing, immigration continues to increase the total population.

Historical Background

The first U.S. census in 1790 counted 3.9 million people. That number almost doubled in the next 20 years and reached 9.6 million by 1820. By 1900, there were more than 76 million people in the United States.

It took 50 years for the population to double again, although the growth rate dropped to an all-time low, roughly 0.5 percent, during the depression years of the 1930s.

Following World War II—in the late 1940s and the 1950s—the number of marriages and babies jumped dramatically. Soldiers returning from the war married, and people felt safe to get on with their lives. Baby boomers—people born between 1945 and 1964—have had and continue to have a significant effect on every aspect of society, from values to shopping to television programming.

When the "boomers" had their children, a smaller, but significant, rise in birth rate occurred. This is sometimes called the "baby boom echo." During the 1990s, the growth rate fell below 1 percent, but the population continued to increase because of the large number of young people. The 2000 population of over 275 million people is expected to climb to nearly 350 million by 2050.

Trends

Although the U.S. population is expected to grow in the near future, the birth rate is decreasing for **three** main reasons.

1. **Economic Factors.** To maintain their standard of living, many couples choose to have a small family.

2. **Lifestyles and Values.** Due to more economic opportunities, women are delaying marriage, limiting the number of children they have, or choosing to remain childless. Large families are no longer necessary to assure that a family survives.

3. **Birth Control.** U.S. families have the education and access to information to help them choose the number of children they have. The government has been spending over $100 million a year to support family planning.

The **replacement rate** is the fertility rate required to replace the parents—generally set at 2.1 children per family to account for early mortality. The fertility rate in the United States at the end of the 20th century was 1.99, below the replacement rate.

Immigration will continue to increase the population. The Census Bureau estimates that legal and illegal immigration will account for about half of the United States' increase in population after the year 2050.

The Environment and Society

Humans depend on the environment for air, food, water, and other resources to sustain life. Early people had little control over their environments. Technology has enabled humans to change the environment. In recent times, people have begun to realize the cumulative effect of those changes.

Ecology and Human Behavior

Ecology is a branch of science that studies the relationship between living things and their natural environment. An **ecosystem**, such as Earth, is a self-contained community of organisms that depend on one another and their environment for survival.

When the human population of Earth was small, resources seemed endless. As populations increased and industrialization developed, people and their machines demanded more energy and resources. People are now aware that:

* Natural resources are limited.
* Nonrenewable resources, such as oil and coal, cannot be replaced.
* Renewable resources, such as trees, must be used carefully and their replacement must be planned.

In understanding the effects of a group of people on the environment, it is not enough just to know how many there are. We also need to know how crowded the people are in a specific location. Six million people spread over 1,000 square miles will have a very different effect from that of the same 6 million in 50 square miles. **Population density**—the number of people in a given area—plays an important role in how quickly resources disappear. In 2000, New York City had a population density of over 24,000 people per square mile. Hong Kong had 270,750 people in the same space!

In every ecosystem, there is a limit to the population of each organism that can be sustained by available resources. This limit—the maximum number of organisms resources can support—is called the **carrying capacity**.

Environmental Concerns

Among the many concerns of ecologists are the loss of biodiversity and habitat, species extinction, depleted resources, and the pollution of existing resources, such as air and water.

Biodiversity

The number of species that share the planet with humans has been estimated at between 3 and 30 million. Fewer than 2 million of those have actually been identified. **Biodiversity** is the term given to this rich variety of life forms. Biodiversity is valuable to humans for many reasons.

EXAMPLES:

* *Genetic diversity* enriches agriculture by producing disease-resistant and high-yielding crops.

* *Species diversity* supplies new medicines and the resources to produce new products.
* *Ecosystem diversity* provides "ecological services," by keeping the water clean, producing oxygen, and preventing soil erosion.

Of equal importance, biodiversity enriches a human's psychological environment, inspiring wonder, curiosity, and respect.

Habitat Loss

The habitat in which an organism lives is critical to its survival. As human populations increase, many habitats are destroyed, diminished, or so altered that native species can no longer survive.

EXAMPLES: In the last 200 years, 53 percent of the wetlands in the United States have been drained and converted to agricultural or commercial land. Seventy-eight million acres of tropical forest are similarly destroyed each year to increase agricultural land or provide resources.

As habitat is destroyed, some species become extinct. Species extinction is a natural process, but it is estimated that human-caused extinction occurs at 1,000 times the natural rate. Between 10 and 20 percent of all species are projected to become extinct in the next 20 to 50 years. Many of those species have never even been identified.

Lake Victoria—A Case Study

Lake Victoria in Africa is the second largest lake in the world. Surrounded by Uganda, Kenya, and Tanzania, the lake is about the size of Ireland. In 1858, the lake was home to more than 500 species of freshwater fish. Four hundred species of cichlid, a small fish, provided 200,000 tons of protein a year for residents. Today, researchers from around the world are trying to keep the lake from dying.

* In the 1860s, a railroad was built into the area. Vegetation around the lake was cleared to plant tea, coffee, and sugar. Agricultural chemicals began washing into the lake during the rainy season. They provided nutrients for unwanted algae.
* Plantations attracted migrant workers. Overfishing became a problem.
* Officials introduced new fish species, including the Nile perch, to remedy the overfishing problem. Nile perch typically grow to several feet and 100 pounds. Commercial fishing fleets and processing plants were introduced to catch and package this new cash crop.
* By 1980, over 200 species of cichlid had been eaten to extinction. The many species of cichlid served a wide range of functions within the ecosystem, functions that the new fish did not perform. For example, disease-carrying snails, once controlled by the cichlids, increased rapidly in number.
* Water hyacinths, another human introduction, multiplied rapidly, choking harbors. By late 1998, nearly 1 million acres of the surface on the Kenyan side of the lake were covered with plants, and the water hyacinth population doubled every two weeks.
* Two hundred thousand tons of fish are exported annually, yet local villagers are threatened with malnutrition.
* Among other programs, researchers are now breeding many species of cichlid in aquariums, looking for ways to kill and control the water hyacinths, and working with local governments to educate the people.

Humans have a choice. They can change themselves to suit the environment, or change the environment to suit themselves. Lake Victoria is an example of what can happen when people make the second choice.

YECCH!

Resource Depletion

Overpopulation can lead to the depletion and eventual shortage of many natural resources, some of which cannot be renewed.

Deforestation

* Logging and clearing land for agriculture is depleting forest habitats at the rate of 2.4 acres per second.
* Seventy-eight million acres of rainforest are destroyed each year. Tropical rainforests cover only 7 percent of Earth's surface, but contain as much as 80 percent of Earth's plant species.
* Thailand, which once had 435,000 acres of forest, now has only 22,000. At the current rate, this will be gone in fewer than 4 years.

Desertification

* As forests are lost, soil washes away; 26 billion tons of topsoil are lost per year.
* For every ton of grain produced in the United States, 6 tons of topsoil are lost.
* It takes between 100 and 1,500 years to replace an inch of topsoil.

Water Shortages

* The amount of water available today is the same as it was when humans first inhabited Earth. It is self-renewing and will not run out.
* Fresh water makes up only 3 percent of all water, and only 1 percent of that is easily accessible.
* Until we learn to convert sea water to fresh water in sufficient quantities for our needs, we must conserve fresh water.

Metals and Fossil Fuels

* If present rates continue, the world's supply of lead, silver, tungsten, and mercury will be depleted in 40 years.
* If present rates continue, the global supply of oil will be depleted in 50 years.
* Solar power and wind power are available as sources of energy to replace fossil fuels, but the technology to use them affordably on a large scale has not yet been developed.

Pollution

In addition to causing shortages of resources, humans influence the environment by polluting air, water, and the land. As humans consume more, they produce more, creating more waste. Nature has mechanisms for transforming some of those wastes, but others, such as dioxin and radioactive waste, are not recycled by natural processes. These result in pollution.

CIVILIZATION IS DOOMED DUE TO OVERPOPULATION POLLUTION MISUSE OF ENERGY & RESOURCES

"They used to be thought of as crackpots."

The chart below describes the effects of common types of pollution.

Our Environmental Future

Here are some ways people are addressing the issues.

Habitat and Species Loss

The United States has laws against the destruction of prime habitat and/or endangered organisms. Around the world, many countries have passed similar legislation or have agreed to address the issue. However, illegal poaching and traditional practices still threaten many species.

Depletion of Resources

Six kinds of ways to address this issue have been found to work. The first three are already happening in U.S. society.

1. Conservation.
2. Recycling.
3. Development of new technologies.

We can look beyond our borders for other solutions. Most European countries consume much less energy than the United States while maintaining a high standard of living. These countries encourage people

Pollution	
Type of Pollution	**Air Pollution**
Sources	* The automobile—it accounts for at least 80 percent of air pollution. * Power-generation facilities. * Refineries. * Chemical plants. * Steel mills. * Coal-, oil-, and wood-burning, which release acid-producing chemicals that dissolve in water and can produce acid rain and carbon dioxide that can trap heat in the atmosphere and cause the "greenhouse effect." * Industrial gases, including those used in aerosol containers, that destroy atmospheric ozone.
Effects	* Irritated eyes, noses, and throats. * Erosion of buildings, destruction of crops, and the "death" of some lakes and rivers. * Global warming. An increase in the average temperature at Earth's surface leads to changes in weather patterns, a rise in sea level, disruption of agriculture, and stress to ecosystems. * More ultraviolet energy from the sun entering the atmosphere. This can damage skin and some crops and wild plants.

to drive smaller cars, lower their thermo-stats, and insulate their homes by offering:

4. Tax credits.

5. Government subsidies.

In addition, not only because its production consumes resources, but also because it adds to pollution, we could:

6. Discourage disposable packaging.

Pollution

Fighting pollution is possible, but it is expensive. One reason SUVs became popular is because they were classified as light trucks and did not have to meet the same emission standards as cars. Therefore, they did not have expensive equipment to control emissions, and buyers could get more car for the money.

Antipollution laws are controversial. Manufacturers don't like them because they increase their costs of doing business.

Workers fear that the laws threaten jobs. How? When a business's costs rise, the officers look for ways to lower them. Often they reach their goal by laying people off or by relocating their plants to regions or other countries where everything—including

Water Pollution	Land Pollution
* Runoff from agriculture—it's the single most important cause of water pollution. * Industrial discharge—including chemicals used or produced in processing paper, textiles, metals, oil, and petroleum. * Domestic wastewater and raw sewage. * Accidental oil spills and the regular dumping of fuels into the oceans during the cleaning of ships' tanks.	Solid waste from: * Agriculture. * Mining. * Industry. * Cities (only about 1.5 percent of the total). * Spent nuclear fuels.
* Poisoning of humans and animals. * Increased algae growth in lakes and streams, which eventually kills other organisms. * Disease among the half the world's population that lacks sanitary facilities. More than a third suffer from water-related diseases. * Death of ocean plants and wildlife.	* Landfills are rapidly filling. Runoff from poorly designed landfills can pollute water sources. * Air pollution from incomplete incineration. * Illness from disease-carrying insects that thrive in the open waste dumps of developing countries.

Noise Pollution

In the 18th century, a crier shouted a fire alarm from the top of a watchtower in the center of town. Today, fire vehicles in large cities must use ear-splitting sirens to be heard. This type of pollution is often overlooked. In many cities, the rumble of trucks, honking horns, jackhammers, air conditioners, factory noises, and even boom boxes have polluted the air as seriously as smog.

The World Health Organization (WHO) lists many physical and psychological problems caused by noise:

* Hearing impairment and ear pain.
* Speech interference.
* Sleep disturbances.
* Cardiovascular effects.
* Performance reduction.
* Psychological stress and annoyance.

These, in turn, can lead to reduced productivity, decreased learning, absenteeism, increased drug use, accidents, and the lowering of property values.

In the United States, laws regulate noise near airports and in factories, but even the noises in some operating rooms are enough to produce physical and psychological damage. A single loud sound can rupture the eardrum and continued exposure, even to loud music, can produce permanent damage in some frequencies.

Rural areas also suffer. Unacceptable noise levels can be produced by snowmobiles and agricultural machinery. WHO recommends stiffer noise-reduction laws as well as increased education of the public on the dangers of noise pollution.

labor— is cheaper. Also, workers fear people will not buy products as their prices rise to absorb the increased expense, and, again, layoffs can result if sales plummet.

Finally, consumers worry that prices will rise. They will have difficulty buying things they need and want when prices go up.

But everyone is in favor of clean air and a clean environment. It takes people with good ideas and good people skills to find solutions. Negotiation will be necessary to resolve these conflicts. Can we do it? What do you think?

Chapter 13 Wrap-up
POPULATION AND THE ENVIRONMENT

Sociologists study human populations and how they change. The census and vital statistics are among their tools. Factors that influence a population include birth and death rates and migration trends.

World population is growing. In nations that are industrialized, birth rates are declining. The U.S. birth rate is below the level needed to maintain a population, but the population is growing nevertheless through immigration.

The relationship between people and the environment is key to human survival on Earth. Natural resources are limited, and traditional energy resources are being depleted. Environmental issues that cause concern are biodiversity and habitat loss, resource depletion, and pollution.

Technology may provide answers to some of these problems. New ideas and strong people skills will be needed to negotiate solutions to problems of conflicting values.

biodiversity—variety of life forms on the planet. *p. 257*

carrying capacity—number of organisms a particular environment can support. *p. 257*

census—official count of the people of a country or district. *p. 248*

demographics—field of sociology that scientifically studies the size, composition, and distribution of populations. *p. 248*

ecology—study of the relationship between organisms and the natural environment. *p. 256*

ecosystem—self-contained community of organisms that depend on one another and the environment for survival. *p. 256*

emigrants—people who leave a country to establish a residence elsewhere. *p. 251*

fecundity—potential number of children that could be born to the average woman of childbearing age. *p. 249*

fertility—actual number of children born per woman between the ages of 15 and 44. *p. 249*

growth rate—difference between the birth rate and the death rate, expressed in annual percentages. *p. 253*

illegal aliens—people who enter or remain in a country against its immigration laws. *p. 253*

immigrants—people who move into a country to live there. *p. 251*

migration—movement of people from one geographical location to another with the intent of establishing a new residence. *p. 251*

migration rate—difference between the number of immigrants and the number of emigrants in a society. *p. 251*

mortality rate—number of deaths in a year per 1,000 members of a population. *p. 250*

political asylum—place offering protection and shelter from persecution for views that are contrary to an established government. *p. 253*

population density—measure of the concentration of people in a given area, usually described as number of people per square mile *p. 257*

refugees—people who flee a region because of its dangers. *p. 252*

replacement rate—fertility rate required to replace the parents. *p. 256*

vital statistics—official records of births, deaths, marriages, divorces, and migration. *p. 249*

CHAPTER 14

Cities and Urban Life

In this chapter, you will learn about:

- **the growth of cities**
- **theories of urban growth**
- **benefits and problems of urbanization**

Kitty Genovese was returning home from work. On the walk from her car to her apartment in a nice, middle-class neighborhood of Queens, a part of New York City, Kitty was attacked by a man with a knife. As she screamed for help, lights went on all over the neighborhood. People stuck their heads out their windows, and one man yelled at the attacker to get away. He did. Unfortunately, he returned before Kitty had time to crawl to safety—not once, but twice. Thirty-eight of Kitty's neighbors saw at least one of the attacks. Not one came to help or called the police until after she was dead.

Why did no one come to help? Were these people afraid for their own lives? Had they seen so much violence that it no longer mattered? Is it a result of living in a city?

Urbanization—the movement of large populations of people to cities—began during the Industrial Revolution. City living has its own unique collection of advantages and problems. People in cities interact with each other differently from people in small towns and rural communities. This chapter will look at the causes and effects of urbanization and at the urban personality.

The Growth of Cities

For more than 40,000 years after the appearance of *Homo sapiens* on Earth, most humans were hunter-gatherers, moving wherever food was easiest to find. Gradually, they began to domesticate animals, grow crops, and live together in larger and larger communities.

The First Cities

Cities are permanent concentrations of a relatively large number of people. The first began thousands of years ago:

* **8000 B.C.**—One of the first human settlements, Jericho, had about 2,500 residents.
* **5000–3500 B.C.**—Agricultural settlements in Mesopotamia between the Tigris and Euphrates rivers developed into cities in what is now Iraq.
* **2925 B.C.**—The Egyptian city of Memphis was founded in Egypt's First Dynasty.
* **2200–1000 B.C.**—Babylon (present-day Baghdad) was founded. The Olmecs built cities in Mexico. Jerusalem was called Urusalim. Anyang and other cities developed along the Huang He River in China.
* **800s B.C.**—Athens, Greece, developed into a city-state with a population of 200,000. The great port city of Carthage on the north African coast (present-day Tunis in Tunisia) developed.
* **753 B.C.**—Rome was founded by twin brothers Romulus and Remus.
* **332 B.C.**—Alexandria, Egypt, was founded by Alexander the Great.
* **100 B.C.**—The great pre-Columbian city of Teotihuacán in Mexico was built.
* **A.D. 900**—The largest cities in the world were Baghdad (in Iraq) with 900,000 people, Changan (Xian, China) with 750,000, and Constantinople (now Istanbul, Turkey) with 300,000 people.

Early European Cities

Cities in Europe developed in waves, moving westward from Greece, from 700 B.C. through A.D. 400, when the first cities developed in Ireland. In A.D. 43 London, England, developed under Roman rule. By the 11th century, London had a population of 10,000 to 12,000.

The Industrial City

Industrialization began in England during the 1700s. When it began, Europe had only a dozen cities with populations of more than 100,000. Over the next century, the size of the population of Europe remained roughly the same, but cities grew as businessmen built factories near them to take advantage of the labor pool. The employment opportunities the factories offered attracted more people to the cities.

As the Industrial Revolution continued, cities rapidly increased in size. Their economic and political importance grew. Social life became more complex. City life became more impersonal. Crime and environmental pollution increased. Some cities grew faster than their resources.

At the beginning of the 19th century, fewer than 50 cities in the world had a population of more than 100,000. Today there are nearly 400 cities with more than 1 million people.

Demographers predict that by 2025, about two-thirds of the world's population will live in cities. One-half of the world's people live in cities today.

U.S. Cities

The first cities in America were:

* St. Augustine, Florida, established by the Spanish in 1565.
* Jamestown, Virginia, established by the English in 1607.
* New York (New Amsterdam), established by the Dutch in 1624.
* Boston, Massachusetts, established by English Puritans in 1630.

Originally, these cities resembled European villages with rambling, narrow streets.

Urban expansion in the United States paralleled that of Europe, increasing rapidly during the 19th century. The exploration of the West and the building of railroads opened urban development west of the Appalachians.

During this time the North grew increasingly urban while the South stayed largely rural. This difference contributed to contrasting values, fueling hostilities during the Civil War.

Types of Urban Areas

While cities are fairly self-contained concentrations of people, urbanization has led to even larger urban areas.

Urbanization in the United States

Urbanization is the movement of people from rural to urban areas. This movement influences all parts of culture and society.

During the census taken in 1790, only 5 percent of the population could be classified as urban. The largest city was New York, with fewer than 50,000 residents. Today, nearly 82 percent of the nation's 281 million people live in urban areas.

Percent of U.S. Population Living in Cities 1790-2000

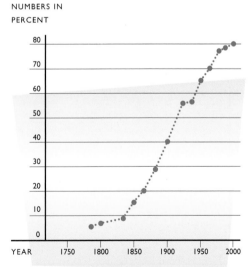

NUMBERS IN PERCENT

Source: U.S. Bureau of the Census

The Metropolis

A **metropolis** is a large urban area that includes the city and its **suburbs**—residential areas on the outskirts of a city. The entire region is tied together culturally and economically.

Three factors influence the movement to suburbs. These include:

1. Movement of middle and upper classes outward as more people migrate to the inner city.
2. Ease of movement produced by cars and mass transportation.
3. Location of more businesses in outlying areas because of space or lower taxes.

The graph below compares the growth of population in Los Angeles to the population growth in its suburbs over a 40-year period. You can see that the bulk of the growth came in suburban areas.

Los Angeles Urban Growth

NUMBERS IN MILLIONS

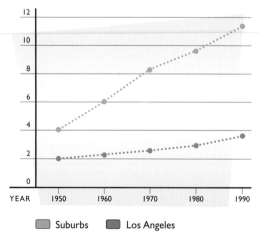

Source: U.S. Bureau of the Census

CMSAs

In some areas where large cities continue to grow, they absorb smaller surrounding cities. The term *urban sprawl* is sometimes used to describe this spread. In the United States, for example, one can drive from Boston, Massachusetts, to Washington, D.C., without leaving the city/suburban complex. Similar areas exist between Detroit and Pittsburgh and from San Francisco to San Diego in California.

Did You Know?

Ten Largest CMSAs

1. New York-Northern New Jersey-Long Island, NY-NJ-CT-PA.
2. Los Angeles-Riverside-Orange County, CA.
3. Chicago-Gary-Kenosha, IL-IN-WI.
4. Washington-Baltimore, DC-MD-VA-WV.
5. San Francisco-Oakland-San Jose, CA.
6. Philadelphia-Wilmington-Atlantic City, PA-NJ-DE-MD.
7. Boston-Worcester-Lawrence, MA-NH-ME-CT.
8. Detroit-Ann Arbor-Flint, MI.
9. Dallas-Fort Worth, TX.
10. Houston-Galveston-Brazoria, TX.

Source: *The World Almanac and Book of Facts, 2001.*

The U.S. Office of Management and Budget, with help from the Census Bureau, identifies a metropolitan area with a population over 1 million as a **Consolidated Metropolitan Statistical Area (CMSA)**. By 1998, there were 40 of these. The largest was New York City-Northern New Jersey-Long Island, New York. This CMSA crosses state boundaries, as do ten others.

The Megacity

A **megacity** is presently defined as one in which the population is greater than 5 million people. Demographers use a variety of terms to describe very large urban complexes. Sometimes you may see the words *urban agglomeration.* The term indicates a

Did You Know?

World's Largest Megacities

1. Tokyo, Japan: over 34 million.
2. New York, U.S.A.: over 20 million.
3. Seoul, South Korea: over 20 million.
4. Mexico City, Mexico: over 19 million.
5. Mumbai (Bombay), India: over 18 million.
6. Sao Paulo, Brazil: over 18 million.
7. Osaka, Japan, nearly 18 million.
8. Los Angeles, U.S.A.: over 16 million.
9. Cairo, Egypt: over 14 million.
10. Manila, Philippines: over 13 million.

huge population of diverse peoples and communities. Most of them are outside the United States. In fact, more than half of the present and future megacities are in developing countries. It is difficult to count the population in such areas. Population counting methods differ and change is constant. What was true the day of the count is no longer true the day the findings are published. By the time you read this book, the numbers will have changed.

Theories of Urban Growth

In the 1920s and 1930s, sociologists at the University of Chicago began a series of studies on how urban centers develop. They were interested in how increasing concentrations of people interacted with their environments. The model they developed is just one that has been suggested over the years. Their observations suggested that cities develop in a certain spatial configuration—zones of concentric circles.

Later scholars proposed other configurations— sectors or multiple nuclei. These models demonstrate *how* cities have grown. They do not explain *why* cities grow in those ways. The way a particular city develops depends on complex factors, including technology, the geography and environment, and the distribution of wealth.

Theories of City Growth

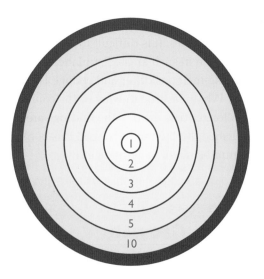

Concentric Zone Theory

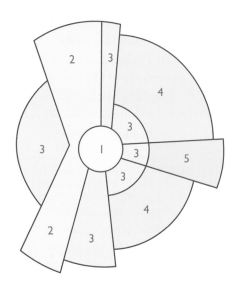

Sector Theory

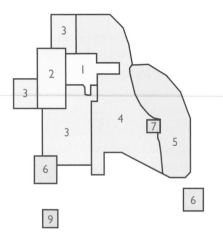

Multiple-Nuclei Theory

Key

1	Central Business District
2	Warehouses/Light Manufacturing
3	Lower-class Residential
4	Middle-class Residential
5	Upper-class Residential
6	Heavy Manufacturing
7	Outlying Business District
8	Residential Suburb
9	Industrial Suburb
10	Commuter Zone

Source: Department of Geography and Earth Sciences, University of North Carolina at Chapel Hill.

The Concentric Zone Theory

Who: Ernest Burgess, Robert Park, and colleagues at the University of Chicago.

When: 1925.

What: Proposed that a city spreads out from the center in *concentric* circular *zones*. Each zone has a different use.

* The innermost zone or central city contains the central business district with shops, banks, offices, hotels, and government buildings.
* The next zone is a transition zone, often rundown and containing factories and deteriorating housing. The crime rate may be high here.
* As one moves away from the city, each zone represents a higher economic class, ending in suburbs—a zone from which people commute to the inner city.

EXAMPLES: This model describes cities heavily influenced by industrial development and use of the automobile such as Chicago and St. Louis. However, many cities do not have concentric zones (for example, Memphis).

The Sector Theory

Who: Homer Hoyt, an urban ecologist.

When: 1939.

What: Agreed that a city grows outward from a central business district. Rather than concentric zones, Hoyt said that wedge-shaped *sectors* extend outward from the center. He proposed a number of ways for these sectors to form, including the following.

* When warehouses are built along a railroad line leading to the central city, low-cost housing will accompany them. The railroad track becomes a border of one sector.
* Businesses or strip malls are built along well-traveled highways leading from the city to the suburbs. These neighborhoods attract people with more money and available cars. The highways form borders.
* Areas that are higher and command better views attract upper-income families. The natural geographic feature provides the border of this sector.

EXAMPLES: San Francisco and Minneapolis exhibit the sector pattern. The pattern depends on geography as well as the growth of industrialization and transportation in the city. The sector model, like the concentric-zone model, is not found in all cities.

The Multiple-Nuclei Pattern

Who: Chauncey Harris and Edward Ullman.

When: 1945.

What: Rather than a particular pattern, cities have a number of specialized areas. Each area acts as a nucleus for similar activities. Many activities have specialized needs.

* Entertainment and restaurants need easy accessibility. Therefore, they will be located near good transportation.
* Businesses locate near other related kinds of business, or near businesses that offer services they need. The Wall

The High Ground

In the United States, high ground is often prized. Such real estate commands the highest prices and generally requires that the residents commute to work. For these reasons, wealthier people occupy the higher areas around a city.

This is not the case in all countries. The city of Cuzco, Peru, is ancient. It was once the capitol of the Inca Empire. It is located at 11,000 feet above sea level and is surrounded by even higher mountains. The mountains have fairly gentle slopes and are grassy rather than treed. This should make them prime locations for wealthier residents of the city. Instead, the hills are home to the poorer people of Cusco. The main reasons for this include the absence of roads or public transportation leading from the hills into the city and the absence of utilities (power and water).

The local government doesn't have the resources to extend roads or city utilities into the hills. There are no developers with the money to create "subdivisions" in those remote areas, particularly because they would have to provide the roads and utilities themselves.

Street area in New York City contains not only the stock markets but many other financial institutions and offices housing workers in related businesses.

✳ Some areas will not be found next to one another because they are not compatible. For example, high-cost housing will not be found near factories and warehouses.

EXAMPLES: Boston and New York.

Urban Culture

One approach to the study of urban culture is to compare urban and rural life. The perspectives of some early sociologists are given in the table opposite.

In cities, encounters tend to be rational rather than emotional. People calculate the "cost" to themselves before allowing their emotions to rule their actions.

Many large cities, such as New York, are famous for the way residents ignore what is going on around them. The case of Kitty Genovese given in the chapter introduction is but one example of the tendency of city dwellers to remain uninvolved in the problems of others.

Sociologist George Simmel defends the "urban personality" as a necessity brought about by the fast pace and stimulation of city life. He sees it as a form of self-protection.

Sociologists are divided in their theories of how city life affects individuals.

Urban Anomie Theory

According to Louis Wirth, city life leads to impersonal relationships, anonymity, and individual problems stemming from loneliness. In addition to creating a sense of alienation (anomie), Wirth argued that **three** factors support his theory:

1. **Population size** prevents intimacy and close relationships common to rural life.

"Boy, look at _his_ personal space!"

Town versus Country	
Principal Sociologist(s)	**Major Ideas**
Ferdinand Tönnies (1887)	**A Rural Society** (Gemeinschaft) is characterized by a community with a relatively small population, a simple division of labor, face-to-face interaction, and informal social control. **An Urban Society** (Gesellschaft) has a large population that forms loose associations, a complex division of labor, and formal social control.
Emile Durkheim (1893)	Agreed with Tönnies but focused on how members of society are bound together. **A Rural Society** is held together by "mechanical solidarity": tradition, unity, similar norms and values, strong informal pressure to conform. **An Urban Society** is held together by "organic solidarity." The complex division of labor makes individuals dependent on one another.
Robert Redfield (1941)	**A Rural Society** is a folk society. It emphasizes tradition, consensus, and primary relationships. **An Urban Society** emphasizes change, diversity, and secondary relationships.
The Chicago School; Robert Ezra Park (1916)	**Established branch of sociology known as urban ecology,** which seeks to identify, study, and explain how city people interact with the environment.
Louis Wirth (1938)	**Described urbanism as a way of life** in which the city affects how people feel, think, and interact.

2. Population density creates stress, particularly when people have different cultural values and social norms. People are bombarded with noise and visual stimulation as well as with the unrelenting presence of people they don't know. In the midst of a crowd, they feel isolated and alone.

3. Social diversity permits more social mobility and breaks down race and class boundaries. Wirth claimed that social mobility makes lasting relationships difficult.

Compositional Theory

Compositional theorists disagree with Wirth and say that, no matter how large a population may be, people will tend to associate with a small, close group of friends and relatives who have similar lifestyles. This social group insulates them to some extent from the impersonal world of strangers.

Sociologist Herbert Gans observed that people in large cities frequently gather in ethnic neighborhoods where there is a strong sense of community loyalty. He calls these *ethnic* or *urban villages*.

Where Would You Live?

In a 1989 Gallup poll, only 38 percent of the people polled would choose to live in urban areas with a population greater than 50,000 people. That includes the 13 percent who preferred the central city and 25 percent who preferred the suburbs.

In 1997, the largest home mortgage lender in the United States, Fannie Mae, ordered another survey on people's attitudes toward cities. This poll looked at whether people perceived cities as centers of business, culture, and progress or of poverty, crime and other social problems.

The survey showed that people's impressions of cities had improved over the past decade. However, the percentage who would choose to live in a large city had not increased.

The survey also found:

* Young adults (ages 18 to 24), married people under 40, and people who grew up in suburbs generally had the most positive view of cities.
* Married renters, with and without children, and African Americans tended to hold negative attitudes toward cities.

Compositional theorists blame the high crime rate in cities on the concentration of people with a tendency toward mental and psychological instability in urban populations.

Recent Trends in Urbanization

In the United States, recent trends in city demographics and culture include shifting populations, the emergence of "edge cities," and urban renewal. Some of these trends have contributed to urban problems.

Shifting Populations

Sociologists have long predicted the movement of the population from Northeastern and Midwestern cities to the "sunbelt" of the South and Southwest. This has occurred, but sometimes not in expected ways.

* Older industrial cities in the South, such as Atlanta and Birmingham, have experienced the same decline and problems as Northern cities.
* The increase in California's population has been unexpectedly high. Seven of the ten fastest-growing large U.S. cities are in Southern California.
* Populations of "sunbelt" cities such as those in Arizona, Texas, and New Mexico have increased as predicted.
* Immigration from developing countries has increased, keeping the population of New York from declining as expected. For the same reasons, Miami has experienced tremendous growth. The following graphs show growth in these two cities.

New York City Urban Growth

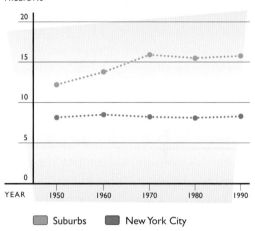

Source: U.S. Bureau of the Census

Miami Urban Growth

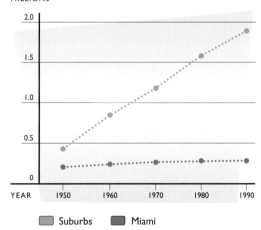

Source: U.S. Bureau of the Census

Edge Cities

By the end of the 20th century, suburbs from which people once commuted to work had sprouted offices, factories, shopping malls, and businesses. They had become *edge cities*—"mini cities" at the edges of their larger counterparts. Unfortunately the traffic congestion, environmental problems, and rising crime rates of the adjacent city accompanied these changes.

Many edge cities are focused on a principal activity, such as computer-related companies, sports or entertainment complexes, or regional medical centers. Commuting patterns that once were directed to the central city have changed. Now you see bumper to bumper traffic in both directions during rush hour.

Urban Renewal

In the 1950s and '60s, in an attempt to provide affordable housing and improve the lifestyles of the poor, cities engaged in "urban renewal" projects. Public housing, usually in the form of high-rise apartment complexes, was built specifically to house the poor.

Many of these projects, such as the Cabrini-Green housing project in Chicago, became social disasters:

* Decisions were made by a distant "housing authority."
* The complexes were poorly maintained and took on the appearance of a giant slum.
* Criminal gangs took over, and drug traffic and gun violence became prevalent.

* The construction of some projects forced the breakup of tightly structured neighborhoods.

A newer form of urban renewal is **gentrification.** This occurs when former working-class neighborhoods or industrial districts are taken over by white-collar professionals who buy and renovate older buildings. Refurbished older homes and converted trendy "loft" apartments attract upscale singles or childless couples.

Gentrification has both positive and negative aspects. It renews rundown areas of the city, improves property values, and creates attractive places where once there was blight. However, it displaces people who cannot afford the new, high-priced residences and does nothing to find them affordable housing. When people are displaced, they lose more than a home. They lose the social network that supports them in their daily life.

Urban Problems

City living has many attractions. It provides business opportunities and an abundance of types of entertainment. City living is "where the action is." Nonetheless, social problems also characterize urban life. Here are **four:**

1. **Housing Segregation Occurs.** Although the government supports individual home ownership, affordable housing is often outside the budget of many low-income families. As wealthier people move to new developments or the suburbs, poorer families are left with aging, inner-city buildings or inferior housing.

Postsuburbia

Sociologists Rob Kling, Spencer Olin, and Mark Poster have explored different theories about edge cities. They suggest that these regions are a new kind of settlement space that can't be described as urban, suburban, or rural. What they term "postsuburban" settlements differ from cities in that they do not have a "center." Shopping, entertainment, and business and industrial "parks" are centers of activity. One sociologist calls them "multi-nucleated metropolitan regions."

People in postsuburban areas rely heavily on private automobiles for transportation. People are as likely to work and interact between postsuburban cities as within them.

In city neighborhoods, people meet and interact while walking to the neighborhood store or church. In postsuburban areas, there are few places where this sort of activity can take place.

In edge cities where people from many different cultures congregate, residents tend to be knowledgeable about, interested in, and appreciative of cultures around the world. Postsuburban areas such as Long Island, New York, and Long Beach, California, have strong arts cultures.

Despite attempts by government to legislate equality in housing opportunity, racial segregation occurs. Realtors often regularly steer minorities away from white neighborhoods. Banks are cautious about granting loans to minority families that want to purchase or rehabilitate homes in primarily white neighborhoods.

2. **Small Businesses Disappear.** In an attempt to revitalize business areas, local governments frequently offer tax incentives to attract businesses to locate within their boundaries. These new businesses may compete with established businesses. "Mom and Pop" businesses are increasingly forced to close because they are unable to compete with larger chain-store prices or variety of items.

3. **Crime and Drug Traffic Spread.** The population density in large cities makes them a breeding ground for crime. Crime rates are also affected by the proximity of wealth and poverty in cities. Although crime *rates* in such major cities as New York have been declining steadily, high *numbers* of crimes are still committed. Cities experience crime related to drug use more often than suburban or rural areas.

There is an interesting trend in large and small cities, such as Chicago,

Illinois, and the smaller state capital Springfield. Chicago had twice as many *violent* crimes per 100,000 people as Springfield. However, Springfield had significantly more *property* crimes, such as burglary, larceny, and auto theft. This same trend is true when comparing New York City with New York State's capital, Albany, and Los Angeles and the California capital, Sacramento.

4. Poverty Increases. The numbers of urban poor are growing. Urban poverty is often a result of declining school quality and a widening gap in education and training in an increasingly technological society. Poverty is accompanied by increases in crime, drug abuse, and the number of people needing welfare services. Homelessness, too, is an aspect of

Did You Know?

Homelessness in the United States

Making an accurate count of homeless people is nearly impossible. Although many homeless people visit shelters where records are kept, many others stay in automobiles, campgrounds, or other places where researchers cannot effectively search. However, various studies have produced some disturbing numbers.

* Several studies indicate that 12 million adult residents of the United States have been homeless at some point in their lives.
* The number of homeless is projected to increase by 5 percent a year.
* Two trends are largely responsible for the rise in homelessness during the past 20 years: a shortage of affordable rental housing and a simultaneous increase in poverty.

* Forty-five percent of urban homeless people are single men; 14 percent are single women.
* Families constitute 38 percent of the homeless population.
* Among urban homeless, children under the age of 18 account for 25 percent of the homeless population. Fifty-one percent of homeless people are between the ages of 31 and 50.
* Forty percent of the homeless have served in the military.
* Approximately 20 to 25 percent of single adult homeless people suffer from some form of severe and persistent mental illness.
* African Americans make up almost half of all homeless people.
* The most common places that homeless people stay are vehicles (59.2 percent) and such makeshift housing as tents, boxes, caves, and boxcars (24.6 percent).

urban poverty. In several large cities, more than three percent of the population used homeless shelters at least once a year. The real proportion of homeless people is higher because not all take advantage of shelters.

Decline of Smaller Cities

Most U.S. cities with populations over 200,000 suffered declining populations in the last decade of the 20th century. While the decline means a smaller demand on city services, it also means:

* A decline in the tax base used to repair aging infrastructures, such as roads and utilities.
* Abandoned buildings that become centers for drug traffic and other crimes.
* Fewer jobs and declining tax revenues because the people who leave are typically middle-class people who also move their businesses.

Sociological Perspectives on Urbanization

Functionalist Perspective

Functionalists focus on the interdependence of people in a city. They have a generally positive view of the social changes that occur in cities. They study the ways that urban organizations meet economic and social needs.

Conflict Perspective

Conflict theorists stress the role of the power elite in making suburbs stronger than cities. They emphasize **three** historic developments:

1. Seeking profit, big construction corporations bought up large tracts of land in rural areas for development as housing, shopping, or industrial complexes. In the process, they drove farmers out of business. The developers were supported by government subsidies, grants, and low-interest loans.
2. As cities expanded into the suburbs, big business "made a killing" in real estate, construction, and banking. The government subsidized the building of many single-family homes in the suburbs, guaranteed mortgages, and offered tax deductions on interest payments, thus encouraging people to purchase the homes.
3. From the 1970s to the present, large corporations have turned suburbs into edge cities, thus avoiding paying high city taxes. Many businesses received large tax breaks from suburban governments to relocate. This drained city revenues, leaving the city to provide for an increasingly larger proportion of needy people.

Interactionist Perspective

Interactionists have studied certain dimensions of urban human interaction and have drawn **three** conclusions.

1. City people tend to interact in superficial and impersonal ways to protect themselves from psychic overload, even to the extent of ignoring a neighbor's calls for help.

2. City people may be respecting each other's desire for privacy by avoiding eye contact in public places.

3. City people tend to be tolerant of diverse lifestyles in such areas as dress, religious practices, or sexual orientations. They are familiar with aspects of cultures other than their own. They tend to refrain from imposing their values on others.

Summarizing Urban Living

Despite the problems of cities, they offer many advantages to residents that rural areas do not, including:

* Wide choice of lifestyles and careers.
* Numerous cultural institutions.

Did You Know?

City Lights

One of the beauties of a city at night is the shimmer and glow of its many lights. City attractions are lit to show them off. Property owners and those concerned with security use high levels of light to protect customers and citizens from crime. However, some warn of a "dark side." Astronomers note that current lighting practices steal the public's view of the night sky. Critics point out that 30 percent of the electricity generated for outdoor lighting is wasted as it is misdirected—upward and outward, rather than down.

One group calls this "trespassing," comparing the spillover of light onto private property with dumping trash on your neighbor's lawn. They cite a study suggesting that high levels of light in a child's bedroom can lead to improper development of the eyes.

Night satellite imagery of the northeastern United States from Chicago to New York City.

* Excellent educational opportunities.
* Specialized medical care.
* Variety in recreational activities.
* Privacy.

The downside of life in cities, however, may include:

* Impersonal social relationships.
* Overstimulation.
* Anonymity.
* High level of competition and conflict.
* Physical danger from crime, smog, easy access to drugs, and the stresses of urban living.

In the foreseeable future, many cities will continue to lose people to the suburbs, the country, and the sunbelt. Because most migrants from the centers of cities are white and middle class, inner cities may become increasingly populated with minorities and the poor.

Will our increasingly information-based society change where businesses locate? We can assume cities will continue to try to attract businesses through incentives and to focus on creating more jobs for the unemployed and underemployed.

Chapter 14 Wrap-up
CITIES AND URBAN LIFE

Urbanization—the movement of people into cities—began about 9,000 years ago. Cities remained rather small until the Industrial Revolution, when improved transportation and the demand for skilled workers drew people to centralized locations. Urban growth in the United States paralleled that in Europe. Today, some enormous population centers around the world include tens of millions of people. Most of these huge population centers are in developing countries.

Sociologists developed three spatial theories that describe how cities have developed—in concentric circular zones, in sectors, and from multiple nuclei. Other sociologists describe urban culture in comparison to rural life. Many are interested in what city life does to personal relationships.

Recent trends in urbanization include shifting populations, edge cities, and urban renewal. Cities have their own particular kinds of social problems. In spite of these, cities offer people advantages that are not found in smaller towns or rural areas.

Sociology — WORDS TO KNOW

city—permanent concentration of a relatively large number of people. *p. 266*

Consolidated Metropolitan Statistical Area (CMSA)—metropolitan area with a population over 1 million. *p. 269*

gentrification—renovation of former working-class neighborhoods or industrial districts by white-collar professionals. *p. 276*

megacity—city with a population greater than 5 million people. *p. 269*

metropolis—large urban area that includes a city and its suburbs. *p. 268*

suburb—residential area on the outskirts of a city. *p. 268*

urbanization—movement of people from rural to urban areas. *p. 267*

Collective Behavior and Social Movements

In this chapter, you will learn about:

- **how and why people in crowds and mobs behave as they do**
- **forms of mass behavior**
- **why social movements occur**
- **how social movements work**

In the last months of the 20th century, people were preparing for the new millennium. Many were concerned with what they called "Y2K" (year two thousand). Their concerns revolved around the massive number of society's activities that are regulated by computers whose software programs were not written to recognize years beginning with the digit 2. The concern was valid, and governments and businesses spent millions reviewing their systems and rewriting computer programs. At the same time, a kind of hysteria arose as people anticipated what might happen. Some began to hoard cash, fearful they wouldn't get access to their bank accounts. Others stored nonperishable food items against the potential failure of warehouses and delivery systems. Cat owners bought up bags of kitty litter. Some people prepared for the end of the world.

What makes people act this way? In this chapter, we'll explore collective behavior, from the activities of "rubbernecks" who form a "gapers' block" when accidents occur on the highway to the more organized group behavior known as social movements. From revolutions to sit-ins and letter-writing campaigns, social movements attempt to bring about change in society.

Collective Behavior

A **collectivity** is an unstructured collection of individuals, with no assigned roles or organized authority, who temporarily engage in an activity. They disperse once the issue that brought them together is over.
EXAMPLES: Onlookers at an accident scene—their interactions are temporary. They may merely gawk or may provide assistance to the victims and help with crowd control or in directing traffic.

Collective behavior consists of the actions, thoughts, and emotions that occur almost simultaneously within a collectivity.
EXAMPLES: Riots, fads, mass hysteria, panic.

Collective behavior is characterized by several factors. It tends to be:

* Unstructured.
* Unpredictable.
* Spontaneous.
* Emotional.

Such behavior differs from the behavior in organizations and institutions where norms and social controls are in place.

Understanding Collective Behavior

A number of approaches have been used to interpret collective behavior. There are **four** prominent theories.

1. **Contagion Theory.** In 1895, Gustave Le Bon proposed that powerful emotions are contagious, particularly in a crowd where people tend to lose their individuality and become anonymous. The "power of suggestion" causes people to behave unpredictably.
   EXAMPLE: Lawyers have argued contagion theory in their defense of some people who acted violently during a riot. They may say that their clients were driven to violence by the powerful influence of other rioters.

   Today, few sociologists believe that there is a common emotion in crowds. Some suggest that the more uncertain the situation, the more likely people are to follow the lead set by others.

2. **Convergence Theory.** This theory states that individuals who participate in mobs are brought together by similar interests and attitudes. These similarities predispose crowd members to collective behavior.
   EXAMPLE: People who attend a rock concert or sporting event share common characteristics and interests.

   Critics of convergence theory point out that it is unlikely that people with similar personalities would be present at fast-developing situations where collective behavior occurs.

3. **Structural Stress Theory.** In 1962, sociologist Neil Smelser argued that collective behavior depends not only on the dynamics of crowds but also on the social context in which the behavior takes place.

Smelser listed **six** conditions that must occur in sequence for collective behavior to happen:

i. *Structural Conduciveness.* Preexisting social organization permits collective acts and sees them as legitimate.

ii. *Social Strain.* There must be a preexisting strain due to previous failures of the government to meet citizens' needs or address social problems.

iii. *Growth and Spread of a Generalized Belief.* Potential participants have formed a belief about the situation that initiates their response.

iv. *A Precipitating Event.* A particular situation or event brings the strain to the breaking point.

v. *Mobilization of Participants for Action.* Leaders emerge, urging people to action.

vi. *Inadequate Social Controls.* Smelser believed this is especially important because once collective behavior occurs, its length and severity are

Sociologist's Perspective

The Rodney King Riots

Riots occurred in Los Angeles in 1992 after a jury found four white policemen not guilty of beating black motorist Rodney King during his arrest. The beating had been videotaped, and TV news programs replayed the scene over and over during the weeks leading up to and through the trial. That event fit Smelser's theory:

Structural Conduciveness. The people who joined the riots lived within the same area of Los Angeles and readily communicated with one another.

Social Strain. There had been a history of police brutality against African Americans.

Growth and Spread of a Generalized Belief. Rioters believed that local police were guilty of mistreating and brutalizing African Americans.

A Precipitating Event. The court found the police officers not guilty.

Mobilization of Participants for Action. Leaders emerged shouting slogans such as "Let's burn!" and setting examples by looting, smashing storefronts, and overturning vehicles.

Inadequate Social Controls. The police were all but absent in the early hours of rioting. Perhaps they felt their presence would further enrage the rioters. Those whose property was destroyed saw their absence as further lack of regard for justice in a minority neighborhood.

determined by the response of "agencies of social control," such as the police or National Guard. When there is no social control, people feel less constrained to behave in ways typically viewed as lawful or acceptable.

4. **Emergent Norm Theory.** This theory states that people in a crowd have the illusion that they share common values and norms, perhaps because they share the interest that brought them together. This illusion predisposes the crowd members to act as a unit and observe a new "norm" of the moment.

EXAMPLE: People who have waited in line for a "big sale" often begin pushing and shoving as soon as the store opens. Once this norm has emerged, they proceed to race from place to place, throwing merchandise around as they grab for bargains before someone else gets them.

Crowds

When people think about collective behavior, they often picture a crowd. Although crowds are not the only type of collectivity, they are an important one. Sociologist Herbert Blumer has described four types of crowds.

Blumer's Crowds	
Type of Crowd	**What It Is**
Casual	A collection of individuals that forms spontaneously because some common event captures their attention. Individuals in a casual crowd engage in little if any interaction with one another. **EXAMPLE:** People watching an accident or a street performer.
Conventional	People gathered for an event such as a performance or a lecture. There is little interaction. While they have a common goal, they pursue it as individuals. **EXAMPLES:** Concerts, lectures, movies.
Expressive	A group coming together for an emotionally charged event. People release emotions in what may not, in other circumstances, be acceptable behavior. **EXAMPLES:** Mardi Gras, New Year's Eve in Times Square, a religious revival meeting.
Active	An excited and emotional group of individuals express their emotions through violent or destructive behavior. **EXAMPLES:** Mobs, rioters, and "hooligans"—what some call rowdy and riotous fans at sporting events.

Sports Fan Behavior

Why do sports fans act the way they do? The social identity theory suggests that sports fans enhance their self-esteem through association with the team. When the team wins, fans bask in the reflected glory of the team. When it loses, they defend the team as if they were defending themselves or family members.

Some sociologists have added a fifth type of crowd, protest crowd, to Blumer's four types. This type is a blend of the conventional and the active crowd, because it is somewhat organized and purposeful. Strikers and protestors are examples.

Emotions and Crowd Behavior

Emotions influence collective behavior.

* *Panic* is a collective behavior that develops when people experience fear that they are in imminent danger. Fleeing from a threat is appropriate behavior, but collective panic leads to irrational and uncooperative behavior in which people can be trampled to death.
* *Frustration and hostility* may lead to mob behavior. Mobs can form spontaneously or through planning. When mob behavior turns violent, it is called a riot.

* *Joy or merriment* accompany celebrations, concerts, and parties. If the collective behavior gets out of hand at these events, it can evolve into mob behavior.

Deindividuation

Psychologists use the term **deindividuation** to describe what happens when a person loses a sense of individuality. **Three** attributes distinguish this state:

1. Loss of self-awareness.
2. Sense of reduced responsibility.
3. Decreased concern about how others view one's behavior.

In an emotional situation, there may be loss of self-awareness as attention is focused on what is happening. When attention is not focused on self, people stop comparing their behavior against normal standards and instead tend to act like everyone else.

Research has shown that being in a crowd decreases an individual's sense of responsibility and accountability. In crowds, people wait for someone else to assume responsibility and act.

Once deindividuation has occurred, some event may push the social arousal level over the threshold. This can be anything from a "bad call" by a referee to the taunts of opposing fans. A few fans start throwing things or fighting. Because people have not only lost self-awareness but also feel anonymous in the crowd, they join in the action. In a mob, no one can be sure who did what, so no one can be blamed.

Mass Behavior

Some collective behavior involves individuals who are not in close proximity to one another. They may live in different parts of the country or the world, but something makes them behave in similar ways. In turn, their behavior influences others to behave in the same way. This is known as *mass behavior*. There are **six** common types of mass behavior:

1. **Fads** are short-term, unexpected behaviors engaged in by one segment of the population, generally adolescents or young adults. Fads often give people the feeling of being part of a group.
   EXAMPLE: Bungee jumping, body piercing, collecting Pokemon cards and slang expressions are fads.

2. **Crazes** are a more serious form of fad that becomes the focus of a person's life or produces negative consequences.
   EXAMPLES: Get-rich-quick schemes and the rapid rise and fall of emerging dot.com companies are crazes.

3. **Fashions** are customs or styles that change periodically but less frequently than fads. More people follow fashions than follow fads.
   EXAMPLES: Style of dress, length of one's hair, home furnishings, and car models are fashions.

4. **Mass Hysteria** is a form of panic in which people reinforce each others' irrational fears about a threat from some powerful force.
   EXAMPLES: In colonial New England, a form of mass hysteria persuaded villagers that their neighbors were witches, resulting in the execution of many innocent people. In 1938, a radio program, *The War of the Worlds*, presented a fictional news broadcast about Martians invading Earth. Although it was announced several times during the program that the show was a dramatization, people in New Jersey, where the Martian landing supposedly was taking place, fled their homes. Listeners with relatives in the area telephoned to warn them.

5. **Rumors** are unverified information from anonymous sources that spreads quickly and informally. Rumors arise and flourish in situations where there is little available information and some anxiety.

Rumors are not necessarily false. However, people rarely take the time to verify their accuracy before passing them on. Later, even when a rumor proves to be false, people continue to believe that "where there's smoke, there must be fire." This is why innuendo (simply hinting things about people or events) is so powerful.

EXAMPLES: Large corporations hurt by false rumors include a fast-food franchise accused of adding earthworms to its burgers and a home-cleaning product line whose logo was said to be a satanic symbol.

6. **Urban Myths** are unsubstantiated stories that are widely circulated and believed. More complex than simple rumors, they often carrying a warning about the hazards of modern life or hidden threats.

EXAMPLES: Alligators in the sewers, rats in soft drink bottles, and poison in the drinking water are all urban myths.

Popular Opinion

Groups in society often seek to influence public opinion, whether to gain sales of a product, persuade voters to elect a candidate, or garner support for a particular social issue, such as reproductive rights, drugs, taxes, or Social Security. Popular opinion, or "public opinion," as expressed in polls and surveys, supposedly reflects the feelings and beliefs of the public. Public opinion can be influenced by propaganda and the mass media.

Propaganda

One tool used to sway popular opinion is **propaganda**—information designed to manipulate public opinion and to influence people to change their beliefs in a particular way. Some propaganda techniques include:

* *Name calling,* associating an opposing idea or product with something undesirable by using such terms as "big spender" or "shoddy" or by juxtaposing images of a race riot or a nuclear bomb with an opponent's picture.

* *Glittering generalities,* associating an idea or product with a vague but highly popular concept, such as democracy or freedom.
* *Transfer,* associating an idea or product with something else that is admired or desired, such as using pets or children in ads.
* *Testimonial,* having a celebrity endorse a product or a national politician endorse a local candidate.
* *Bandwagon,* creating the impression that "everyone else" supports an idea or product. Have you noticed how quickly positive poll results or endorsements by major unions or newspapers are announced by political candidates?

Mass Media

The mass media exert influence on public opinion. For example:

* When the media report something, people are likely to believe it.
* If a commentator says something that we already believe, our belief is validated.
* When ideas that are out of the mainstream are reported, they seem legitimate.
* When media reporters use phrases such as "crime wave" and "police brutality," the vague anxieties people may have become more real.
* The media establish the importance of an idea or issue by the degree to which they cover it.

Social Movements

Social movements are collective efforts to bring about social or political change. Compared to collective behaviors, social movements:

* Are goal-oriented.
* Are more structured.
* Are longer-lasting.
* Have more participants.
* Have official leaders.

Social movements are temporary, making them different from institutions. A social movement can become an institution if and when it is accepted by society.

Characteristics of Social Movements

All social movements share **three** major characteristics.

1. **Ideology.** A set of beliefs unifies the members of a movement and determines the social process the movement wishes to influence. Though it is sometimes vague, the ideology provides a rallying cry for the movement.
   EXAMPLE: Women's movements believe that women have a right to be treated fairly and equally and to make their own decisions about their lives.
2. **Organization.** Social movements have social structure. They have a core group of leaders, a group of active participants, and others who support the cause of the organization in a variety of ways.

EXAMPLES: Large and successful social movements may become formal organizations, such as the NAACP or Greenpeace. These organizations have paid staff and, often, huge fund-raising capabilities. They exert political influence through lobbying or political action committees. Major causes such as protecting the environment or animal rights may have hundreds of separate organizations working on their behalf.

3. **Goals and Tactics.** A social movement has one or more goals or objectives that are clearly defined. These goals are reached through the use of tactics that vary depending on the cause and the goals. Tactics may include:

* Community action, such as setting up recycling programs.
* Voter registration programs.
* Letter-writing drives.
* Lobbying and political action groups.
* Direct action, including protests and civil disobedience.

The working members of social movements are called activists. An **activist** is one who engages in assertive, sometimes militant, action as a means of supporting or opposing a controversial issue.

Frequently, activism takes the form of civil disobedience. **Civil disobedience** is a form of nonviolent protest in which individuals or groups deliberately and publicly disobey a law they believe is unjust.

Although they are breaking a law, their behavior is not lawless. They respect laws and expect to be punished for breaking them. They resign themselves to the consequences for the sake of the opportunity to call public attention to an injustice.

Most social movements do not condone violence. On occasion, they have proved unable to prevent their supporters from resorting to violent acts. Further, when activists begin a civil action, there is no guarantee that other people, untrained in nonviolence, won't join them and engage in violent or unlawful behavior. This was the case in 2000 when people seeking to protest a meeting of the World Trade Organization in Seattle, Washington, attracted a large number of others who were mainly interested in provoking mayhem.

▲

A cartoonist questioned the motives of "protestors" at the Seattle meeting of the World Trade Organization.

Types of Social Movements

Social movements can be characterized by the type of change they promote. The following chart describes six major types of social movements.

Social Movements	
Type	**Characteristics**
Expressive	Aims at individuals rather than society. Encourages individuals to replace their behaviors with behaviors deemed more desirable. **EXAMPLES:** Alcoholics Anonymous, religious movements.
Progressive	Attempts to improve society by making positive changes in institutions and organizations. Advocates that society try new ways of doing things. **EXAMPLES:** Labor Movement, Civil Rights Movement.
Regressive/ Resistant	Responds to efforts at social change by trying to prevent change or by advocating a return of society to a previous state. Triggered by strong disapproval of social trends. **EXAMPLES:** Efforts to oppose affirmative action, feminism, and homosexual rights.
Reform	Attempts to make a major change to some aspect of society or politics without completely transforming it. Often attempts to gain rights and protection for some segment of society without changing other aspects. **EXAMPLES:** Efforts to end the death penalty, efforts to increase gun control, the consumer rights movement.
Revolutionary	Advocates a radical shift in the fundamental structure or practice of a society. Often involves violence. Arises when a segment of the population is strongly dissatisfied with the existing society. **EXAMPLES:** American Revolution, Bolshevik Revolution in Russia, Castro-led revolution in Cuba.
Utopian	Seeks to create an ideal social environment from an image of a perfect society. Rejects violence as a method to gain its goal. **EXAMPLES:** Puritan society in colonial America, counterculture movement of the 1960s and 1970s.

Social Movements

Three great U.S. social movements have produced widespread social change: the Labor Movement, the Civil Rights Movement, and the Women's Suffrage Movement. Smaller social movements have focused on:

* Abortion.
* Animal Rights.
* Black Power.
* Consumer Protection.
* Death Penalty.
* Drugs.
* Environmental Protection.
* Health Care.
* Nuclear Weapons.
* Peace.
* Pornography.
* School Busing.
* Smoking.
* Temperance.
* Welfare Rights.
* White Supremacy.
* Women's Liberation.

Perspectives on Social Movements

Sociologists who study social movements have **two** major explanations for how and why they become organized.

1. **Relative Deprivation Theory.** Social movements arise when people feel deprived relative to other people or to their own expectations of what society should provide. You might think that social movements would arise in societies experiencing poverty. In reality, they occur more often in fairly wealthy societies. Often, they occur in societies in which improvements underway are not moving as quickly as people believe they should. Therefore, the explanation is not that people are deprived, but that they are *relatively* deprived.

2. **Resource Mobilization Theory.** Social movements begin when deprived groups have found the resources to sustain organized action. Resources include money, facilities, leadership, influential contacts, and the people necessary to do the work.

There is some evidence that relative deprivation theory helps explain "crisis movements," such as those dealing with issues of race, poverty, or unemployment. Resource mobilization theory explains why the anti-slavery movement could not take place among the slaves themselves, but began when those with resources were moved to take action.

The Ruckus Society's Boot Camp for Activists

The Ruckus Society takes its name from the expression "to raise a ruckus." (A *ruckus* is a "noisy disturbance.") The society seeks to help environmental and human rights organizations achieve their goals. Since its beginning in 1995, the Ruckus Society has trained activists in the "arts and crafts" of nonviolent civil disobedience. At Ruckus Society Action Camps, activists are trained in:

* Nonviolent actions and protests.
* Scouting and planning civil action.
* Basic climbing skills for protest situations, such as tree sits, bridge blockades, and building climbs.
* Communication technology.
* How to set up blockades.
* Media techniques, such as "spin control," sound bites, and media delivery.
* How to create banners for specific site conditions.
* Political theater—humor, drama, and pageantry to enhance campaigns.

People don't all agree that such training is a good thing for society. Trained protestors have generated a fair amount of criticism. Some activists "protest for hire." Their actions don't reflect their personal beliefs. Rather, they work for any activist group that will pay them and spend their time moving from protest to protest.

Criteria for Success

The success of a social movement depends on leadership, loyalty, and social conditions.

Leadership

A successful leader must have the ability to involve masses of people in support of an ideology and a particular goal. She or he must have the ability to reach compromises among members with different views and to maintain a sense of cohesion within the movement.

Movements need charismatic leaders, such as Martin Luther King, Jr., who lead through their personal enthusiasm and dedication to the ideology of the movement. Such leaders help members take the belief system of the movement to heart.

They also need administrative leaders to tend to the practical matters of organization, such as recruitment, fund-raising, and public relations.

Loyalty

The loyalty and dedication of members in a successful movement are constantly reinforced through propaganda, slogans, speeches, and such artifacts as buttons or bumper stickers. If member interest wanes, achieving the goal of the movement is less likely.

Social Conditions

Conditions that tend to improve a movement's chances of success include widespread discontent, frustration, social disorganization, and financial or social insecurity. When other issues become more pressing than the one addressed by the movement, people may lose interest. When a major incident occurs, interest is revived.

Stages of a Social Movement

Although every social movement is different, sociologists have identified **four** stages common to their development:

1. **Emergence.** A relatively small group of activists stirred by a problem begins to agitate for action or change.
2. **Coalescence.** More individuals become interested and join together in an organized activity. In this stage:
   * A small leadership group emerges.
   * Goals and tactics are adopted.
   * Plans are made and action begins.
   * A rally or demonstration may be used to increase public awareness.
   * Organizations with common interests may join together to strengthen the movement.
3. **Bureaucratization.** A hierarchical structure emerges among the leaders and the active members. Now the organization takes on the characteristics of a bureaucracy:
   * Participants take on specialized roles.
   * Rules become more extensive.
   * These changes add to the strength of the organization, but may also drain off some of the momentum.

Across **Cultures**

Social Movements in China

Mao Zedong, leader of the Chinese Communist Party (CCP), gained the support of 600 million Chinese by promising protection of human rights, equal distribution of land and profits, and a prosperous future. Mao understood the power of social movements. The CCP sponsored dozens of groups, including the All-China Federation of Democratic Youth and the All-China Federation of Trade Unions, to teach CCP ideology and keep the revolutionary movement alive.

Forty years later, a social movement emerged that did not have CCP support. While socialism had produced some improvement in economic conditions, the people were frustrated. Human rights violations were common.

In April 1989, Hu Yaobang, a former general secretary of the CCP, died. Hu had become a hero to Chinese students by refusing to stop demonstrations in 1987. To honor him, students began peaceful memorial demonstrations in several cities.

These demonstrations grew into a prodemocracy movement. Protesters demanded the removal of China's Communist leaders. The government ordered the demonstrations to stop, but they continued. On May 20, the government declared martial law. Troops marched to Tiananmen Square in Beijing, where protesters had erected a statue called the Goddess of Democracy. It resembled the Statue of Liberty. On June 3 and 4, the People's Liberation Army killed hundreds of demonstrators, injured another 10,000, and arrested hundreds of students and workers. The reform movement was squashed.

In 2000, when the CCP celebrated the Republic of China's 50th anniversary, there were no major incidents. While China has acknowledged to the international community that human rights are important and has taken steps to improve its record, "serious problems remain," says the U.S. State Department.

4. **Decline** The end of the social movement can take place in several ways:

* The movement accomplishes its goals, and members see no point in continuing their efforts. This was the case with the Women's Suffrage Movement.
* The movement fails, and members leave.
* The leadership is "co-opted" by those in power. When this happens, the movement loses its ability to enact change and can no longer be effective.
* Factions develop within the organization, dividing the attention of members and weakening the overall effort.
* Members lose interest in the movement's goals.

* The movement becomes so accepted by society that the group becomes a social institution. This happened to the NAACP with the success of the Civil Rights Movement.

Look to the Future

Some sociologists believe that issues in U.S. society will continue to be addressed through numerous single-issue social movements. But the technology of movements will certainly change. Recent years have seen the Internet being used to plan "spontaneous" demonstrations at events.

How effective are social movements in forcing social change? In the next chapter, we'll explore that topic.

Chapter 15 Wrap-up
COLLECTIVE BEHAVIOR AND SOCIAL MOVEMENTS

Collective behavior consists of the relatively short-lived actions, emotions, and thoughts that occur spontaneously in a group of people. This behavior may be restrained, such as the behavior of crowds at lectures or the theater, or it may be the unruly and sometimes illegal violence that erupts in a mob.

In mass behavior, people in various locations are moved by some stimulus to behave in the same way. Fads, fashions, rumors, and urban myths are examples of mass behavior.

Many groups try to influence popular (or public) opinion. Propaganda and the mass media are often used for this purpose.

Social movements are an organized form of collective behavior. Social movements are characterized by having an ideology, goals and tactics, and organizational leadership. Two theories have been proposed to explain social movements, the relative deprivation theory and the resource mobilization theory.

activist—person who engages in assertive, sometimes militant, action as a means of supporting or opposing an issue. *p. 291*

civil disobedience—form of protest in which laws are deliberately and publicly disobeyed out of a belief that they are unjust. *p. 291*

collective behavior—actions, thoughts, and emotions that occur almost simultaneously within a collectivity. *p. 284*

collectivity—unstructured collection of individuals with no assigned roles or organized authority who temporarily engage in activity together. *p. 284*

deindividuation—individual's loss of a sense of individuality. It is characterized by loss of self-awareness, sense of reduced responsibility, and decreased concern about how others view one's behavior. *p. 287*

propaganda—information designed to manipulate public opinion and to influence people to change their beliefs in a particular way. *p. 289*

social movement—collective effort to bring about social or political change. *p. 290*

Social Change

In this chapter, you will learn about:

- **modern and traditional societies**
- **theories of social change**
- **factors that influence social change**

The time: Imagine the beginning of the 21st century, anywhere in the world. Joanie is feeling a bit bored and a little lonely, too, if the truth be told. She sits at her computer, cruising the information highway and looking for something that will pique her interest. Suddenly, she has an idea. She will start her own country! She'll declare herself President—or Monarch—or Dictator—and make up all the rules. Then she'll invite people to become citizens of her country. What fun!

As bizarre as the idea sounds, it's something that is already happening. Virtual communities are springing up every day. How will these societies influence "real" societies with "real" geographies, economies, politics, and citizens? How will this social change mix with other social changes?

This chapter explores how and why social change occurs. Various theories of social change and the factors that influence it are examined. Finally, the roles people might play as society moves into the future are explored.

Explaining Social Change

Social change occurs when there is a significant shift in the patterns of social and cultural behavior, relationships, institutions, and systems.

Change in a world where there are more than 6 billion individuals is clearly complex. Sociologists have a number of different approaches to understanding how and why social change takes place.

Traditional and Modern Societies

Much social change has taken place as societies have moved from traditional ways of life to the highly technological ways of the modern world.

Traditional Societies

Society in much of the developing world is traditional. In the agricultural communities, life is based on the rhythmic cycles of nature such as day and night and the changing seasons of the year. Spiritual values and cooperation among community members keep the society functioning smoothly. Ancestors and families are also important. People tend to look to the past for wisdom rather than to modern experts. Daily work is done as it has always been done. Decisions are made based on tradition.

In most of these societies, people have little opportunity to improve their lives economically. When goods are traded, the trade is part of the personal relationships between those who make the exchange. A traditional society tends to remain unchanged over long periods of time.

Modern Society

A modern society, in sociological terms, is one that has moved from an agricultural to an industrial focus. Its time orientation is linear and progressive rather than cyclical. Values of efficiency and productivity are added. Formal organizations rather than family units predominate. There is a rational-scientific basis to decision making.

Modernization is the process of change from a traditional to a modern society. Some sociologists argue that modern societies have lost tradition and with it the feeling that members are a part of something larger and have the ability to live in harmony with nature. However, societies such as India and Japan have undergone significant modernization and yet have maintained and, in some cases, strengthened, their traditional cultures.

Types of Social Change

Social change can be examined by asking questions such as:

* What are the differences between the original society and the one into which it has changed?
* When societies change, do they become more like each other or more different?
* What is the difference between large, systemwide changes and smaller, more rapid social changes?

Each of these questions has been addressed by sociologists.

Convergence or Divergence

As traditional societies become more industrialized, do they become like modern societies? **Two** theories pose opposite answers:

1. **Convergence** theorists say modernization will eventually erase cultural differences. Societies will come together—will converge—to produce a global society. They argue that norms and values change with major changes in technology and that exposure to Western technology and lifestyles will cause non-Western cultures to adopt Western values. They see the leadership in developing countries changing and expect that those who understand new technologies will gain economic advantages and will become a new "elite."

2. **Divergence** theorists point to the growing conflicts between Western and non-Western cultures. They argue that modernization will not override cultural differences. They note the ways in which some Muslim societies protect their culture from Western influence. In Saudi Arabia, for example, movies and dancing are forbidden, Western publications are censored, and Islamic law is rigidly enforced. Some countries reject the idea of a "global village" and see the incursion of Western fast-food franchises and theme parks as a form of "cultural imperialism."

Societies that are not hostile to the West, such as South Korea and Taiwan, however, have modernized and yet retained their unique cultures. They are very different societies from ours.

Macro- versus Micro- Social Change

Macro-change characterizes the gradual alterations in a society as it shifts from simple to more complex. These changes affect the entire society and occur over one or more generations. Some examples of macro-changes include:

* The shift from hunter-gatherer societies to agricultural societies.
* Industrialization.
* Modernization.
* The shift from an industrial economy to an information and services economy.

Micro-changes occur within small social institutions such as the family or a business. They are based on day-to-day situations. Although they may appear insignificant, these changes accumulate and eventually affect society as a whole. One example is the use of personal computers, which started very slowly in the 1970s. Today, at least in the Western world, it may be difficult for a person not to use something created or controlled by computer technology.

Some people look forward to change, and others fear it. Every society changes in its own way and its own time; it cannot help but move toward its future. The culture, traditions, and institutions currently in place in a given society both enable and limit the types of social change that can occur. In a country such as the United States where there is freedom of speech, social movements arise much more easily than in countries where it is dangerous to speak against the government or important people.

Theories of
Social Change

The sociological perspectives you have been studying have application to macro-change at the societal level because it encompasses change in all social institutions. Sociologists have developed a number of specific theories to describe how and why social change occurs.

Functionalist Perspective

Functionalists assert that changes in society take place to maintain harmony in the social order. Society shifts in whatever way is necessary to maintain balance or equilibrium and stay on course. These changes take place gradually.

Functionalists use **three** different metaphors to further explain these changes:

1. **Functional Evolution.**
   Influenced by Darwin's theory of evolution, early sociologists proposed that societies evolve through stages from simple to complex. Such change is a **unilinear process**—one that "progresses" in one direction through stages, such as savagery, barbarism, and civilization.

   Auguste Comte referred to these stages as:
   * *Theological:* Society is governed by spiritual explanations and such notions as the divine right of kings.

* *Metaphysical:* Such concepts as the social contract, the equality of persons, and popular sovereignty describe people's relationship to government.
* *Positivist:* People take a scientific approach to political organization. Comte envisioned the ultimate society governed by a scientific elite using the methods of science to solve human problems and improve social conditions. He argued that this final stage was the most evolved, the ultimate stage of human development.

Herbert Spencer argued that the survival of societies, as well as that of organisms, depended on their ability to adapt to a changing environment. Spencer believed that industrialized societies were better adapted to 19th-century conditions, and therefore were more "advanced." Spencer also supported the idea that more "civilized" societies had a moral duty to help more "primitive" societies advance.

Ferdinand Tönnies disagreed that industrialization was the ultimate stage of development. Modern societies might offer people more opportunities and material wealth, but these benefits are offset by an increased sense of isolation and powerlessness that could lead to disenchantment and the decline of the society.

Emile Durkheim argued that economic competition could lead to chaos. According to Durkheim, society would evolve from mechanical to organic solidarity. This transformation would maintain social order.

Neo-evolutionists have replaced the simplistic linear progression of society from one stage to the next with a more complex evolutionary theory. **Neo-evolutionary theory** argues that:

* The level of social complexity increases with the degree of **social differentiation:** As family, politics, economy, and religion become increasingly separate entities, society becomes more complex.

* There are many different ways in which society can develop and change. There is no "ultimate" state that is superior to others.

* **Gerhard and Jean Lenski** suggest that, rather than being a "natural" process through which all societies become transformed, social change is precipitated by such external forces as technology, population changes, and new ideologies.

* Change does not necessarily mean improvement.

2. **Cyclical Theory.**

Other functionalists describe social change as moving through cycles, not proceeding on a straight line.

Oswald Spengler, a German historian, believed that societies, like organisms, go through cycles of birth, adolescence, maturity, old age, and eventual death. He found examples to support his ideas in the decline and fall of the great empires of Rome, Greece, and Egypt.

Although sociologists found Spengler's ideas lacking in scientific proof, his cyclical theory influenced later theoreticians.

Arnold Toynbee, a British historian, agreed with the idea of the rise and fall of societies, but disagreed that such movements were part of a natural process. Toynbee proposed that social change resulted from environmental challenges. The way in which people dealt with the challenges influenced the direction in which the society moved. Toynbee suggested that the severity of the challenge is important. For example, when food is plentiful, the challenge is mild, humans can become complacent, and civilization declines. However, a severe food shortage may either strengthen or destroy the civilization. Toynbee argued that a moderate challenge produced the greatest stimulation to growth and change.

We cannot measure the severity of a challenge until it is over. Nonetheless, many sociologists feel Toynbee's theory helps people understand past events.

▲
The End of Roman Civilization

Pitirim Sorokin, a Russian sociologist, theorized that society fluctuates between two opposing forms of culture. Similar to the traditional and modern society and the first and last of Comte's stages, the forms are:

* **Ideational culture**, in which faith or religion is the source of knowledge, and people value a spiritual life.
* **Sensate culture**, in which scientific evidence is the source of knowledge, and people value a practical, materialistic life.

Sorokin introduced a new concept, the **principle of imminent change**—the idea that a shift from one form of culture to another occurs when sufficient forces build within the society itself. Like Toynbee's theory, Sorokin's is more easily applied "after the fact."

3. **Equilibrium Theory.**
Rather than describing social change as linear or cyclical, one U.S. sociologist theorized that change occurs in an effort to keep balance within the society.

Talcott Parsons pointed to the importance of social institutions in the change process. According to his **equilibrium theory**, every institution in society has specific functions. Because the institutions are interdependent, a change in one evokes changes in the others in order to maintain the equilibrium of the society.

Parsons proposed that society, rather than shifting from one extreme to the other or through various stages, is constantly seeking balance.

EXAMPLE: Rising prices in the economic sector cause a shift in family structure as both parents seek employment. This in turn produces a need for more child-care services. The government gets involved through tax benefits and increased services. Similar changes in various social institutions occur in a constant attempt to maintain a harmonious social order.

Critics of equilibrium theory say that, while it takes an integrated look at the roles played by various social institutions, it doesn't explain revolutionary change. In addition, it tends to characterize societies as more stable and harmonious than they really are.

Conflict Perspective

Rather than focusing on the harmonious functioning of society and its institutions, conflict theorists emphasize the role of conflict, tension, and strain as sources of social change. These arise among individuals, groups, states, and, particularly, among social classes.

Karl Marx shared some of the ideas of the functionalists in explaining social change. He agreed that:

* Societies have to adapt to a changing world to survive.
* Social change is linear, proceeding in one direction.
* Societies move from simple to complex—in his model, from a class to a classless society.

Marx's Theory of Revolutionary Change

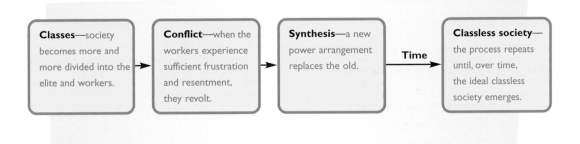

The diagram above describes how Marx thought the evolution to a classless society would occur.

Marx wrote in the mid-1800s. He did not anticipate the rise of a large middle class or the ways in which governments have worked to improve the status of workers. Later conflict theorists broadened Marx's approach by adding social conflicts, such as conflicts over race and religion, to the economic conflict that interested Marx.

Interactionist Perspective

Interactionists view social change in terms of how people's self-images and social interactions change as a result of major shifts in society.

In a traditional society, self-image and roles are determined by an individual's family, ancestors, and the collective needs of the society. Because little value is placed on acquiring power or wealth, the way people interact is natural and informal, as in primary groups (see Chapter 3).

In a modern society, where individual achievement is a fundamental value, people are expected to define their own roles. There is more uncertainty than in a traditional society, so people may be less self-confident. Their interactions outside of close friends and family are tentative and more formal.

The change from an industrial to an information-based society has raised new issues of identity and created new ways to interact. New tools, such as computers and the Internet, hold much interest for interactionist sociologists. The social networks open to individuals with access to these have no national borders. Communicating across age, gender, and social class barriers is facilitated because we cannot "see" the people we chat with or send e-mail messages to. New symbols are added to our language.

Will these tools break down social barriers? Most certainly they will. Will people erect new ones? Many sociologists worry that the biggest barrier is the economic one that keeps such tools out of the reach of many.

Virtual Communities

Worldwide, at any hour of the day or night, over 100,000 people are "talking" on-line. The Internet gives sociologists a laboratory for studying society in the making.

The Internet allows people to create their own social environments. For some, the fact that others in the community don't know who they "really" are is important. They use nicknames. They create themselves anew.

For others, the opportunity to connect with others who share a particular passion or need is their goal. Parents of a child with a disease so rare there are only 20 others in the country can find each other on the Internet. They can share ideas about how to cope with the problems their children face undergoing treatment. They can give each other moral support.

Virtual communities arise around issues, ideas, and common interests. Hobbyists discuss tools and techniques, activists organize social movements, scientists discuss their latest findings, and game players take part in ongoing tournaments. Just as in "real" society, friendships are maintained, power struggles and reasoned arguments take place. Norms have developed to control those who abuse the medium.

The emerging culture responds to the same pressures and achieves the same successes and failures as any other culture.

Because a virtual community can change rapidly, interactionists find it a useful tool for investigating society.

Comparing Perspectives

Each sociological perspective on social change offers insight into particular types of change. Each also has its limitations:

* Evolutionary theory provides little help in understanding internal social changes, such as political changes.
* Cyclical theories apply to many Western cultures but less well to societies in other parts of the world.
* Functionalist theories focus on stability and tend to ignore conflict.
* Conflict theories focus almost exclusively on economic strain and ignore other factors, such as technology.
* Interactionist theory provides little help in understanding macro-changes.

Several theorists have attempted to integrate the views, such as introducing tensions into the functionalist perspectives or describing the functions of conflict. As yet, no comprehensive theory of social change has emerged.

Causes of Social Change

A variety of factors influence change. Natural disasters produce unplanned changes. Technological change can totally transform society. Economic factors can produce fads, which are short-term, or the rise of capitalism, which is a relatively permanent change.

The Physical Environment

The economy and much of the culture of a society are shaped by its geography. If something happens to change the physical environment, the society must change in response. Floods, hurricanes, tornadoes, and earthquakes all have the potential to destroy the economy of a society. Cities, such as the ancient Greco-Roman city of Pompeii, have been eliminated by natural disaster.

Global warming is of concern to society in general. If, as some predict, Earth's atmosphere warms sufficiently to melt polar ice, sea levels will rise and coastal communities will be destroyed. Natural habitats will change, and some species will not survive. Changes in temperature will result in changes in precipitation and growing seasons. Such changes will affect the trade of food and other resources among countries and have the potential to influence the population of the entire planet, not just single communities or societies.

Population Changes

Rapid changes in population size or make-up can place great pressure on society to change. There are **four** main demographic events that can lead to change.

1. **Population Growth.** Depending on the wealth and resources of a society, population growth can produce anything from a great weakening of society to rapid social improvements.
   EXAMPLES: The rapid growth in population in Bangladesh combined with the country's inability to produce sufficient food led to the starvation of millions of people. The baby boom in the United States during the 1940s led to an expansion of educational facilities.

2. **Loss of Population.** Decreasing population or population growth that is too slow may threaten a society because there are too few workers to perform the necessary jobs.
   EXAMPLE: In Montana, there are few opportunities for technological employment in many communities. Graduates interested in those positions have to move to find jobs. As a result, the communities cannot attract many businesses because they lack a skilled work force.

3. **Migration.** Movement of people forces changes in social institutions.
   EXAMPLE: The immigration of workers and their families from Mexico to the United States has increased pressure on U.S. institutions, such as schools. It has also challenged norms regarding the status and rights of illegal aliens. The

question of whether or not such individuals should be granted driver's licenses, for instance, is debated as society questions whether public safety is not more important than immigration law.

4. **Age Distribution Change.** An increase in the number of older or younger people in society can shift the emphasis of social programs.

   EXAMPLE: In the United States, changing age demographics have made Social Security and the cost of health care hot topics in political campaigns.

Social Structure

Conflict among competing members of society can lead to social change. The revolutionary wars in France and Russia arose out of conflicts between social classes. Following the wars, both societies changed radically.

In the United States, a social structure that included slaves was the argument over which the Civil War was fought. Out of it came major social change—no one was enslaved any longer; former slaves and their descendants moved into all strata of society.

Other changes growing out of conflict between groups occupying different places in the social structure include the gains won by the Women's Suffrage Movement and the Civil Rights Movement. While the social structure works to perpetuate itself, in democracies, severe strain among different groups generally leads to social change.

The Role of Technology

Since the invention of the wheel and the discovery of fire, technology has been responsible for tremendous social change. In just the 20th century, the world accessible to humans grew to the moon and beyond.

The invention of the automobile transformed society, enabling people to work at a distance from their homes and to develop social relationships with those whom they otherwise might never have met.

Other technological developments that created pervasive social change include the:

* Printing press.
* Cotton gin.
* Steam engine.
* Camera.
* Assembly line.
* Electricity.
* Telegraph and telephone.
* Airplane.
* Nuclear reactor.
* Television.
* Computer.

New technologies in genetic engineering, wireless communication, biotechnology, and electronics offer the promise (or the threat) of even more profound changes. Potential changes range from the ability to feed more people and improve health to having a society where corporations know the brand-name preferences of every citizen and governmental agencies know their whereabouts at all times.

How the Axe Changed a Society

Sometimes, it takes a very small advance in technology to create a very large social change.

The first white people who encountered the aborigines of Australia were amazed at the hard stone axes they produced. The stone came from only one area, and the men controlled the making and use of the axes, passing the knowledge down from father to son.

When the missionaries gave the aborigines steel axes, the women no longer needed to ask permission to use an axe. They could have their own axes. As a result, men lost both power and status in the society.

Modernization and Economic Development

The economic development that brings modernization is ongoing in the developing countries of the world. Different theorists have tried to explain what is needed for the process to work successfully:

* *Modernization theorists* say that developing countries need democratic institutions, money for development, and an economic system that encourages personal initiative among its citizens. All these are lacking in many countries.

* *Dependency theorists* maintain that the industrialized nations of the world must take responsibility for improving conditions in the developing countries. They argue that the success of industrialized countries has come at the expense of poorer countries. Resources were taken and cheap labor was exploited, first from the colonialism of the 19th and early 20th centuries and later through the activities of big businesses.

* *Marxist theorists* focus on the class structure of developing countries and the appropriation of resources by the dominant class. Often, those in charge use a community's resources for their own personal gain. When the resources of a country are not properly used, the society stagnates and fails to modernize.

Human Action

Another factor in social change is the actions of individuals, either alone or in groups. In the history of the world, there have been any number of individuals who played a very large role in social change:

* Julius Caesar.
* Harriet Beecher Stowe.
* Karl Marx.
* Adolph Hitler.
* Martin Luther King, Jr.
* Add your favorites here.

While recognizing their contributions to social change, sociologists maintain that such individuals were products of their social and cultural environments. Their actions may have gone unnoticed had other factors not been present in society. The American patriot Patrick Henry stirred people with his "Give me liberty or give me death!" speech when the colonies were on the brink of war. Many found him a downright nuisance during peacetime. Revolutionary social change requires some major strain in the fabric of society.

Social movements are a major factor in social change. From revolutions to activism on local issues, collective action works to change society. Social change, like any activity humans engage in together, takes leaders. But it would not happen without the group of people who together share a different vision of society.

The Processes of Social Change

Sociologist William Ogburn proposed **three** processes that produce change:

1. **Invention** occurs when existing elements are combined to provide new ones. Invention is not only technological. Social inventions include bureaucracies and corporations.

2. **Discovery** involves a new way of seeing reality. Discovery produces social change only when other conditions are right. Viking Leif Eriksson's "discovery" of the North American continent preceded Columbus, but Viking settlements disappeared and the native populations remained largely unchanged. Not until Columbus did the huge transformation we call the Columbian Exchange begin to take place.

3. **Diffusion** is the spread of an invention or discovery throughout society. Diffusion also includes the spread of ideas, values, and social institutions. Ogburn maintained that cultural and social institutions in a society are slower to change than technology. He called this "cultural lag."

We can look at the introduction of the computer into the social institution of education to see an example of how cultural change lags behind technological change. While educators were quick to put computers into the schools, the uses of those computers mirrored the way teaching was traditionally done. Computers were primarily used for drill and practice. Computer

An End to Privacy?

People have grown accustomed to seeing security cameras in stores and remotely controlled cameras in offices. Such surveillance makes some people feel more secure. However, few people realize the degree to which personal privacy has become a thing of the past—thanks to technology.

* Grocery chains determine your buying habits when you check out. If you use a store's membership card to get discounts on your purchases, chances are good the store will sell information about you to other businesses.
* If you make a donation to a candidate for a national office or to a political action committee, your name, address, employer, and job title are by law reported to the Federal Election Commission and are published on their web site. Right-to-privacy advocates point out this information could be abused by an employer in making hiring or promotion decisions.
* When you cruise the web, the sites you visit are monitored and recorded. The next time you're on, ads pop up for products in which your "profile" suggests you are interested. If you actually register on a site, you have released even more information about yourself into the public domain.

The people who develop and use these technologies argue that they are providing services or acting in the public interest. There is no guarantee, however, that the technology won't be used by less scrupulous people. Hackers who have broken into highly secured government and business computers have shown us how difficult it is to protect our privacy.

classes involved programming and such basic skills as how to use a mouse, a word-processing program, or floppy disks. The unique possibilities the computer offered to the process of learning—as a tool to let students investigate the world outside the classroom, as a tool to use in developing interactive projects, as a tool for exchanges with students and others around the world—were not tapped until much later.

The Future Is Now

When it comes to social change, the future is now. Ethnic conflicts in the Balkans, environmental movements in the United States, and unrest in other parts of the world are all evidence of ongoing change.

As societies modernize, people become more focused on individual rights. The news is filled with demands for:

* Human rights.
* Civil rights.
* Criminals' rights.
* Victims' rights.
* The rights of the unborn.
* Children's rights.
* The right not to go hungry.
* The right to strike.
* The right of free speech.
* Nonsmokers' rights.
* The right to own assault weapons.
* The right to privacy.

Any list of rights should be accompanied by a discussion of the responsibilities of individuals to their communities, to their countries, and to future generations.

The choices that people make today cannot help but influence the future. Among those choices is the role that each of us will play in society.

Individuals play **four** different roles in social change.

1. **Supporters** actively participate in social movements, from taking on leadership roles to volunteering their services, making contributions, engaging in letter writing, and helping with fund-raising.

2. **Resisters** oppose changes that violate their value systems or that threaten their present sense of security. They may use any of the same methods that supporters use.

3. **Passives** have no interest in change, but they do not actively fight it either. They are generally satisfied with society as it is. They ignore the processes of change that occur around them.

4. **Adaptives** are also indifferent to change and have neither strong resistance nor strong support for it. However, unlike passives, they do not ignore it; they adapt to it. They "go with the flow."

For some people, only a direct attack on their values or an event that threatens their personal sense of well being can trigger their involvement in social change. Others have a highly developed social conscience and take a global view of change. They recognize their role in the larger society and are willing to get involved, even when they have no obvious personal stake in an issue. What role will you play in creating the society of the future? The choice is yours.

Something to Think About

If the 600 million people in the world are represented by a group of 100 people, then:

* 60 are Asian.
* 12 are Europeans.
* 5 are North American.
* 8 are from Latin America.
* 13 are Africans.

The April 1997 issue of *Women's Press* reported further that:

* 51 are females, 49 are males.
* 70 are non-white.

* 70 are non-Christian; 30 are Christian.
* 17 live in industrialized countries.
* 6 individuals control 50 percent of the world's wealth—all Americans.
* The richest 20 would consume 86 percent of the world's goods and services.
* The poorest 20 would consume about 1.3 percent of the world's goods and services.
* 70 are unable to read.
* 50 suffer from malnutrition.
* 1 is near death and 1 is about to be born.
* And only 1 would have a college education.

Chapter 16 Wrap-up
SOCIAL CHANGE

Societies are constantly in a state of change, although not at the same rate or in the same direction. Types of social change include convergence, divergence, macro-change, and micro-change. Sociologists have proposed a number of theories to explain how change occurs, including functionalist theories—evolutionary, cyclical, equilibrium; conflict theories of social and economic tensions; and the interactionist theories that examine individual roles and relationships.

Social change is influenced by the physical environment, population shifts, conflict, technology, and economics as well as by individuals and groups.

convergence theory —sociological theory that through modernization societies will come together and be more alike than they were before it. *p. 301*

divergence theory —sociological theory that modernization will not override cultural differences. *p. 301*

equilibrium theory —Talcott Parsons's theory that social change is a result of the interdependence of social institutions. *p. 304*

ideational culture —culture with faith or religion as the source of knowledge. People value a spiritual life. *p. 304*

macro-change —gradual alterations in an entire society that take place as it shifts from simple to more complex. Macro-change takes place over several generations. *p. 301*

micro-change —change within small social institutions, such as the family or a business. Cumulatively, micro-changes affect society as a whole. *p. 301*

modernization —process of change from a traditional to a modern society. *p. 300*

neo-evolutionary theory —sociological theory about how societies become more complex with an increase in social differentiation. *p. 303*

principle of imminent change —Pitirim Sorokin's idea that a shift from one form of culture to another occurs when sufficient forces build within the society itself. *p. 304*

sensate culture —culture where scientific evidence is the source of knowledge. People value a practical and materialistic life. *p. 304*

social change —significant shift in the patterns of social and cultural behavior, relationships, institutions, and systems. *p. 300*

social differentiation —in functionalist neo-evolutionary theory, the increasing specialization of different systems within a society that occurs with modernization. Thus the institution of family becomes separate from that of the world of work, for instance. *p. 303*

unilinear process —change that proceeds in one direction through different stages. *p. 302*

SKILLS

"Back of its use [sociological imagination] there is always the urge to know the social and historical meaning of the individual in the society and in the period in which he has his quality and his being."

—C. Wright Mills
The Sociological Imagination, *1959*

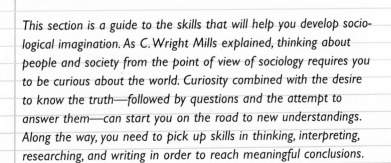

This section is a guide to the skills that will help you develop socio-logical imagination. As C. Wright Mills explained, thinking about people and society from the point of view of sociology requires you to be curious about the world. Curiosity combined with the desire to know the truth—followed by questions and the attempt to answer them—can start you on the road to new understandings. Along the way, you need to pick up skills in thinking, interpreting, researching, and writing in order to reach meaningful conclusions.

Thinking and Interpreting Critically

Good sociology students have a special "mindset" when they study society, groups, and individual interactions. Developing the mindset begins with an issue or social question about which you really want to know more. This interest in social questions can come from almost anywhere. For example, you may have a friend who surprises you by getting a tattoo. Then another friend gets one, and so on, until several of your friends have tattoos. You could just shrug your shoulders and not think much about it.

But the sociology student would begin to ask questions. Why did so many students begin getting tattoos at the same time? How is modern tattooing different from tattooing in the past? Does tattooing have different meanings to different people? All these questions reflect a curiosity and a desire to understand a social truth—a sociological "mindset." Once you begin to ask sociological questions, you must find evidence to answer them and interpret your findings. This depends on objective thinking.

Objective Thinking

Objective thinking requires that you look at a sociological phenomenon from the outside in. That doesn't mean that you should take a "cold" approach to human interactions. It just means that it is important to recognize personal feelings and put them aside enough to consider other possibilities. For example, say you are riding on a train, and you observe an African-American passenger in an argument with a white conductor. Your subjective self may immediately assume that the conductor is a racist and is picking on the passenger. The mindset of sociology requires you to put the assumption aside and consider other possible reasons for the argument. Your original reaction may be correct, but your conclusion will be based on a deeper understanding of the interaction.

Objective thinking may be divided into **two** categories:

1. **Inductive thinking** is reasoning from particular instances to general principles. This type of thinking allows you to identify broad societal patterns based on specific observations.
   EXAMPLE: You may observe that a friend's parents get a divorce. A few months later another friend's parents get a divorce. Then you may think about how many friends' parents have divorced over the past several years. Inductive thinking will lead you from specific families to a general principle: Divorce is a pattern in modern U.S. society. Careful observers do not identify general principles until they have seen enough particular instances to justify calling a behavior a pattern.

2. **Deductive thinking** is reasoning from the general to the particular. A person with a broad question may go in search of specific evidence to answer it.
   EXAMPLE: You may wonder if people who live on farms lead deeper spiritual lives than city dwellers. A deductive thinker would look for ways to measure

spiritual depth and then set about looking for specific attitudes of particular people to either support or refute the broad question.

The thing to remember about both types of objective thinking is that they try to make a connection between the individual and the broad societal influence—a characteristic of the sociological imagination.

Interpreting Graphics

Social observations are often reflected in cartoons or compiled into graphs, maps, and tables. They combine words, numbers, and drawings to help communicate how sets of information relate to one another. The ability to interpret—and create—graphics can help you come to thoughtful conclusions about patterns of behavior in society.

Graphs

Graphs summarize information by combining text with drawings and/or lines.

Two skills are involved in using a graph: reading and interpreting. Careful reading of a graph simply means that you understand the information presented. The most important part of using a graph is interpreting it. What does it mean? How does it increase your understanding of an issue?

The graph at right is a bar graph, which uses "bars" or columns to represent people, places, or things. A bar graph is often used to compare quantities.

Growth of Population 65+

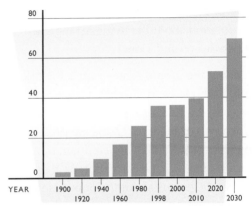

Source: U.S. Bureau of the Census (1998)

Reading the graph. Always study *all* the parts of a graph carefully. Start by looking at the title of the graph. It tells you the subject and helps frame the information. Be sure to look at information measured vertically and horizontally. What do the numbers on the left mean? Look at the words on the graph for the clue. The numbers represent millions of people 65 and older. Look at the numbers going horizontally across the bottom of the graph, and notice that they represent years from 1900 to 2030. The graph measures the numbers of older people at ten different points in time, including projections into the future.

Interpreting the graph. What does the graph tell us about older people as a group? Clearly, their numbers increased significantly during the 20th century. But what is even more striking are the projections for the future. What implications does this information have for society? Who could use it and how?

The graphs below are pie charts. A pie chart is a particularly effective way to show percentages or proportions, like portions of a real pie. These pie charts give us information about the living arrangements of persons 65 and older.

Reading the graph. Again, notice the title first. Each pie chart also has a legend, or a text-based guide, to explain the diagrams. When two or more diagrams are presented together, be sure that you compare the information. What information do these pie charts give us about the population of older people?

Interpreting the graph. Notice the differences between the pie charts for men and women. What are some possible reasons for the differences? What implications does the information have for society?

Maps

Map skills are useful not just for studying history, geography, and politics. Reading and interpreting maps can help develop the sociological imagination as well. The two maps opposite give us information about the distribution of older U.S. residents.

Living Arrangements of People 65+

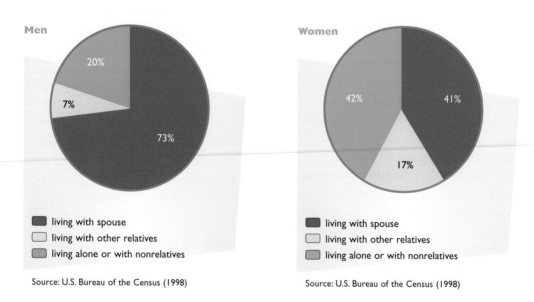

Men

20%

7%

73%

☐ living with spouse
☐ living with other relatives
☐ living alone or with nonrelatives

Source: U.S. Bureau of the Census (1998)

Women

42%

41%

17%

☐ living with spouse
☐ living with other relatives
☐ living alone or with nonrelatives

Source: U.S. Bureau of the Census (1998)

Both are political maps. In other words, they show us boundaries drawn by the government. These maps show us states. Read the titles and legends carefully. How are the two maps different? How do you interpret the information? What are the implications for the states and for U.S. society as a whole?

Percent Increase 65+

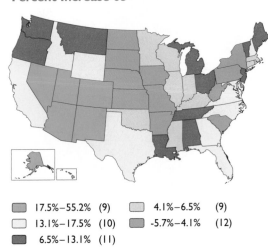

	17.5%–55.2% (9)		4.1%–6.5% (9)
	13.1%–17.5% (10)		-5.7%–4.1% (12)
	6.5%–13.1% (11)		

Source: U.S. Bureau of the Census (1998)

Percent 65+ by State

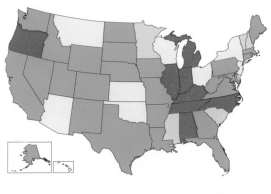

	13.7%–18.4% (14)		12.0%–6.5% (5)
	13.2%–13.7% (9)		5.4%–12.0% (14)
	12.4%–13.2% (9)		

Source: U.S. Bureau of the Census (1998)

Tables

A table organizes words and numbers so that the observer can see how they relate to each other. The table below summarizes income information about older people in the United States.

Family Income Distribution, 65+

Family Income Distribution, 65+	
Under $10,000	6%
$10,000–$14,999	8%
$15,000–$24,999	23%
$25,000–$34,999	19%
$35,000–$49,999	18%
$50,000–$74,000	13%
$75,000 and over	13%

Source: U.S. Bureau of the Census (1998)

What information does the table give you about the incomes of older people? How do you interpret the information? What implications does this information have for U.S. society and for the future? What other information might help you better understand this table?

Cartoons

Cartoons are meant to be funny, of course. But they also have more serious purposes, particularly when they address social and political issues. They are a good medium for the cartoonist to express a point of view, often much more effectively than in prose. The cartoon here makes some comments about older people.

Cartoons are often much more sophisticated than they appear to be at first glance. This cartoon came out when the 77-year-old former astronaut (and senator) John Glenn made a return voyage into space. Carefully study *everything* the cartoonist draws and says. A good cartoon will include many subtleties that not only make it funnier, but serve to increase the power of the social comments. What is Pat Oliphant (the cartoonist) saying about attitudes of older and younger people in the United States?

Graphs, maps, tables, and cartoons are rich sources of information about society and groups within it. If you develop your skills with all of them, you can combine information that each provides so that your observations become more thoughtful and accurate. For example, think about the combination of graphs, maps, tables, and cartoons you have just seen. All address characteristics of older people. You could use them for many purposes—family and class discussions, essay writing, and perhaps doing your own research project.

Oliphant by Pat Oliphant

Determining Cause and Effect

Understanding the relationship between cause and effect is an important thinking skill in sociology. Suppose that you observe two *social facts*—activities or situations—that occur at the same time. Imagine that you observe more police cars patrolling in poor city neighborhoods than in well-to-do areas. First, of course, you would want to be sure that your observation is correct.

Then, as sociologists do, you would begin to think about two *variables* (social facts that may change): income levels in neighborhoods and the amount of police patrolling. Does one cause the other? You might speculate that the *independent variable* is the income level and the *dependent variable* (which changes according to the independent variable) is the amount of police patrolling. In other words, the "poorness" of the neighborhood causes the police to patrol more frequently (the effect).

The biggest problem with cause and effect is that the relationship can be very complicated. Think about the example above. Sociological curiosity could lead you to ask, "*Why* do police patrol more in poor neighborhoods?"

You may speculate that the police are acting on previous experience—more crimes have occurred in poor neighborhoods in the past. Or there could be some geographical factor that you don't know about. Or the patrolling levels could be caused by a societal desire to protect poor people or a bias against poor people.

Investigating cause and effect must be combined with objective thinking in order to reach conclusions that will deepen your social understanding. Especially in seeking the less obvious, more long-term root causes, objective thinking allows you to think of possibilities beyond your own opinions.

Recognizing Bias

A *bias* is a tendency or inclination that draws a person away from objective thinking. All people have biases that are based on personal preferences learned from experience. Sociology students recognize that biases exist, both in the observer and the observed, that can invalidate a relationship between variables that they find.

Observer Bias

If a person is interested enough in a topic to study it sociologically, you can be fairly confident that he or she has some built-in biases about it. It is up to observers to recognize their biases and react to correct them. Otherwise, observations are probably not valid because the assumptions behind them skew the conclusions.

For example, if you are studying income levels of medical doctors in the United States, ask yourself why you chose the topic. Be honest. What did you think when you began your study? If you believed at the beginning that doctors are overpaid, were you looking only for statistics that proved your assumption? If so, you almost certainly will produce a biased study.

Sociology students may avoid biased thinking by:

* Becoming aware of their own biases.
* Asking other people to review their work.
* Recognizing that biases of people they observe may be affecting their behavior.

Biases of the Observed

If you are investigating a topic, whether you are conducting a research project or just satisfying your sociological interests, you need to recognize that the people you talk to also have biases. It is not always easy to detect bias, especially if you don't know the people you are questioning. You can't assume that they are thinking objectively.

For example, a few years ago some researchers at the University of Cincinnati asked 1,200 local residents whether they favored passage of the Monetary Control Bill of 1983. About 21 percent said that they favored the bill, 25 percent said that they opposed it, and the rest said they didn't know or hadn't thought about it. These are astonishing responses, since the Monetary Control Bill of 1983 doesn't exist. Why did nearly half the respondents pretend that they knew about it? To save face or save time? To tell the researchers what they thought they wanted to hear? Whatever the reasons, many of the answers were obviously biased.

Distinguishing Fact From Opinions

Whether you are reading about a social topic, discussing it with friends or family, or conducting your own research, the ability to distinguish fact from opinions can help you. Facts represent the truth and

can be checked for accuracy. Opinions, on the other hand, are expressions of people's attitudes and beliefs. Opinions may be based on fact, but they cannot be proved to be right or wrong. Careful thinkers are able to make sound judgments partly because they can tell the difference between the facts and the opinions in what they are reading or hearing.

Sometimes facts are easy to distinguish from opinions. For example, a person may say, "Your dress is blue." That is a fact. Or the person may say, "Your blue dress is pretty." That is an opinion. However, it isn't always that easy. Opinion can be communicated in subtle ways so that it comes across as fact. Consider the following example from a fictitious tour guide's description of a room in a small museum:

"This is the ballroom where people from all over the state gathered on festive occasions. Many famous people came here, including Robert E. Lee, Andrew Jackson, and John C. Calhoun. If you look carefully at the wall in front of you, you can see the outline of a beautiful balustrade that once was in the room. Also, in the 19th century the room had ornate floor and ceiling moldings and a large chandelier. All of these things are gone now because a museum in New York City stole them from us."

If you read carefully and critically, you will recognize that the word *stole* suggests an opinion, not a fact. It would be important to follow up and determine what actually happened.

Doing Research

Students with a well-developed sociological imagination will find that they frequently think about links between specific behaviors and situations and the broader social world. They will interpret things they observe with a critical, objective eye, finding cause and effect, recognizing bias, and distinguishing facts from opinions. However, sometimes a relationship is so intriguing, confusing, or compelling that it becomes important to do formal research on the topic. Research is not limited to professionals. Still, as with critical thinking and interpreting, doing research requires special skills if connections and conclusions are to be valid and insightful.

Using the Scientific Method

The scientific method is crucial to the success of any sociological research. Even if you don't do a full, formal study, it is important to understand the process and apply it to your work. The **five** basic steps to follow are:

1. **Defining the Problem.** The questions may come from almost anywhere—personal experience, previous sociological research, and common beliefs.

2. **Reviewing the Literature.** Studying what research has already been done on your topic will give you some good ideas and can save you some steps.

3. **Formulating the Hypothesis.** Make a statement that represents your best answer to your research question(s). Be as thoughtful as possible.

4. **Designing a Research Plan and Collecting the Data.** Design a plan for testing your hypothesis, and collect your data carefully. You must be able to determine what the data mean in terms of how well they support the hypothesis.

5. **Analyzing the Data and Developing the Conclusion.** The data support the hypothesis or they do not. If the data do not support the hypothesis, you will need to come up with a new hypothesis and a new research design.

Designing Your Research

Thinking skills, such as inductive and deductive thinking, reading and interpreting graphs and tables, finding cause and effect, and recognizing bias, are important guides throughout the entire research process. But other special skills are needed to design a good research plan.

A *research design* is a detailed plan or method for collecting data scientifically. Selecting a good research design is a critical step for sociologists. It requires creativity as well as solid thinking skills. Understanding some commonly used research designs can help you select one that works best for your research questions.

Surveys

A survey is a study, often in the form of an interview or questionnaire, that provides information about how people think and act. Most people in the United States

have responded to a countless number of surveys, on topics from laundry detergent preferences to dating preferences to voting preferences. And, of course, polls before a presidential election have become an important tool in political life. Some types of surveys, such as "person-on-the-street" interviews and call-ins on television shows, are not based on scientific method. A scientifically designed survey follows **three** principles.

1. **Representative Sampling.** The people surveyed must accurately represent the wider population being studied. For example, if you are studying middle-class families in the Midwest, the people you survey should accurately reflect everyone who fits that category. Your sample should have almost exactly the same proportions of different groups (gender, race, income levels, rural, urban, and so on) if it is to represent the whole.

2. **Random Sampling.** An important technique for getting a representative sampling is collecting a random sample. In a random sample, every member of a population being studied has the same chance of being selected. To select people at random from a small group, such as your class, you could invite people to roll dice and interview only those who rolled a predetermined number.

3. **Creating Well-worded Questions.** An effective survey question should be simple and clear enough for people to understand. Also, it should be as free from bias as possible. For example, avoid a question like, "Do you favor

brutal police tactics to prevent jaywalking on city streets?" People will respond much differently to a question like, "Do you agree with the mayor's new policy to fine jaywalkers on city streets?"

The **two** main forms of survey are:

1. **Interview.**
2. **Questionaire.**

Each has advantages and disadvantages. An interview can probe deeply into a respondent's underlying feelings and reasons. A person talking usually reveals more than he or she will on a written questionnaire. Because it's easy for a recipient to throw a questionnaire away, response rates are generally low. However, a questionnaire is cheaper and easier to do than one-on-one interviews and can generally target a much larger portion of the population.

Observations

Careful observations of social behaviors and situations are an integral part of the sociological imagination. Sociology students may observe and accurately record events they encounter in their daily lives. What if the subject you want to study needs objective observation, but it is not a part of your daily routine? Logically, you have to go out of your way to do the observations.

In some cases, observations can be inconspicuous, such as watching pedestrians at a busy intersection. However, sometimes *participant observation* is necessary. For example, if you wish to observe religious services where the congregation is actively involved, you would call attention to yourself if you didn't participate, too. Otherwise, you risk ruining the spontaneous behavior you want to observe.

William F. Whyte conducted a famous participant-observation study in Boston in the late 1930s that he named *Street Corner Society.* Whyte moved into a low-income neighborhood and for four years was a member of a group of "corner boys." Most of the previous research on poor neighborhoods had been gleaned from records of social services, hospitals, and courts. Whyte's research was unique because he joined in neighborhood conversations and activities. He listened and observed carefully, and according to his own account, he answered questions that he would not otherwise have thought to ask.

Experiments

Experiments are particularly well suited to studying cause-and-effect relationships. They are artificially created situations that allow researchers to test variables.

Using a Control Group. In order for an experiment to show cause and effect, variables must be isolated. This means the researchers need to eliminate all but one factor (variable) that might cause a particular social behavior. One way to do this is to assign subjects to one of two groups, the experimental group and the control group. The conditions should be exactly the same for both groups—the same room size and temperature, the same time of day, equal numbers of men and women, and everything else. With the experimental group the researchers introduce only the variable in question, and with the control group they do not.

EXAMPLE: An advertiser who seeks to discover whether people will respond to a particular phrase will use that phrase with the experimental group and leave it out of the message shown to the control group.

Being Ethical. It is important to consider ethical questions when designing an experiment, because the effects on the participants are sometimes dramatic.

EXAMPLE: In the early 1970s, Philip Zimbardo conducted a controversial sociological experiment with students at Stanford University. He wanted to study the impact of prison life on both guards and inmates. He believed that conducting the experiment with actual prisoners and guards would limit his results because prison rules would restrict him. Also, in a real prison, he could not easily control for differences in individual backgrounds of the subjects. So he decided to do an experiment with 24 student volunteers.

Zimbardo constructed a "prison" in the basement of the psychology building at Stanford and divided the students into two groups, "guards" and "prisoners." The two groups were matched for socioeconomic background, education, and race.

One night 12 students dressed as guards collected the 12 other students as prisoners in a simulated surprise arrest, handed out their prisoner uniforms, and put them

behind bars. Two days later, rumors of a prison rebellion began to spread. The guards reacted with surprising brutality, and the prisoners submitted with little resistance. The students became so deeply involved in their roles that Zimbardo had to stop the experiment before it was completed.

The ethical question he had to answer was whether his need to know outweighed the possible psychological damage to his subjects. By stopping the experiment, he chose their well-being over his research.

Use of Existing Information

Sometimes research questions can best be answered by compiling evidence from sources that already exist. Someone else may have already gathered data that can be used to support or challenge new hypotheses. Sociologists may study newspapers, magazines, radio and television tapes, diaries, songs, or folklore as well as previous research. For example, you could use magazines to help you reach conclusions about the effects of the modern women's rights movement on women's self-images. You could compare modern films to those from 40 years ago to help determine changes in smoking and the use of alcohol in U.S. society.

Using existing information is obviously the best method for studying societies and social relationships from the past. This method also has an advantage of not influencing people's behavior as you might in an experiment, or even in an observation or survey. Data in Emile Durkheim's classic study of suicide patterns in Europe was gathered primarily from existing information.

Organizing and Interpreting the Data

The data a researcher collects do not usually speak for themselves, but must be classified. Trends and relationships have to be identified for a study to be meaningful. For example, a list containing the height of every student in your school is useless unless this information is divided into categories—4'–5', 5'1"–5'6", 5'7"–6', 6'1"–6'6", 6'7" and over, for instance. The researcher must decide what tables and graphs to use, what categories to display, and whether to use maps or other graphic organizers to illustrate the findings.

Once the data are organized, the researcher must decide what the facts mean—a job that is full of hazards. For example, crime statistics can be very deceptive. You may study a police department's records and discover that many more crimes have been recorded in recent years than in past decades. A less-careful researcher may use the data to conclude that crime rates have increased dramatically in the city. However, good interpretive skills require that you think about possible alternative explanations. The police department may keep better records than it did before, or it may be better staffed and therefore able to catch more criminals than before. Unless the research has been designed to control these other possible variables, the data cannot be used to prove an upsurge of crime in the city.

Whether or not you carry out a full research study on your own, learning research skills can help you understand the connections between specific behaviors and situations and larger societal influences.

Writing Effectively

Writing is important for organizing and explaining your research, and it is also critical for communicating your ideas or for developing debate positions. Writing effectively consists of breaking the process down into **four** key steps:

1. Planning your writing.
2. Expressing the main idea.
3. Using evidence to support the main idea.
4. Making generalizations and drawing conclusions.

Planning Your Writing

Before you begin, you should organize your writing in an outline, list, flowchart, or graph—anything that helps you think through what you are going to say and how you will organize it. If you need to read about or research your topic before you write, do so and think about what information you will use and where. Planning involves thinking and interpreting skills. Use your sociological imagination while you plan.

Expressing the Main Idea

Writing a good *thesis statement* that captures the main idea of your paper will get you off to a strong start. It is harder than it seems. Your thesis statement should not just repeat the research questions or the issue about which you are writing. It should give an overview of the answers that your paper will give.

Suppose you are researching the factors that influence people in the United States to strive for financial success. Consider this thesis statement:

"There are many factors that influence people in the United States to strive for financial success."

Notice that this statement only repeats the question. It gives the reader no idea about the evidence and the arguments that your paper will make.

Part of the secret of expressing your main idea effectively is being sure that you know what your paper is going to say before you begin to write it. In your reading and research, what factors did you find? Which ones do you think are most important—ones that you want to include in your paper? Your thesis statement should provide an overview of the answers to these questions. A better thesis statement would be:

"Factors that influence people in the United States to strive for financial success include encouragement from family and friends, a positive attitude toward life developed in childhood, and a stimulating work environment."

Using Evidence to Support the Main Idea

Effective writing in sociology includes the ability to choose and use evidence to back up main ideas.

When you are relying on research, be sure that your sources are reliable and be sure that you understand what the authors are saying.

When you are writing a position essay or preparing for a debate, you may be organizing many of your own thoughts to support your thesis.

Whatever you are writing, it is very important that you don't confuse your own ideas with the ideas you've picked up from your reading and research. Whether you use your ideas or someone else's, be sure that your evidence is based on objective thinking. Make it clear that you have considered alternatives, and that the evidence you are using is strong and reliable.

You may present evidence gathered from other sources in **three** ways:

1. **Summaries.** You may present the main idea, including only enough details or examples to make your point clear. When you are summarizing someone else's work, rephrase it in your own writing style. Use quotation marks around any words you feel you must quote from the study. When you summarize, give credit to your source in the body of your paper.

2. **Paraphrases.** A paraphrase is similar to a summary, but it includes more details and descriptions, and it is closer in length to the original source. Just as with a summary, change both the vocabulary and the sentence structure so that your work sounds different from the source. Cite the source in your paper. You don't need

quotation marks when you are using your own words. You *must* use quotation marks when you are picking up phrases or longer passages from the source.

3. **Quotations.** Direct quotes are effectively used when the author's words make a powerful point. If the author is well respected or famous, the effect may be even greater. For example, if you are writing about financial success in the United States, a quote from Bill Gates or Donald Trump could add credibility to your arguments. Keep the quotes short and to the point, and be sure that you identify the author.

Making Generalizations and Drawing Conclusions

A good paper states its main idea strongly and clearly, presents solid evidence, and then brings it together to make a powerful set of points. It does not merely summarize. After specific pieces of evidence are pulled together to support the thesis statement, the paper generalizes and draws conclusions that are directly related to the evidence.

Generalizations and conclusions are more effective if they follow these guidelines:

* *Be sure that you have enough evidence to support the generalizations.* Before you begin your conclusion, look over the evidence that you have compiled to be sure that your examples directly lead to the generalizations that you make.

* **Avoid using inclusive words, such as every, no, or all.** For example, if you say that "all successful people in the United States come from supportive families," you are almost certainly wrong. Your argument loses effectiveness when your claims are exaggerated. Instead use words like *most, many,* and *usually.*

* **Avoid false or flawed conclusions that won't stand up to close inspection.** In many ways, this point goes back to thinking critically. Don't come to a conclusion that obviously ignores evidence that you conveniently don't present. For example, if you use the evidence gathered about financially successful people to argue that families are to blame for people's lack of success, your argument won't be very convincing. Most people realize that financial success or failure is more complex than that.

The rewards of developing a sociological imagination are great. You can develop a new awareness of the relationships between individuals and the wider society. You can better comprehend the links between your immediate, personal social settings and the seemingly impersonal social world that surrounds and helps shape you. Your understanding of public issues broadens and becomes more profound. However, these rewards cannot be realized unless you learn and perfect the necessary skills. Sociology students build their understandings and new insights step by step: thinking and interpreting critically, researching carefully, and writing effectively.

References

CHAPTER 1

"ASA Code of Ethics." http://www.asanet.org

Campbell, I. C. "The Lateen Sail in World History." *Journal of World History,* Spring 1995.

Lengermann, Patricia Madoo, and Niebrugge-Brantley, Jill. *The Women Founders: Sociology and Social Theory. 1830–1930.* Boston: McGraw-Hill, 1998.

Mills, C. Wright. *The Sociological Imagination.* New York: Oxford University Press, 1959.

Ritzer, George. *The McDonaldization of Society.* Thousand Oaks, CA: Pine Forge Press, 1993.

CHAPTER 2

Barlowe, Arthur. *Voyages and Travels by John Pinkerton,* vol. 12. London: Longman, 1812, p. 604.

"Fragment on the History of the Linapis since about 1600," in *Walam Olum or Red Score, The Migration Legend of the Lenni Lenape or Delaware Indians. A New Translation.* Indianapolis: Indiana Historical Society, 1954.

Murdock, George Peter. "The Common Denominator of Culture," in Ralph Linton, ed., *The Science of Man in World Crisis.* New York: Columbia University Press, 1945, p. 124.

The National Election Studies, Center for Political Studies, University of Michigan.

"Numbers." *Time Magazine,* July 31, 2000, p. 17.

Ogburn, William F. *Social Change with Respect to Culture and Original Nature,* rev. ed. New York: Viking, 1950.

Rubenstein, Harriet. "Protecting the Health and Safety of Working Teenagers." *American Family Physician,* August 1999.

Southgate, Eliza. *A Girl's Life Eighty Years Ago: Letters of Eliza Southgate.* Clarence Cook, ed. New York, 1887.

Williams, Robin. *American Society,* 3rd ed. New York: Alfred A. Knopf, 1970.

CHAPTER 3

Asch, Solomon E. "Effects of Group Pressure upon the Modification and Distortion of Judgments," in H. Guetzkow (ed.) *Groups, Leadership, and Men.* Pittsburgh: Carnegie Press, 1951.

Bales, R. F., et al. "Channels of Communication in Small Groups." *American Sociological Review* 16, 1951, pp. 461–468.

Michels, Robert. *Political Parties* (1915). Glencoe, IL: Free Press, 1949.

Parkinson, C. Northcote. *Parkinson's Law.* Boston: Houghton Mifflin, 1957.

Peter, Laurence J., and Hull, Raymond. *The Peter Principle.* New York: William Morrow, 1969.

CHAPTER 4

Benedict, Ruth. *Patterns of Culture.* New York: New American Library, 1959 (originally 1934).

Cloud, John. "A Kinder, Gentler Death." *Time Magazine,* September 18, 2000, pp. 60ff.

Davis, Kingsley. *Human Society.* New York: Macmillan, 1948, pp. 204–205.

Kubler-Ross, Elisabeth. *On Death and Dying.* New York: Macmillan, 1969.

McLane, Daisann. "The Cuban American Princess." *New York Times Magazine,* February 26, 1995, pp. 42–43.

Mead, Margaret. *Sex and Temperament in Three Primitive Societies.* New York: Morrow, 1935.

Statistical Abstract of the United States. 1992, pp. 392–394.

CHAPTER 5

Amir, Menachem, and Berman, Yitzchak. "Chromosomal Deviation and Crime," *Federal Probation* 34 (June 1970), pp. 55–62.

Bellesiles, Michael A. *The Origins of a National Gun Culture.* New York: Alfred A. Knopf, 2000.

Black, Donald J. "The Social Organization of Arrest." *Stanford Law Review* 23, 1971.

Bonner, Raymond, and Fessenden, Ford. "States with No Death Penalty Share Lower Homicide Rates." *The New York Times,* September 22, 2000, p. A1.

Cohen, Albert K. *Deviance and Control.* Englewood Cliffs, NJ: Prentice Hall, 1966.

Crime in the United States, 1997. Washington, DC: U.S. Government Printing Office, 1998.

Hooten, Ernest A. *Crime and the Man.* Cambridge, MA: Harvard University Press, 1939.

Kerbo, Harold, and McKinstry, John A. *Modern Japan.* Boston: McGraw-Hill, 1998.

Lacy, Marc, and Bonner, Raymond. "Pervasive Disparities Found in the Federal Death Penalty." *The New York Times,* September 12, 2000, pp. A1, A18.

Lombroso, Cesare. *Crime: Its Causes and Remedies.* Boston: Little, Brown, 1918.

Lyons, Richard D. "Ultimate Speck Appeal May Cite Genetic Defect." *The New York Times,* April 22, 1968.

Merton, Robert K. *Social Theory and Social Structure.* New York: Free Press, 1968.

Russell, Cheryl. "Murder is All-American." *American Demographics* 17, September 1995, pp. 15–17.

Sheldon, William H. *Varieties of Delinquent Youth*. New York: Harper & Bros, 1949.

Simmons, Ann M. "Where Fat Is a Mark of Beauty," *Los Angeles Times*, September 30, 1998, pp. A1, A12.

Terry, Don. "Cleaning Graffiti-Scarred Areas, A Wall at a Time." *The New York Times*, October 20, 2000, p. A18.

"Uniform Crime Reports, Summary 1999" http://www.fbi.gov/ucr/Cius_99/99crime/99cius1.pdf

CHAPTER 6

Blau, Peter, and Duncan, Otis Dudley. *The American Occupational Structure*. New York: Wiley, 1967.

Cratsley, John. "The Crime of the Courts," in Bruce Wasserstein and Mark J. Green, eds., *With Justice for Some*. Boston: Beacon Press, 1972.

Fussell, Paul. *Class: A Guide Through the American Status System*. New York: Summit Books, 1983.

Gertner, Jon. "What Is Wealth?" *Money Magazine*, December 2000, pp. 94ff.

"Health and Income Equity" http://depts.washington.edu/eqhlth/

Hodge, Robert W., Siegel, Paul M., and Rossi, Peter H. "Occupational Prestige in the United States: 1925–1963," in Reinhard Bendix and Seymour Martin Lepset, eds., *Class, Status, and Power*, 2nd ed. New York: Free Press, 1966, pp. 324–325.

Holmes, Steven A. "Incomes Up and Poverty Is Down, Data Show." *The New York Times*, September 27, 2000.

Johnston, David Cay. "Gap between Rich and Poor Found Substantially Wider." *The New York Times*, September 5, 1999.

"Poverty Rates" http://adaction.org/99incineq.html

Rytina, Joan Huber, Form, William H., and Pease, John. "Income and Stratification Ideology: Beliefs about the American Opportunity Structure." *American Journal of Sociology*, vol. 75, January 1970, pp. 703–716.

CHAPTER 7

Adorno, T. W. *The Authoritarian Personality*. New York: Harper & Row, 1950.

Bureau of the Census 1998d, 1998e; also http://www.census.gov/population/estimates/nation/intfile3-1.txt
http://www.census.gov/PressRelease/cb96176.html
http://www.census.gov/population/estimates/state/srh/srhus96.txt

Bureau of Labor Statistics 1998b

Dunn, Ashley. "Southeast Asians Highly Dependent on Welfare in the U.S." *The New York Times*, May 19, 1994, pp. A1, A19.

"Hate Crime." http://www.ncvc.org/special/hatec.htm

Lotke, Eric. "Young African American Men in D.C.'s Criminal Justice System Five Years Later," http://www.ncianet.org/ncia/hobb.html

Navarro, Mireya, and Sengupta, Somini. "Arriving at Florida Voting Places, Some Blacks Found Frustration." *The New York Times*, November 30, 2000, pp. A1ff.

Roy, Daniel L. "Summary Results from the Latino Ethnic Attitudes Survey." http://falcon.cc.ukans.edu/~droy/

Sugimoto, Yoshio, *An Introduction to Japanese Society*. Cambridge, UK: Cambridge University Press, 1997.

CHAPTER 8

Belluck, Pam. "A Bit of Burping is Allowed, If It Keeps Parents on the Job." *The New York Times*, December 4, 2000, pp. A1ff.

Bureau of the Census 1998c, pp. 419–421, 476.

Bureau of the Census 2000. http://www.aoa.dhhs.gov/aoa/STATS/profile/default.htm#older

Crossette, Barbara, "'Oldest Old,' 80 and Over, Increasing Globally." *The New York Times*, December 22, 1998, p. 7.

Draper, Patricia. "!Kung Women: Contrasts in Sexual Egalitarianism in Foraging and Sedentary Contexts," in *Toward an Anthropology of Women*, ed. R. Reiter. New York: Monthly Review Press, 1975, pp. 77–109.

Fischer, David. *Growing Old in America*. New York: Oxford University Press, 1977.

"The Global Infectious Disease Threat and Its Implications for the United States." http://www.cia.gov/cia/publications/nie/report/nie99-17d.html

"Life Expectancy at Birth." http://www.cia.gov/cia/publications/factbook/fields/life_expectancy_at_birth.html

"Living Arrangements of Elderly Men and Women" and "United States with Distribution of 65+ Population." http://www.aoa.dhhs.gov/aoa/STATS/profile/default.htm#older

Martin, K., and Voorhies, B. *Female of the Species*. New York: Columbia University Press, 1975.

Money, John, and Ehrhardt, Anke. *Man and Woman, Boy and Girl*. Baltimore, MD: Johns Hopkins Press, 1972.

United Nations Human Development Report, 1995.

CHAPTER 9

Bureau of the Census. "Household and Family Characteristics." March 1998.

Bureau of the Census, "Population and Housing," detailed tables, 1990 data.

Bureau of Justice Statistics, 1998.

The Evan B. Donaldson Adoption Institute. "Adoption in the United States." March 2000. http://www.adoptioninstitute.org/research/ressta.html

Dowd, Frances Smardo. "Library Latchkey Children." ERIC Digest, 1992. http://ericeece.org/pubs/digests/1992/dowd92.html

For Shelter and Beyond. Boston: Massachusetts Coalition of Battered Women Service Groups, 1990.

Glazer, Sara. "Violence Against Women." *CQ Researcher*, Congressional Quarterly, Inc., 3:8, February 1993.

IBSA. "African Traditions & Customs: Marriage in Hausa Tradition, Part 1." http://www.ibsa-inc.org/customs.htm

Journal of the American Medical Association, August 22/29, 1990.

Pasley, Kay, and Lipe, Emily. "How Does Having a Mutual Child Affect Stepfamily Adjustment?" Stepfamily Association of America, Research Findings, Summer 1998. http://www.stepfam.org/faqs/findings/1.htm

"Statistics Supporting the Equal Shared Parenting/Kids Need Both Parents Bill." http://www.execpc.com/EqualSharedParenting/stat.htm

ThinkQuest team 16645. "The People: Hausa." 1998. http://library.thinkquest.org/16645/the_people/ethnic_hausa.shtml

"Who's Minding Our Preschoolers?" (series). *Census and You* 33:4, April 1998, p. 5.

CHAPTER 10

Adherents.com Home Page, http://www.adherents.com.

Baylis-Heerschop, Christen. "Federal Aid to Education." http://www.nd.edu/~rbarger/www7/fedaid.html

Center for Education Reform. "CER National Charter School Directory 2000 Now Available." http://www.edreform.com/press/ncsd2000.htm

Chase, Bob. "Voucher System Would Hurt Schools Not Help." http://www.nea.org/society/vouchers/vouchers.html

Coleman, James S., et al. "Equality of Educational Opportunity." Washington, DC: National Center for Educational Statistics (DHEW), 1966.

"Coleman, James S(amuel)" *Encyclopedia Britannica Online*. http://www.britannica.com

Collins, Bethany D. "Brown v. Board of Education." http://www.nd.edu/~rbarger/www7/brown.html

"The Condition of Education 2000, Supplemental Table: School Choice and Parental Satisfaction." http://www.nces.ed.gov/pubs2000/coe2000/section4/s_table46_1.html

Cotton, Kathleen. "School Size, School Climate, and Student Performance." School Improvement Research Series. Northwest Regional Education Laboratory. http://www.nwrel.org/scpd/sirs/10/c020.html

Global Learning @ Home. "Statistics on Home Schooling." http://www.g-learn.org/homestats.htm

Grocke, Vicky. "Compulsory Education." http://www.nd.edu/~rbarger/www7/compulso.html

Hoff, David J. "Echoes of the Coleman Report." Education Week on the Web, March 24, 1999. http://www.teachermagazine.org/ew/vol-18/28coleman.h18

Lightcap, Brad. "The Morrill Act of 1863." http://www.nd.edu/~rbarger/www7/morrill.html

Miller, Tonjia. "Impact of Business and Industry." http://www.nd.edu/~rbarger/www7/impbusin.html

Ort, Tamara L. "Plessy v. Ferguson." http://www.nd.edu/~rbarger/www7/plessy.html

Scherer, Melissa. "A Nation at Risk: The Imperative for Educational Reform, 1983." http://www.nd.edu/~rbarger/www7/nationrs.html

"The Scopes 'Monkey Trial,'" http://xroads.virginia.edu/~UG97/inherit/1925home.html

U.S. Department of Education. "Educational Innovation in Multiracial Contexts: The Growth of Magnet Schools in American Education." 1996.

VanZant, Kevin. "The Land Ordinance of 1785 and Northwest Ordinance of 1787." http://www.nd.edu/~rbarger/www7/ord17857.html

CHAPTER 11

Bureau of the Census. *Historical Income Tables—People* http://www.census.gov/hhes/income/histinc/p01.html

Bureau of the Census. *Reasons for Not Voting . . . November 1998*. http://www.census.gov/population/socdemo/voting/cps1998/tab12.txt

Bureau of Labor Statistics, 1990

Dahl, Robert. *Who Governs?* New Haven, CT: Yale University Press, 1961.

General Motors. *1999 Annual Report—Financial Highlights*. http://www.gm.com/company/investors/ar1999/fh/index.htm

IDEA: Voter Turnout from 1945. http://www.idea.int/voter_turnout/voter_turnout_pop2,2.html

Mills, C. Wright. *The Power Elite*. New York: Oxford University Press, 1956.

Ritzer, George. *Expressing America: A Critique of the Global Credit Card Society*. Thousand Oaks, CA: Pine Forge Press, 1995, p. 177.

"This Nation." *Processes: Public Opinion* http://www.thisnation.com/processes-opinion.html

United Nations *United Nations Member States* http://www.un.org/Overview/unmember.html

U.S. State Department, *Independent States of the World* http://www.state.gov/www/regions/independent_states.html

Weber, Max. *The Theory of Social and Economic Organization*. New York: Free Press, 1957.

CHAPTER 12

Advertising Age, September 29, 1997.

American Medical Association. Statement on Television Violence: Hearings before the U.S. Senate Committee on Commerce, Science, and Transportation, July 12, 1995. http://www.nfhs.org/Area_III.htm

Bagdikian, Ben. *The Media Monopoly*, 5th ed. Boston: Beacon, 1997, pp. xlv–xlvi.

Ballard, S. "A show that has the goods." *Sports Illustrated*, February 20, 1989, p. 38.

DeFleur, Melvin L., and Dennis, Everette E. *Understanding Mass Communication*. Boston: Houghton Mifflin.

Dunning, Eric G., et al. (eds.) *The Sports Process: A Comparative and Developmental Approach*. Champaign, IL: Human Kinetics Publishers, 1993, pp. 20–38, 131.

"Estimated Probability of Competing in Athletics Beyond the High School Interscholastic Level." NCAA Online. http://www.ncaa.org/research/prob_of_competing

Fouke, Janie (ed.). *Engineering Tomorrow: Today's Technology Experts Envision the Next Century*. New York: IEEE Press, 2000, pp. 4–6.

"*H. Sapiens*, Sport, and a Theory: A look at the development through figurationalism." http://clam.rutgers.edu/~jkl30/archaeology.html

Huffman, Richard. "The Media Goliath's War on Democracy." 1997. http://www.wolfe.net/~lzerfred/LFPS/Resume/Samples/Media.html

Huizinga, Johan. *Homo Ludens: A Study of the Play Element in Society*, referenced in Hart, Marie (ed). *Sport in the Sociocultural Process*. Dubuque, IA: Wm. C. Brown Co., 1976, pp. 5–7.

"Interview: Ben Bagdikian." http://www.pbs.org/wgbh/pages/frontline/smoke/interviews/bagdikian.html.

Lapham, Lewis. *Bad News Sells Good News*. Excerpts from an address to Public Radio News Directors. Minneapolis, August 5, 1995. http://www.americanreview.net/badnews.htm

Levine, Madeline. *Viewing Violence*. New York: Doubleday, 1996.

McPherson, Barry D., et al. *The Social Significance of Sport: An Introduction to the Sociology of Sport*. Champaign, IL: Human Kinetics Books, 1989.

NCAA. http://www.ncaa.org/research

National Federation of State H.S. Associations. Hollis, Gay. *Murder, Mayhem, Politics and Commerce: The Influence of the Media in the United States*. http://www.nfhs.org/Area_III.htm

National Violence Study. Mediascope, Inc. *Two New Studies on Television Violence and Their Significance for the Kids' TV Debate*. February 1996. http://www.cep.org/tvviolence.html

Naughton, Jim. "Women's Teams in NCAA's Division I See Gains in Participation and Budget." *The Chronicle of Higher Education*, April 3, 1998: pp. A42–48.

Postman, Neil. *Amusing Ourselves to Death*. New York: Viking Penguin, Inc., 1986.

Sadler, William A., in Hart, Marie (ed.) *Sport in the Sociocultural Process*, pp. 173–174.

Sherman, Len. *Big League, Big Time: The Birth of the Arizona Diamondbacks and the Power of Sports in America*, 1998, quoted in Ohanion, Susan. *One Size Fits Few*. Portsmouth, NH: Heinemann, 1999, p. 127.

"Violence in television." *CQ Researcher* 3, Congressional Quarterly, Inc. 1993, pp. 274–276.

Westall, Tim. "High School Sports." http://www.soc.sbs.ohio-state.edu/cfp/sport2/HS2.htm

Westall, Tim. "Social Class and Sport." http://www.soc.sbs.ohio-state.edu/cfp/sport2/class1~1.htm

CHAPTER 13

Bureau of the Census. Guide to 1997 Economic Census. http://www.census.gov/epcd/www/g97/intro.htm

Bureau of the Census. Historical National Population Estimates: July 1, 1900, to July 1, 1999. http://www.census.gov/population/estimates/nation/popclockest.txt

Bureau of the Census. Statistical Abstract of the United States. Washington, DC: U.S. Government Printing Office, 1998.

Bureau of the Census. World Vital Events. http://www.census.gov

Demographia. Top 85 World Urbanized Areas: 1985: Population, Land Area and Density. http://222.publicpurpose.com/dm-iua85.htm

Fornos, Werner. "1996 Population Overview." http://www.population-institute.org.1997.

Kumin, Judith. "Europe: the debate over asylum." *Refugees Magazine,* Issue 113, 1999. http://www.unhcr.ch/pubs/rm113/rm11302.htm

Lemonick, Michael D. "The Ozone Vanishes," *Time Magazine,* February 17, 1992, pp 60–63.

Mitchell, Jennifer D. "Before the Next Doubling." *World Watch 11* (January/February) 1998, pp. 21–27.

New England Aquarium. Research Cornerstones. Freshwater Biodiversity: Lake Victoria Cichlids. http://www.neaq.org/corner/res/lakevic.html

People and the Planet. Lake Victoria: a sick giant. http://www.oneworld.org/patp/pap_victoria.html

Rainforest Action Network. "Rates of Rainforest Loss." http://www.ran.org/info_center/factsheets/04b.html

Rocky Mountain News, September 17, 1896. http://www.iberia.vassar.edu/1896/0917rmn.html

Shcherbak, Yuri M. "Ten Years of the Chernobyl Era." *Scientific American,* April 1996.

"Solid Waste." http://www.dne.wvnet.edu/c/env100/sessions/solwaste.html

Union of Concerned Scientists. "Frequently Asked Questions About Biodiversity." http://www.ucsusa.org/resources/biodiv.faq.html

United Nations. Determinants and Consequences of Population Trends, 2nd ed. New York: United Nations, 1973.

United Nations Human Development Report. New York: Oxford Press, 1996.

United Nations Population Division, World Population Prospects: The 1998 Revision and Below-Replacement Fertility. http://www.popin.org/pop1998/7.htm

U.S. Committee for Refugees. News Release, September 9, 1999. http://www.refugees.org/news/press_releases/1999/090999.htm

U.S. Department of Commerce. World Population Growth Rates: 1995–2005. http://www.imcglobal.com/cropsalt/popgrowth.htm

U.S. Immigration and Naturalization Service. Percent Foreign-Born and Emigration from the U.S. http://www.ins.usdoj.gov/graphics/aboutins/statistics/301.htm

Wilson, Edward O. *The Diversity of Life.* Cambridge, MA: Harvard University Press, 1992.

Wrong, Dennis H. "The oversocialized conception of man in modern sociology." *American Sociological Review* 26, 1959, pp. 183–193.

CHAPTER 14

Center for Advanced Spatial Technologies. University of Arkansas, Fayetteville. *Population Density—1990.* http://www.cast.uark.edu/local/catalog/national/html/Population.htmldir/Uspop1990.html

CNN.com. "Night-light may lead to nearsightedness." May 13, 1999. http://www.cnn.com/HEALTH/9905/12/children.lights/index.html

Fisher, Christy. "What We Love and Hate about Cities" *American Demographics,* October 1997. http://www.demographics.com/publications/ad/97_ad/9710_ad/ad971029.htm

Harris, Chauncey D., and Ullman, Edward L. "The Nature of Cities." *The Annals* 242, 1945, pp. 7–17.

Hoyt, Homer. *The Structure and Growth of Residential Neighborhoods in American Cities.* Washington, DC: U.S. Government Printing Office, 1939.

The International Dark Sky Assoc. "Light Pollution." http://maple.lemoyne.edu/~mcmahon/LP.html

Kling, Rob, Olin, Spencer, and Poster, Mark (eds.). "Beyond the Edge: The Dynamism of Postsuburban Regions" in *Postsuburban California: The Transformation of Postwar Orange County, California* (2nd ed.) University of California Press, 1995. http://www.ics.uci.edu/~kling/postedge.html

National Coalition for the Homeless. "How Many People Experience Homelessness? And Who Is Homeless?" *NCH Fact Sheet #2 and #3.* http://nch.ari.net/numbers.html and http://nch.ari.net/who.html

Park, Robert E., et al. *The City.* Chicago: University of Chicago Press, 1925.

Rotstein, Arthur H. "Light Pollution Debate Splits Arizona." http://dailynews.yahoo.com/h/ap/20000824/sc/dimming_the_lights_2.html

Simmel, Georg. *The Sociology of Georg Simmel.* Kurt H. Wolff (tr.) New York: Free Press, 1950.

Slippery Rock University of Pennsylvania. *Urbanization of the United States.* http://www.sru.edu/depts/artsci/ges/discover/d-6-10.htm

CHAPTER 15

BBC News. "UK Soccer fans organise riot on the Web." http://newssearch.bbc.co.uk/hi/english/uk/newsid_414000/414543.stm

Blumer, Herbert G. "Collective Behavior," in A. M. Lee (ed.), *Principles of Sociology*, 3rd ed. New York: Barnes and Noble Books, 1969.

Blumer, Herbert. "Elementary collective groupings," in Louis E. Genevie (ed.), *Collective Behavior and Social Movements*. Itasca, IL: Peacock, 1978.

Diener, E. "Deindividuation, self-awareness, and disinhibition." *Journal of Personality and Social Psychology* 37, 1979, pp. 1160-1171.

Hall, J. G., et al. "Self-awareness—reducing effects of alcohol consumption." *Journal of Personality and Social Psychology* 44, 1983, pp. 461–473.

LeBon, Gustave. *The Crowd: A Study of the Popular Mind.* New York: Viking Press, [1895] 1960.

Mann, L. "The baiting crowd in episodes of threatened suicide." *Journal of Personality and Social Psychology* 41, 1982, pp. 703–709.

Mann, L., et.al. "A test between deindividuation and emergent norm theories of crowd aggression." *Journal of Personality and Social Psychology* 42, 1982, pp. 260–272.

McAdam, Doug, et al. "Social Movements," in Neil J. Smelser (ed.), *Handbook of Sociology*. Newbury Park, CA: Sage, 1988.

Microsoft *Encarta 99.* "China" and "Tiananmen Square Protest."

"Modern China: The Chinese Communist Party." Washington State University. http://www.wsu.edu:8001/~dee/MODCHINA/COMM2.HTM

"NC State Sociologist Examines What Turns Fans into Fanatics." North Carolina State University. http://www2.ncsu.edu/ncsu/univ_relations/releases/fans.html

The Ruckus Society. http://ruckus.org

Schultz, D. P. *Panic Behavior.* New York: Random House, 1964.

Smelser, Neil J. *The Theory of Collective Behavior.* New York: Free Press. 1971/1962.

Tajfel, H. and Turner, J. C. "The social identity theory of intergroup behavior." In S. Worchel and W. G. Austin (eds.), *Psychology of Intergroup Relations*. Chicago: Nelson-Hall, 1985.

Tesser, A. *Advanced Social Psychology.* New York: McGraw-Hill, 1995.

Tilly, Charles. *From Mobilization to Revolution.* Reading, MA: Addison-Wesley, 1978.

Turner, Ralph H., and Killina, Lewis M. *Collective Behavior*, 3rd ed. Englewood Cliffs, NJ: Prentice-Hall, 1987.

CHAPTER 16

Barber, Benjamin R. *Jihad vs. Mc World.* New York: Times Books, 1995.

Barnett, Richard J., and Cavanagh, John. *Global Dreams: Imperial Corporations and the New World Order.* New York: Simon and Schuster, 1994.

"Demography." Trinity College. http://www.trinity.edu/~mkearl/demograp.html

Isbiter, John. *Promises Not Kept: The Betrayal of Social Change in the Third World*, 4th ed., Chapter 3. West Hartford, CT: Kumarian Press, 1998.

Lenski, Gerhard, and Lenski, Jean. *Human Societies: An Introduction to Macrosociology*, 5th ed. New York: McGraw-Hill, 1987.

Lenski, Gerhard, Lenski, Jean, and Nolan, Patrick. *Human Societies*, 7th ed. New York: McGraw-Hill, 1995.

Leo, John. "Community and personal duty." *U.S. News & World Report*, January 28, 1991, p 17.

Ogburn, William Fielding. *Social Change.* New York: Viking, 1922.

Regnery, George M. "Even the smallest political gift can open your life for all to see." *Hartford Courant*, reprinted in *The Missoulian*, September 21, 2000, p. A4.

Rheingold, Howard. *The Virtual Community.* Chapter 6. Online book. http://www.rheingold.com/vc/book/6.html

Sharp, Laurison. "Steel Axes for Stone-Age Australians." In *Down to Earth Sociology: Introductory Readings*, 8th ed., James M. Henslin, ed. New York: Free Press, 1995.

SKILLS SECTION

Mills, C. Wright. *The Sociological Imagination.* New York: Oxford University Press, 1959.

"Profile of Older Americans:1999" The Administration on Aging. http://www.aoa.dhhs.gov/aoa/stats/profile/

Credits

Index

N

S